RARE BITS

Unusual
Origins

of

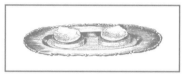

Popular
Recipes

Patricia Bunning Stevens

OHIO UNIVERSITY PRESS   ATHENS

Ohio University Press, Athens, Ohio 45701
© 1998 by Patricia Bunning Stevens
Printed in the United States of America
All rights reserved

Ohio University Press books are printed on acid-free paper ⊗ ™

05 04 03 02 01 00 99 98   5 4 3 2 1

Book design by Chiquita Babb

Library of Congress Cataloging-in-Publication Data

Stevens, Patricia Bunning.
    Rare bits : unusual origins of popular recipes / Patricia Bunning
Stevens.
        p.   cm.
    Includes bibliographical references and index.
    ISBN 0-8214-1232-9 (cloth : alk. paper). — ISBN 0-8214-1233-7 (paper)
    1. Cookery. 2. Cookery—History. I. Title.
TX714.S7812 1998
641.5—dc21   98-4672

In memory of
John Spencer
and
John Bunning

CONTENTS

Sweets

Stirred or Shaken

PREFACE

History is my field, and I began reading cookbooks when I was about eleven years old. As it turned out, that combination of interests was good preparation for this book.

My first interest, as I began this project, was simply in the unusual names of many well-known recipes, but this soon led me to the whole history of foods and cooking. I found that culinary history was often written by nonhistorians, who repeated everything and checked nothing, so it was important to turn to standard reference works whenever possible. Most useful in this regard were the twenty volumes of *The Oxford English Dictionary*.

Recipes seemed an essential addition to the investigation, for to describe a dish one must also describe how it is made. And the recipes came from everywhere—the labels on cans and packages, old magazines and newspapers, out-of-print cookbooks and old fund-raising cookbooks. If I were to single out one never-failing source of inspiration, however, especially for baked goods, it would be the oldest editions of the General Mills cookbooks. When I was a young cook, Betty Crocker was my mentor, and Betty never let me down!

Occasionally, too, I turned to current cookbooks for ideas, adapting recipes that in their turn have been copied and recopied for decades or even centuries. Frequently I took two or three versions of a recipe and rearranged the proportions of the ingredients for a combination I thought would be especially delicious, for that is the way I tend to cook. If my version then turned out to be as good as I hoped it would be, that was the version I used.

In every case my goal was to find recipes for these classic

dishes that were at once authentic, pleasing to modern tastes, and manageable in the home kitchen.

So let us offer a tribute to all the cooks, whether they cooked for love or cooked for a living, who created something new to please the ones they served. Each, in his or her own small way, was making the world a more pleasant place for all the generations to come.

THE STAFF OF LIFE

CHAPTER 1

BREADS

Grain made civilization possible. No group of people has ever gone directly from a hunting and gathering economy to cities and empires and the more complicated way of life that goes with them. First there must be agriculture and especially the cultivation of grains, crops that can be stored to provide sustenance for all in every season of the year, stored even to provide for years of bad harvests and the possibility of famine. Wheat and barley flourished in Egypt, in Mesopotamia, and along the Indus river, millet and rice in China, and maize or Indian corn in the Americas; without these vital crops there could have been no progress.

Porridge or gruel may be older than bread, at least in some parts of the world, and if it was not too appetizing it did at least fill hungry bellies. Milling stones made possible the production of coarse meal or flour, and then bread baking began. The earliest breads were hearth cakes, unleavened and baked on hot stones set in the embers of the fire. The best-known example today of such an ancient bread might be the tortilla; though its name is Spanish (little cake), its ancestry is Indian.

Bread raised by yeast was first made in Egypt. Spores of wild yeast, naturally present in air, readily contaminate wet dough, and the first raised breads were the product of the resultant spontaneous fermentation. Real progress occurred with the discovery that a piece of old dough could be saved to leaven the new dough, a technique still used in many parts of the world. Later, beer brewers found that the sediment from the fermentation process, which contains yeast, also worked as a leavening agent. Although Egyptian peasants no doubt continued to bake coarse hearth breads long after the advent of yeast-risen breads, the wealthy, by 2000 B.C., had professional bakers to serve them raised breads.

The Greeks and Romans were slow to learn the art of bread baking. The Greeks grew mostly barley and baked it in flat, unleavened loaves, while the Romans ignored the vast potential of bread in the early days of their republic, preferring instead to make a simple porridge or mush called *pulmentum*. The obvious forerunner of polenta, *pulmentum* was made first from crushed millet, then from barley, then from an early form of wheat called *far*. Sternly plain and practical, perhaps *pulmentum* suited the austere farmers and soldiers of the first centuries.

When milling methods improved, the crushed grain was made into farina, genuine flour. The Romans probably learned about leavened bread from the Egyptians, but in time the most highly prized yeast was a cultivated type imported from Gaul, where it was used to make beer. Professional bakers began to appear in Italy around 170 B.C.

The problem of feeding the proverbial Roman mob led to the introduction of bread doles. The number of recipients on the dole roster rose from 40,000 in 72 B.C. to 200,000 by the time of Caesar and to an estimated 300,000 in 275 A.D. Huge shipments of wheat came regularly from North Africa. The large rotary mills turned by donkeys, oxen, or slaves were superseded by immense water-driven mills, some of which were capable of producing an estimated twenty-eight tons of flour in a ten-hour day. Public bakeries did the baking, for the poor lived in such hideous tenements as to make cooking at home almost impossible. When the poet Juvenal accused the Romans of wanting nothing but "Bread and circuses!" he was speaking the literal truth.

To the north the barbarians still depended on oats and rye, raised in clearings in the woods. With their simple hearthcakes our story begins.

BANNOCKS OR SCONES
4 servings

The Celts emerge, as the Victorians would have said, from the "mists of antiquity." They are the first people north of the Mediterranean whom we know by name. Before them Western Europe must be left to the archaeologists, who can identify people only by burial customs, battle axes, or pottery styles.

The Celts are a branch of the great family we call Indo-European, for strictly speaking, Celtic is a linguistic term; a Celt is someone who speaks a Celtic language. Nevertheless, the ancient writers noted their height, their fair skin, and their red-golden hair and described them as a brawling, sprawling race of barbarians who inhabited a vast area between the Alps and the North Sea. Their languages today can be found only on the fringes of Europe, in western Ireland, northern Scotland, Wales, and Brittany.

The Celts, wherever they settled, divided the year into four quarters, with four festivals to mark their beginnings. February 1 and August 1 were relatively minor feasts, while May 1 and November 1 were the most sacred days of the year. (Curiously, these dates were called witches' sabbaths in the Middle Ages, proof that European witchcraft, where it really existed, was simply the last dying gasp of European paganism.)

To commemorate this division of the year the Celts invented the sun wheel, a circle divided into four parts, quite similar to the equally ancient *swastika*. This symbol remains in the Celtic Cross and can also be detected in the hearth breads of the British Isles.

The oldest of these breads is probably the bannock. Before there were bannocks made of wheat flour there were bannocks made of oats and barley, and special bannocks for each of the traditional feasts. The bannock was mixed quickly, always stirring to the right, as the sun was thought to move, and put on a griddle at the hearth. It was always round, for women in primitive times knew nothing of loaf pans, and always cut into four quarters, forming the ancient symbol. In time such hearth breads also came to be called scones and today the words are almost interchangeable.

1 ½ cups flour

2 tablespoons sugar

1 ¼ teaspoons baking powder

¼ teaspoon baking soda

⅜ teaspoon salt

6 tablespoons butter or margarine

½ cup buttermilk

1. Preheat oven to 425°F.

2. In a large mixing bowl combine flour, sugar, baking powder, baking soda, and salt. Cut in butter with pastry blender or two knives until mixture resembles fine crumbs.

3. Add buttermilk. Mix only until the dry ingredients are moistened. Gather the dough into a ball and press so it holds together.

4. Turn the dough out onto a lightly floured surface. Knead quickly twelve times. Pat the dough into a circle ½ inch thick. Cut the dough into four quarters. Place 1 inch apart on an ungreased baking sheet. Bake 12–15 minutes, or until tops are browned. Serve hot, with butter or margarine, and jam.

Note: *Bannocks or Scones may be baked on a griddle, in the old way, if preferred. The griddle should be preheated, and dusted with flour, not greased. Some experimentation may be needed to regulate the heat so that the Bannocks or Scones are cooked through before becoming too brown. They should be turned only once.*

IRISH SODA BREAD
1 round loaf

In Ireland a hearth bread similar to bannocks is called Irish Soda Bread. It, too, is always marked with a deep cross cut into the dough before it is baked. Modern Irish cooks rationalize the custom as intended to ensure even distribution of heat, or to make the loaf easier to break apart, but really it is the old pagan symbol of long, long ago.

2 ½ cups all-purpose flour

2 tablespoons sugar

1 teaspoon baking soda

1 teaspoon baking powder

½ teaspoon salt

3 tablespoons butter or margarine, softened

½ cup raisins (optional)

1 teaspoon caraway seeds (optional)

¾ cup buttermilk

1. Preheat oven to 375°F. In a large mixing bowl combine flour, sugar, baking soda, baking powder, and salt. Cut in butter with pastry blender or two knives until mixture resembles fine crumbs. Stir in raisins, caraway seeds, and just enough buttermilk so dough leaves side of bowl.

2. Turn dough onto lightly floured surface. Knead until smooth, 1–2 minutes. Shape into round loaf about 6 ½ inches in diameter. Place on greased cookie sheet.

3. With a floured knife, cut a cross about ½ inch deep through top of loaf. Bake until golden brown, 35–45 minutes. Brush with butter or margarine, softened, if desired.

Note: It is not advisable to try to bake Irish Soda Bread on a griddle. In historic times Irish women have always baked soda bread in a heavy, three-legged iron pot called a bastable. Glowing turf (peat) sods are put on top of the close-fitting cover while baking, making the bastable an improvised oven.

HOT CROSS BUNS
24 buns

Hot Cross Buns, too, recall Britain's ancient past. They once must have been part of one of the Celtic spring festivals, for in historic times they were baked only on Good Friday. Well into the nineteenth century hundreds of poor children and frail elderly people would converge on the bakeries at dawn, eager to spend the morning hours selling the buns from large, covered baskets. Their cry was so familiar it became a nursery rhyme,

Hot cross buns!
Hot cross buns!
One a penny, two a penny,
Hot cross buns!
If you have no daughters,
Give them to your sons.

The common folk carefully dried a bun and saved it, for the belief persisted that even a few crumbs from a bread baked on Good Friday would cure any ailment. The crosses, originally cut into the dough, are now usually made with vanilla icing.

1 package active dry yeast
¼ cup warm water (105–115°F)
1 cup lukewarm milk (scalded, then cooled)
⅓ cup sugar
⅓ cup butter or margarine, softened
1 teaspoon salt
1 teaspoon ground cinnamon
¼ teaspoon ground nutmeg
1 egg
1 egg yolk
3¾–4¼ cups all-purpose flour
¾ cup dried currants
1 egg white, slightly beaten
1 tablespoon water

Note: *For vanilla icing, mix 1 cup confectioners' sugar and ½ teaspoon vanilla with enough cream or milk to give a spreading consistency.*

1. In a large mixing bowl dissolve yeast in warm water. Stir in milk, sugar, shortening, salt, cinnamon, nutmeg, egg, egg yolk, and 2 cups of flour. Beat on low speed until smooth. Stir in currants and enough remaining flour to make dough easy to handle.

2. Turn dough onto lightly floured surface; knead until smooth and elastic, about 5 minutes. Place in greased bowl; turn greased side up. Cover; let rise in warm place until double, about 1 ½ hours. (Dough has doubled when two fingers, pressed into it, leave an indentation.)

3. Punch down dough; divide into 4 equal parts. Cut each part into 6 equal pieces. Shape each piece into a ball; place about 2 inches apart on greased cookie sheets. Cover; let rise until double, about 40 minutes.

4. Preheat oven to 375°F. Mix egg white and 1 tablespoon water; brush tops of buns with egg white mixture. Bake until golden brown, about 20 minutes. Cool. Make crosses on buns with icing.

LUSSEKATTER (LUCY CATS)
16 rolls

Across the North Sea the Germanic peoples, too, had their festival breads that have long outlasted their pagan origins. The Germans had a little-known goddess named Berchta, who, like many goddesses, could assume different forms. In one of these forms she was a "white lady," bright, shining, beautiful. In this role Berchta lives on in the Lucia Day celebrations in Sweden. December 13 in the church calendar is the Feast of St. Lucia. The real Lucy or Lucia was a Sicilian Christian who died for her faith early in the fourth century. But the name means light, and Lucy's feast day came at the time of the longest nights of the year. Inevitably the saint's day celebration became mixed with far older pagan customs, and Lucy took on Berchta's identity.

Traditionally, in Sweden, Lucy is represented by the oldest daughter of the family. Before dawn she dressed in white and cautiously placed on her head a crown of lighted candles. Thus arrayed, she went to her parents' bedside and offered them steaming cups of coffee and special breakfast rolls called *Lussekatter* (Lucy cats). Just why the rolls are called cats is an intriguing question. True, the raisins placed in the whirls of sweet bread do look vaguely like cat's eyes, but that alone is not enough to explain the unusual name.

Domestic cats were still a novelty in northern Europe in late pagan times, and were often associated with goddesses, as later they would be associated with witches. Today's Lussekatter, delicious, intricately shaped sweetrolls, unknowingly recall the long-forgotten cats that once were said to be the companions of Berchta-turned-Lucy.

1 package active dry yeast

6 tablespoons warm water (105–115°F)

½ cup lukewarm milk (scalded, then cooled)

1 ½ teaspoons grated orange peel

6 tablespoons sugar

½ teaspoon salt

¼ cup butter or margarine, softened

1 egg

¼ cup finely ground blanched almonds

½ teaspoon ground cardamom

3 ¼ cups flour

Raisins

1 egg yolk

1. Dissolve yeast in warm water in a large mixing bowl. Stir in milk, orange peel, sugar, salt, butter or margarine, egg, almonds, cardamom, and 2 cups of flour. Beat on low speed until smooth. Stir in enough remaining flour to make dough easy to handle.

2. Turn dough onto lightly floured board. Knead until smooth and elastic, about 5 minutes. Place in greased bowl, turning to bring greased side up. Cover and let rise in warm place until double, about 1 ½ hours. (Dough is ready if impression remains when touched).

3. Punch down dough. Turn out and divide in half, then fourths, etc., till 32 equal lumps of dough are obtained. With palm of hand, roll each into a pencil-thin strip, 6–7 inches long. On greased large cookie sheet, cross 2 strips to make an X; curl each end to the right to form a small coil. Press a raisin in center of each coil. Cover and let rise until double (40–50 minutes).

4. Preheat oven to 400°F. Brush buns with 1 egg yolk mixed with 1 tablespoon water. Bake 12–15 minutes or until golden brown. Cool on wire rack.

KUGELHUPF
12–16 servings

Not all European breads and rolls are so ancient—the Kugelhupf dates from only the seventeenth century! It was a time when Austria stood virtually alone, the last outpost of the west, steadfastly resisting the Ottoman Turks. In the summer of 1683 a Turkish army of two hundred thousand men was besieging Vienna. The emperor and his family had fled, but the citizens, courageous and disciplined, were determined to defend their city. The Turkish commander, knowing he did not have guns heavy enough to batter down the city's ancient walls, intended to mine them, opening breaches, and then rushing his troops in for a final assault. The Viennese say that it was a young baker, beginning his day's work as the city slept, who first heard the noise of tunneling and gave the alarm, and the story at least could be true.

At any rate, the city and its walls stood firm, and the Turks were finally driven off by an army raised by the king of Poland. To celebrate the great victory, the bakers of Vienna designed the Turk's head mold, its fluted, elaborate convolutions intended to represent the folds in a sultan's head dress.

Today the mold is used for cakes of various sorts, but originally it was intended only for Kugelhupf (sometimes spelled Kugelhopf or Gugelhupf; literally, "ball head"), a sweet, yeast-raised bread that would eventually become a favorite not only in Austria but also in Germany and Poland and even in France.

1 package active dry yeast

¾ cup warm water (105–115°F)

½ cup sugar

½ teaspoon salt

¼ cup butter or margarine, softened

2 eggs

2 ½ cups flour

½ cup raisins

2 teaspoons grated lemon peel

½ teaspoon vanilla

3 tablespoons fine dry bread crumbs

¼ cup chopped almonds

Confectioners' sugar

1. Dissolve yeast in warm water in a large mixing bowl. Add sugar, salt, butter or margarine, eggs, and 1 ¼ cups of the flour. Blend ½ minute on low speed of electric mixer, scraping bowl constantly. Beat 2 minutes on medium speed. Stir in raisins, lemon peel, and vanilla. Add remaining flour and mix thoroughly. Scrape batter from sides of bowl, cover and let rise in warm place until double, 1 ½–2 hours.

2. With a pastry brush, thoroughly butter a fluted 1 ½-quart Turk's Head Mold, a Bundt pan, or an ovenproof ring mold, making sure all indentations are coated. Dust with dry bread crumbs. Sprinkle bottom of mold with chopped almonds.

3. Stir down batter by beating briskly with a wooden spoon. Spoon carefully into mold. Let rise until almost double, about 1 hour.

4. Preheat oven to 350°F. Bake about 35–40 minutes, or until Kugelhupf is light golden brown. Cool 10 minutes in pan. Turn out onto a cake rack to finish cooling. Dust lightly with confectioners' sugar before serving.

SALLY LUNNS
12 buns

Bath, in the south of England, became a fashionable spa in the eighteenth century. Queen Anne, always in ill health, went in 1702 to "take the waters" at the old Roman town, and the royal visit set off a wave of popularity. Everything from Bath was fashionable: Bath olivers (a commercially made biscuit or cracker named for Dr. William Oliver, a Bath physician who founded what is now the Royal National Hospital for Rheumatic Diseases), Bath buns, and Sally Lunns. It is the last of these, light little tea buns, that became the best known, both in Britain and in the American colonies.

According to British tradition, Sally Lunn was a baker who kept a shop in Lilliput Alley and "cried" her wares in the streets. A not-too-reliable writer who lived a half century later states this, and adds that a baker named Delmar bought the recipe and made his fortune with the buns.

Alas for legend, various early spellings for the bread include such distinctly French-derived versions as Soli lume, Solileme, and Soel Leme, and in France a virtually identical brioche-style bread is called Solilem or Solimeme. Whatever their origins, Sally Lunns did become a traditional English treat. Carlyle and Dickens both mention them in their writings and Thackeray slyly recalls a certain meal that was made up of "green tea, scandal, hot Sally Lunns, and a little novel reading."

1 package active dry yeast

¼ cup warm water (105–115°F)

½ cup lukewarm milk (scalded, then cooled)

¼ cup sugar

1 teaspoon salt

1 egg

¼ cup butter or margarine, softened

2 ¼ cups flour

1. Dissolve yeast in warm water in large mixing bowl. Stir in milk, sugar, and salt. Add egg, butter or margarine, and 1 cup of flour.

2. Beat on low speed, scraping bowl constantly, 30 seconds. Beat on medium speed, scraping bowl occasionally, 2 minutes. Stir in remaining flour. Scrape batter from side of bowl. Cover and let rise in warm place (85°F) until double in bulk (about 1 ¾ hours).

3. Stir down batter by beating about 25 strokes with a large spoon. Drop spoonfuls into 12 well-greased muffin cups, dividing evenly. Let rise until dough rounds slightly above tops of cups (24–30 minutes).

4. Preheat oven to 400°F. Bake buns 12–15 minutes or until tops are browned. Serve hot with butter or margarine.

SALLY LUNN, AMERICAN STYLE
1 10-inch loaf

Sally Lunn became a favorite, too, in the southern colonies, and it was only in America that it became tall, spectacular, and almost cake-like.

2 packages active dry yeast
½ cup warm water (105–115°F)
1 ½ cups lukewarm milk (scalded, then cooled)
2 tablespoons sugar
1 ½ teaspoons salt
2 eggs
¼ cup butter or margarine, softened
5 ½ cups flour

1. Dissolve yeast in warm water in large mixing bowl. Stir in milk, sugar, and salt. Add eggs, butter or margarine, and 2 cups of flour.
2. Beat on low speed, scraping bowl constantly, 30 seconds. Beat on medium speed, scraping bowl occasionally, 2 minutes. Stir in remaining flour. Scrape batter from side of bowl. Cover and let rise in warm place (85°F) until very light (about 1 hour).
3. Stir down batter by beating about 25 strokes with a large spoon. Pour into well-greased 10-inch tube pan. Let rise to within 1 inch of top of pan (45 minutes).
4. Preheat oven to 350°F. Bake 45–50 minutes, until golden brown and crusty. Slice into wedges and serve hot, with butter or margarine.

BATH BUNS
24 buns

Bath's other specialty, the famed buns, never caught on in the colonies, but they enjoyed tremendous popularity all over England. Then in the late nineteenth and early twentieth centuries the Bath Bun got a reputation for stodginess. The commercial, mass-produced rolls beloved by schoolboys were a bit too large and substantial for the tastes of most adults. But Bath Buns made properly, at home or by a good neighborhood bakery, are light and delectable little creations, a treat for either brunch or tea.

Make dough as for Hot Cross Buns (page 7), omitting the cinnamon and nutmeg and substituting *¾ cup diced candied lemon peel*, finely chopped, for the currants. Bake at 400°F 15–20 minutes. While buns are baking, warm *½ cup sugar* with *¼ cup milk* until sugar is melted. After buns have been taken from the oven, use a pastry brush to coat the tops with the warm sugar mixture. Sprinkle on *granulated* sugar generously and put back into oven for a minute or two, until sugar begins to melt and glaze. Allow to cool.

CHELSEA BUNS
18 buns

London's bakers, jealous of Bath's reputation, countered with the Chelsea Bun. Various bakers made the buns and hawked them in the streets, but the real home of the Chelsea Bun was the Old Original Royal Bun House, at the end of Pimlico Road. The House, which was really both shop and restaurant combined, stood for almost 150 years before being torn down in 1839 and replaced with another that stood until 1888. For four generations the Hand family maintained the Royal Bun House, and it did, indeed, enjoy royal patronage.

Make dough as for Hot Cross Buns (page 7), omitting cinnamon, nutmeg, and currants. After dough has risen, punch down and roll out into an oblong 9 inches by 18 inches. Spread with *2 tablespoons softened butter or margarine.* Sprinkle with *½ cup sugar and 1 cup dried currants.* Roll up tightly, beginning at wide side. Seal well by pinching edges of roll together. Stretch to make roll even. Cut into 1-inch slices. Place well apart on a greased cookie sheet. Cover and let rise until double in bulk (35–40 minutes). Preheat oven to 375°F. Bake 25–30 minutes, until golden brown and completely baked through. Allow to cool and then drizzle with icing. For icing, mix *2 cups confectioners' sugar* and *½ teaspoon vanilla* with enough *milk* or *cream* to give a spreading consistency.

JOHNNYCAKE
8–10 servings

In the meantime, while the English drank their tea and enjoyed their favorite delicacies, a whole new kind of breadmaking was being invented in the American colonies.

Often close to starvation, the earliest colonists learned to depend on Indian corn or maize, so closely identified with the Indians that cornmeal was often just spoken of as "Injun," a colloquialism now remembered only in Indian pudding. If the cornmeal itself was "Injun," the bread might be called pone, ashcake, hoecake, or Johnnycake. It is the latter term, of course, that is best known today.

It has often been stated that Johnnycake is a corruption of journeycake, cakes baked especially for travelers, but that seems most unlikely. Cornbread in any form is notoriously crumbly, a poor choice for carrying about, and besides, corn bread was everyday fare, unceasing and everlasting, not a specialty to be baked for those starting out on a journey. Another suggestion is that the word began as Shawneecake and gradually slurred into Johnnycake. But modern scholars have also found *joniken*, an American Indian word meaning corn cake, and there seems little doubt that it was adopted by the early settlers and became first jonnycake and then Johnnycake.

¼ cup butter, margarine, or bacon drippings

1 cup yellow cornmeal

1 cup flour

2–4 tablespoons sugar (optional)

4 teaspoons baking powder

½ teaspoon salt

1 cup milk

1 egg, beaten

1. Preheat oven to 400°F. Place butter, margarine, or bacon drippings in an 8- or 9-inch square baking pan or 10-inch oven-

proof skillet and melt in oven; tilt pan to coat bottom evenly, and set aside.

2. Combine dry ingredients in a large bowl. Add milk, beaten egg, and reserved melted shortening. Mix with a spoon just until blended, then beat vigorously for 30 seconds.

3. Pour into pan. Bake 20–25 minutes or until golden brown and wooden pick inserted in center comes out clean. Serve hot, with butter or margarine.

Note: Northerners traditionally put sugar in their Johnnycake; Southerners emphatically do not!

BOSTON BROWN BREAD
4 small loaves

Cornmeal may have saved the colonists' lives, but the New Eng-landers never particularly liked it. They could not use it for yeast breads, for one thing, and besides, they got tired of it. As times improved they mixed it with rye flour, for rye was easier to grow than wheat, creating "rye 'n Injun." Then, when the wheat crops became more abundant, they used all three flours to create Boston Brown Bread. When the thrifty Puritan women of Massachusetts, who would waste nothing, discovered that dry bread crumbs could be substituted for some of the flour, the popularity of the bread was secure. It takes its name, of course, from Boston, the city that was the heart of the Massachusetts Bay Colony from the earliest times.

1 cup rye flour
1 cup yellow cornmeal
1 cup whole wheat flour
2 teaspoons baking soda
1 cup seedless raisins (optional)
2 cups sour milk or buttermilk
¾ cup molasses

1. Thoroughly grease 4 empty 16-ounce tin cans.
2. Combine rye flour, cornmeal, whole wheat flour, and soda in a large bowl. Mix well. Stir in raisins, if used. Stir in milk and molasses.
3. Divide bread batter equally between the cans. Cover cans tightly with aluminum foil. Set on rack in heavy kettle or steamer. Pour boiling water into pan to within 1 inch of top of cans. Place a heavy weight on top of cans to prevent them from tipping over. Cover kettle.
4. Steam 2 hours, keeping water at the simmering stage. Add hot water if needed. Remove cans from water. Remove foil. Place in a slow oven (300°F) 15 minutes to dry loaves. Cool bread in cans 5 minutes. Remove from cans and finish cooling on a wire rack.

PARKER HOUSE ROLLS
24 rolls

Boston is also the home of the Parker House Roll, a creamy-white yeast roll with a creased center. It was created at the Parker House Hotel in Boston soon after its opening in 1855 by the kitchen's head baker, a German immigrant named Ward. One story holds that Ward, angry at a guest's belligerence, merely threw some rolls into a pan, clenching each one in his fist as he did so. In another version of the tale, he was upset over a quarrel with his sweetheart. Whatever the circumstances, he had come up with a light, puffy little bun that would make his employer, Harvey Parker, famous.

1 package active dry yeast	1 teaspoon salt
¼ cup warm water (105–115°F)	1 egg
¾ cup lukewarm milk (scalded, then cooled)	¼ cup shortening, butter, or margarine, softened
¼ cup sugar	3 ½–3 ¾ cups flour

1. Dissolve yeast in warm water in a large mixing bowl. Stir in milk, sugar, salt, egg, shortening, and 2 cups of the flour. Beat on low speed until smooth. Stir in enough remaining flour to make dough easy to handle.

2. Turn dough onto lightly floured board. Knead until smooth and elastic, about 5 minutes. Place in greased bowl, turning once to bring the greased side up. Cover and let rise in a warm place until double, about 1 ½–2 hours. (Dough is ready if impression remains when touched lightly with two fingers.)

3. Punch down dough and let rest a few minutes. Roll out dough to ¼-inch thickness. Cut into 3-inch circles with a cookie cutter or water glass. Brush with melted butter.

4. Make a crease slightly off center across each circle with handle of dinner knife. Fold so top half slightly overlaps bottom half. Press edges together firmly to seal. Place about 1 inch apart on an ungreased cookie sheet. Cover and let rise until double (20–30 minutes) before baking. Preheat oven to 400°F. Bake 15–20 minutes or until golden brown.

PHILADELPHIA STICKY BUNS
15 buns

But if Boston can claim two famous breads, Philadelphia can boast of at least one. Somewhere along the way an anonymous baker in the old Quaker city created Philadelphia sticky buns. Often known in other parts of the country as caramel buns, they are made like an upside down cake and then flipped over, allowing the gooey syrup to trickle down the sides and into the crevices of the simple roll.

1 package active dry yeast
¼ cup warm water (105–115°F)
¼ cup lukewarm milk (scalded, then cooled)
¼ cup sugar
½ teaspoon salt
1 egg
¾ cup butter or margarine, divided
2 ¼–2 ½ cups flour
½ cup brown sugar

1. Dissolve yeast in warm water. Stir in milk, sugar, salt, egg, ¼ cup butter or margarine, softened, and 1 ¼ cups flour. Beat on low speed until smooth. Stir in enough remaining flour to make dough easy to handle.

2. Turn dough onto lightly floured board. Knead until smooth and elastic, about 5 minutes. Place in a greased bowl, turning once to bring the greased side up. Cover and let rise in a warm place until double, about 1 ½ hours. (Dough is ready if impression remains when touched lightly with two fingers.)

3. While dough is rising, melt remaining ½ cup butter or margarine in a 9 by 13-inch baking pan. Sprinkle ½ cup brown sugar over butter or margarine.

4. When dough is ready, punch down and roll out into a rectangle 15 by 9 inches. Roll up, beginning at a wide side, to make a roll 15 inches long. Pinch edge of dough into roll to seal well. Stretch roll to make even. Cut roll into 15 slices. Place slightly apart in prepared pan. Let rise until double, about 40 minutes.

5. Preheat oven to 375°F. Bake 25–30 minutes, or until golden brown. Remove from oven and place a large tray over pan. Holding tray and pan *firmly* together, turn upside down. Let remain a minute so caramel drizzles down over rolls.

GRAHAM GEMS
9 medium muffins

America prospered in the first half of the nineteenth century. Food was cheap and, for all but the poorest of the urban poor, abundant. Alarmed by the lavish meals and heavy eating of the period, a few reformers called for simplicity. One of these prophets was Sylvester Graham.

It was an era of reform, and Graham found a ready audience in a society concerned with abolition, temperance, women's rights, and free public education. A former minister, he now preached a gospel of plain living, cold baths, and—most important of all—coarse, unrefined whole wheat bread. Graham's rhetoric was far from temperate—he insisted that condiments such as catsup and mustard could cause insanity—but he did attract a number of followers. Whole wheat flour became Graham flour; Graham crackers were invented; and one recipe, for Graham gems or muffins, proved so popular that it was included in the first edition of Fannie Farmer's celebrated *Boston Cooking-School Cook Book*.

Graham's message enjoyed a brief vogue and then was quickly forgotten; he influenced the breakfast food industry that was beginning in Battle Creek, Michigan, but for the most part he was dismissed as a faddist. Only recently has a new interest in both natural foods and fiber caused nutritionists to look back at his often polemical writings with new respect.

2 cups whole wheat flour

⅓ cup sugar

3 teaspoons baking powder

1 teaspoon salt

¾ cup milk

½ cup vegetable oil

1 egg

1. Preheat oven to 400°F. Grease bottoms, sides, and rims of 9 medium muffin cups.
2. In a bowl, thoroughly mix flour, sugar, baking powder, and salt. In a separate large bowl, beat milk, oil, and egg.
3. Add flour mixture to liquids, all at once, stirring just until flour is moistened. Do not overmix.
4. Divide batter among muffin cups. Bake until golden brown, 18–20 minutes. Immediately remove from pan. Serve hot, with butter or margarine.

KAISER ROLLS
16 rolls

Over twenty million immigrants came to the United States in the half century following the Civil War. Each group brought the foods of its homeland to the rapidly growing nation, and of course this included breads and rolls, several with unusual names.

The Kaiser roll was created in Vienna and brought to America by Austrian bakers. It takes its name from the German *kaiser*, "emperor," which comes from the Latin Caesar, referring to the appearance of the roll, which does indeed resemble the high, ornate, velvet-filled crowns of the nineteenth-century monarchs.

1 package active dry yeast
1 cup warm water (105–115°F)
1 ½ teaspoons salt
1 tablespoon hydrogenated shortening
3 ½–3 ¾ cups flour

1. Dissolve yeast in warm water in a large mixing bowl. Add salt, shortening, and 1 cup of the flour. Mix. Continue to add flour and mix, first with a spoon and then by hand, till dough begins to leave the sides of the bowl. Turn out onto a lightly floured board.
2. Knead until the dough is smooth and elastic, and does not stick to the board. Place the dough in a greased bowl, turning once to bring the greased side up. Cover and let rise in a warm place (80–85°F) until double in bulk, about 1–1 ½ hours. (Dough has doubled when two fingers, pressed into it, leave an indentation.)
3. Punch down and then let rise again until almost double, 30–45 minutes. Turn out and divide into 16 equal parts. Form each into a little bun. Allow to relax for a few minutes, then flatten to ⅜ inch thick.

Note: *Kaiser rolls, unless you have a Viennese baker by your side, are tricky. If you are dexterous and lucky, your first batch may be beautiful. If you are not so dexterous or lucky, they may not be beautiful, but they will be crusty and delicious.*

4. Hold the flattened dough in the left hand, with the thumb near the center. With the right thumb, fold a section of dough back into the center of the bun. Repeat four times, as the left hand turns the dough clockwise. Each fold of dough should overlap, and the center should remain unbroken. The last fold is pressed into the center of the roll, where the left thumb was.

5. Allow the rolls to rise on a greased baking sheet, *upside down*, for one hour. Preheat oven to 425°F. With a spatula carefully turn rolls right side up and use a pastry brush to brush with cold water.

6. Bake rolls for 10 minutes. Again brush gently with cold water and bake 10–15 minutes more, until golden and crusty.

BISMARCKS
24 doughnuts

German immigrants to America brought their yeast-raised, jelly-filled doughnuts. Back home in Germany they had begun as *Fastnachkuchen*, a treat made on Shrove Tuesday, the day before Ash Wednesday, to feast before the coming fast and to use up the fats that would not be allowed during Lent. Later, for reasons unknown, they began to be called *Berliners*.

In the United States they first appeared in German bakeries and quickly acquired a new name, as Americans associated everything German with Otto von Bismarck (1815–1898), the "Iron Chancellor," who dominated German politics for almost thirty years. They remain an odd memorial to the man who told the German people they must choose between "guns and butter."

1 package active dry yeast

¼ cup warm water (105–115°F)

¾ cup lukewarm milk (scalded, then cooled)

¼ cup sugar

1 teaspoon salt

1 egg

¼ cup hydrogenated shortening

3 ½–3 ¾ cups flour

Vegetable oil

1 ½ cups jelly or jam

Additional sugar

1. Dissolve yeast in warm water. Stir in milk, ¼ cup sugar, salt, egg, shortening, and 2 cups of flour. Beat on low speed until smooth. Stir in enough remaining flour to make dough easy to handle.

2. Turn dough onto lightly floured board. Knead until smooth and elastic, about 5 minutes. Place in greased bowl, turning greased side up. Cover and let rise in a warm place until double, about 1 ½ hours. Punch down dough and let rise again until almost double, about 30 minutes.

Note: *If preferred, roll dough ½-inch thick and fry without filling. When cool, cut a short slit in the side of each fried ball through to the center. Thrust a teaspoonful of jelly or jam into the center and close slit tightly. Roll in sugar.*

3. Roll dough to ¼-inch thickness. Cut into 4 dozen 3-inch rounds. Place a generous teaspoonful of jelly or jam on top of half of the dough circles. Top with remaining halves, pinching edges closed and sealing with water or egg white. Let rise for 40 minutes or until doubled in bulk. Check to make sure edges have stayed sealed, and carefully repinch where necessary.

4. Heat vegetable oil (3 or 4 inches deep) to 375°F in deep fat fryer or kettle. Lift Bismarcks with a spatula and lower into hot fat, a few at a time. Do not crowd. Fry 2–3 minutes or until golden brown on both sides, turning once. Remove with a slotted spoon and drain on paper towels. While warm, roll in sugar.

CHALLAH
1 loaf

Challah (sometimes spelled "hallah") means sacrifice and this Jewish bread, made throughout Europe, recalls the twelve sacrificial loaves placed on the high altar in Jerusalem, long before its destruction. The white loaves are always braided for the sabbath, in three, four, six, or even more strands, and usually two are made, one to be eaten warm on Friday evening, the other to be saved for the following day. But at Rosh Hashanah the bread is baked as a coiled round loaf, to represent the completeness of the year and the hope that the New Year will be rounded out and perfect.

Variation: To form a braid, as for the sabbath, divide dough into three or four parts and form each part into a long rope. Pinch all ropes together at one end and braid. Bake as directed, putting challah on a cookie sheet oiled and sprinkled with cornmeal.

1 package active dry yeast	1 egg
¼ cup warm water (105–115°F)	1 tablespoon hydrogenated shortening
½ cup lukewarm water	2 ½–2 ¾ cups flour
1 tablespoon sugar	1 egg yolk
1 teaspoon salt	2 tablespoons cold water

1. Dissolve yeast in warm water. Stir in lukewarm water, sugar, salt, 1 egg, shortening, and 1 ¼ cups of the flour. Beat on low speed until smooth. Stir in enough remaining flour to make dough easy to handle.

2. Turn dough onto lightly floured board. Knead until smooth and elastic, about 5 minutes. Round up dough in greased bowl, turning to bring greased side up. Cover. Let rise in warm place until double, 1 ½–2 hours.

3. Punch down dough. To shape for Rosh Hashanah (round challah): Form dough into a large rope, 12–15 inches long and several inches thick, with tapered ends. Starting in the center, coil the rope in concentric circles until a large snail-like shape is created. Seal ends. Oil a 9-inch round cake pan and sprinkle it generously with cornmeal. Place the challah in the prepared pan, cover, and let rise until double, about 40–50 minutes.

4. Preheat oven to 375°F. Beat egg yolk and cold water until blended. Brush over bread. Bake 25–30 minutes, or until golden brown.

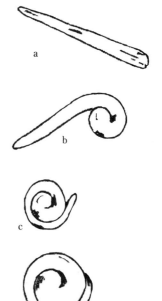

CHAPTER 2

SANDWICHES

The sandwich is named for John Montagu, fourth Earl of Sandwich and an inveterate gambler. The word was coined in 1762, when Sandwich spent twenty-four hours straight at a gaming table, ordering his servants to bring him food he could hold in one hand so as not to interrupt the game.

Although he held several posts in the various governments formed by King George III, and by most accounts proved himself an able administrator, John Montagu faced criticism for corrupt practices in office. Gambling was only one of his many vices, but despite his own notable decadence he led the charges of obscenity against the journalist and politician John Wilkes, champion of the common man, turning viciously on his erstwhile friend. Their hatred provoked an exchange unique in the annals of Parliament: Sandwich, in a fit of anger, predicted that Wilkes would die "either on the gallows or of the pox," and Wilkes immediately replied, "That depends, my lord, on whether I embrace your principles or your mistress."

In 1771 Sandwich resumed the post of first lord of the admiralty, his second extended tour of duty in this office. Although he faced bitter criticism for the unprepared state of the navy during the American Revolution, he did have a real interest in exploration and sponsored Captain James Cook's three voyages to the South Pacific. In 1778, on his last voyage, Cook named the Sandwich Islands (now Hawaii) for his patron.

Islands in the far-off Pacific, however, were not what made Sandwich's name a household word, but rather his simple food innovation. Incidentally, the fact that his name became attached to the meal-in-one-hand does not mean that his "invention" was truly original. For centuries, farmers going to the fields had carried a lunch of cheese between two slices of bread. Sandwich merely made the idea fashionable among the upper classes. Undoubtedly it was his notoriety that gave the combination a name and an identity, and nowhere did it become more popular than in the United States.

America's favorite sandwich, of course, is the hamburger, and numerous cookery experts have stated, over and over again, that it is a truly homegrown innovation unknown in Germany. But the plain fact of the matter is that Germany does have and always has had a hamburger of its own, predating the American version. Just as Frankfurt has the frankfurter and Vienna the wiener (short for Wienerwurst), Hamburg's special sausage was the hamburger, a large, plain sausage, today made of coarsely ground pork but formerly made of coarse ground beef. Moreover, German street vendors have always sold sausages wrapped in buns, usually with a dab of sharp mustard to complement the spicy sausage. When the two traditions are considered together, it becomes obvious that around the turn of the century, when the German community in the United States was still a large and distinct ethnic group, the German hamburger was easily transformed into the American hamburger.

Similarly, it is not really surprising that Hamburg steak appears in print well ahead of the now better-known burger on a bun. The old German port of Hamburg, noted for its eel soup, also has a ground beef specialty, today called simply *Deutsches Beefsteak* (in French, *Bifteck à la Hambourgeoise*), ground beef made into patties, fried, and served with fried onions.

It has been suggested that the hamburger first gained national recognition at the St. Louis World's Fair held in 1904. So many foods are said to have been invented at the fair that it would seem its only purpose was to introduce new dishes to the American public. Still, there were a great many Germans living in St. Louis and many of the concessionaires were no doubt of German descent. Twelve million people visited the Exposition; there is at least a possibility that many of them went home talking about a new sandwich called the hamburger.

As Americans began to take to the roads in newly affordable automobiles, the "hamburger stand" became a national institution. Not even the Depression could dim enthusiasm for the hamburger because it was, after all, one of the cheapest meals that could be purchased away from home. Variations came, and usually went, but one proved durable: the cheeseburger appeared in the 1930s and has steadfastly maintained its popularity.

The sausages sold by German street vendors became a part of American life in yet another way. They were introduced to the ball parks by Harry Stevens, a well-known concessionaire, in 1900. It was a cold April day, and the crowd at New York City's Polo Grounds, home of the New York Giants, had no interest in ice cream, so Stevens sent out for sausages and buns. They went over well, and he continued to supply them at later games, telling his vendors to call them "hot dachshund sausages," and to yell "get 'em while they're hot." Inevitably, the name was shortened to "hot dogs."

The dachshund bit referred to the long, skinny shape of the sausages, which resembled the newly introduced canine breed from Germany; the sausages were still considered a German food. Perhaps, too, Stevens wanted to discredit a persistent rumor by turning it into a joke. The story had circulated for years that the cheap sausages sold in the streets contained dog meat.

Tad Dorgan, sports cartoonist for *The New York Evening Journal*, began to draw cartoon characters of the sausages, giving them faces, tails, and feet. His immensely popular work soon had the whole nation clamoring for "hot dogs."

America's fascination with sandwiches of all sorts has continued unabated. From the quite elegant club sandwich to the peanut butter and jelly beloved of small children to the ham and cheese on rye that finds its way into countless brown bags and lunch buckets, we are a nation of sandwich lovers. When noontime comes and we pause to renew our energy, many more times than not we turn to the sandwich, simple, available, and appetizing.

CONEY ISLANDS
8 sandwiches

The vendors at New York's famed Coney Island, sensitive to the charge that cheap sausages contained dog meat, disliked the term hot dog and refused to use it. Instead they called their wieners encased in rolls "Red Hots," or "Coney Islands." The New York–style Coney Island, traditionally served with a spicy meat sauce, was the forerunner of the now ubiquitous chili dog.

¼ pound ground beef	1 ½ teaspoons chili powder
¼ cup chopped onion	½ teaspoon salt
¼ cup water	8 wieners
1 clove garlic, minced	8 wiener buns, warmed
1 can (8 ounces) tomato sauce	Chopped onion for garnish (optional)

1. In a heavy skillet, over low heat, cook ground beef and onion, stirring with a fork until beef begins to brown and onion is tender. Pour off all fat.
2. Mix in water, garlic, tomato sauce, chili powder, and salt. Simmer, uncovered, 10 minutes, or until sauce is thick.
3. Meanwhile, place wieners in a saucepan, cover with cold water, bring to a boil, and simmer for 5 minutes. Place wieners in warmed buns and top with hot sauce. Top with additional raw onion if desired.

SLOPPY JOES
4 servings

Sloppy Joes, yet another variation on the theme of ground beef on a bun, take their name either from the large, bulky sweaters popular in the early 1940s or from the occasional use of "sloppy Joe," like the better-known "greasy spoon," as a name for a far-from-elegant eatery. The delicious, but rather messy, sandwich has inspired other versions, such as the Sloppy Tom (ground turkey, usually in a sauce other than tomato) and the Sloppy José (ground beef in a chili-flavored sauce) but none has proven as long-lasting as the original sweet and spicy Sloppy Joe.

1 pound ground beef
½ cup chopped onion
½ cup chopped green pepper
1 can (6 ounces) tomato paste
¾ cup water
⅓ cup barbecue sauce
4 hamburger buns, split

1. In a heavy skillet, over low heat, cook ground beef, onion, and green pepper, stirring with fork and breaking up the ground beef, until beef begins to brown and onion is tender. Pour off all fat.
2. Mix in tomato paste, water, and barbecue sauce. Simmer over low heat, stirring constantly, 10 minutes or until mixture is thick. (Mixture must be watched carefully, as it burns easily.)
3. Spoon over bottom halves of 4 buns; cover with top halves, or serve open-faced.

DENVER SANDWICH
4 sandwiches

The origins of the Denver or Western Sandwich are obscure. Certainly the Denver or Western Omelet preceded the sandwich of the same name, but little beyond that can be said with certainty. Students of culinary lore have suggested that many of the cooks at the ranches and logging camps of the Old West were Chinese, and that the mixture closely resembles Egg Foo Yong. On the other hand, it is also very like the flat, unfolded omelets or frittatas of Spain and southern France. (The name omelet itself is of somewhat obscure origin, and has undergone countless variations in spelling, some almost unrecognizable; it probably comes from the French word *alemette* or *alumelle* (literally "thin plate"), reflecting the omelet's thin, flat shape, but a Latin origin has also been suggested, from the classic Roman dish *ova mellita*, beaten eggs cooked with honey on a flat clay dish.)

Men from all over the world, and some adventurous women as well, poured into the American West with each loudly heralded gold and silver strike, so international culinary influences abounded. At any rate, whatever its origin, the Denver is an excellent sandwich.

Butter or margarine
¼ cup chopped onion
¼ cup chopped green pepper
4 eggs
½ cup chopped ham
8 slices bread

1. In heavy skillet, melt 2 tablespoons butter or margarine. Add onion and green pepper and cook over low heat, stirring until onion is tender. Beat eggs and add ham.
2. Pour egg mixture into skillet. Cook over low heat until set. Cut into four wedges and turn. Brown slightly. While eggs cook, toast and butter bread slices. Serve wedges of egg mixture between slices of buttered toast.

REUBEN SANDWICH
6 sandwiches

The Reuben is one of America's most popular sandwiches, but its history has caused a considerable amount of controversy. Most New Yorkers (and some dictionaries) take for granted that its name was derived from the once famed but now defunct Manhattan institution, Reuben's Restaurant and Delicatessen. A number of versions of the story exist. According to one of these, the now famous combination was originally the handiwork of William Hamerly, businessman and bachelor cook, who is said to have first made the sandwich in the 1950s and named it for Arnold Reuben, founder of the restaurant, to honor him for his many charitable endeavors.

But Arnold Reuben, Jr., the son of the restaurant's founder, believes that the sandwich was first made "in 1927 or 1928" by one of the chefs who, telling him he ate too many hamburgers, promised to make him a "really good sandwich."

To further complicate matters, Patricia B. Taylor, daughter of the restaurant's founder, remembers that her father made the first Reuben in 1914. She described the incident to Craig Claiborne of the *New York Times.*

> Late one evening a leading lady of Charlie Chaplin's came into the restaurant and said, "Reuben, make me a sandwich, make it a combination, I'm so hungry I could eat a brick." He took a loaf of rye bread, cut two slices on the bias and stacked one piece with sliced Virginia ham, roast turkey, and imported Swiss cheese, topped off with coleslaw and lots of Reuben's special Russian dressing and the second slice of bread. (The bias cut bread made his sandwiches a sandwich and a half).
>
> He served it to the lady who said, "Gee, Reuben, this is the best sandwich I ever ate, you ought to call it an Annette Seelos Special." To which he replied, "Like hell I will, I'll call it a Reuben's Special." (*Craig Claiborne's* The New York Times *Food Encyclopedia*, p. 365)

There is no reason to doubt Taylor's recollections, but it should be noted that the sandwich she described is *not*, by any stretch of the imagination, the Reuben sandwich of today.

James Beard, writing many years later, recalled that the first Reubens he ate, when the deli was at Madison Avenue and 59th Street, "were not toasted. They were made with corned beef, Swiss cheese, cole slaw, and Russian dressing on pumpernickel, and I think sometimes there was a slice of turkey breast, too" *(Beard on Food*, p. 206).

There is yet another school of thought that totally ignores the New York claims and insists that the Reuben was created sometime between 1920 and 1935 by Reuben Kay, a wholesale grocer in Omaha, Nebraska. Kay belonged to a weekly poker group whose members apparently enjoyed fixing their own sandwiches every bit as much as they enjoyed the cards. One of the players, a man named Schimmel, operated the Blackstone Hotel in Omaha. Either he or his son put the "Reuben" on the hotel menu, and there it stayed until 1956, when Fern Snider, a waitress at the hotel, entered the combination of corned beef, sauerkraut, and Swiss cheese on rye in the National Sandwich Contest held that year. The Reuben won first place and almost immediate national fame.

What we seem to have here is not an attempt on anyone's part to deceive, but a number of recollections of quite an array of different sandwiches. The New York Reuben was constantly creating and naming sandwiches. Damon Runyon noted that they were "regular productions, not just slabs of bread with things between them. For years it has been Arnold's custom to apply to these masterpieces of the sandwich architect's skill the names of persons of more or less notoriety in our fair city" (quoted by Claiborne, p. 365). What was the Reuben's Special in 1914 might have been quite different than the Reuben of the 1920s or the Reuben of the 1950s. And evidently two quite different Reuben sandwiches were evolving in different cities during approximately the same years. Only when the Nebraska Reuben became known from coast to coast did the identities fuse. Curiously, the companion sandwich now known as the Rachel (from the old song, "Reuben and Rachel") is very much like the earlier New York version.

Note: *The chili sauce referred to here is a sweet tomato relish, more robust than ketchup and usually commercially prepared. It does not contain chili peppers or chili powder. Ketchup can be substituted if preferred.*

½ cup mayonnaise or salad dressing

2 tablespoons chili sauce (see note)

12 slices rye bread or pumpernickel

½ pound Swiss cheese, sliced

½ pound cooked corned beef, thinly sliced

1 can (16 ounces) sauerkraut, chilled and drained

Butter or margarine (optional)

1. In small bowl, mix mayonnaise or salad dressing and chili sauce. Spread on 6 slices of bread. Arrange cheese, corned beef, and sauerkraut on spread slices. Top with remaining bread.
2. If desired, butter both sides of the finished sandwiches and grill.

Variation: *For Rachel Sandwiches, omit sauerkraut and substitute 1 ½ cups cole slaw. Do not grill.*

SOUPS & SALADS

CHAPTER 3

SOUPS

Soup is as old as the first cooking pot. In ancient times, with food often scarce, any available scraps of meat went into the pot, along with odds and ends of vegetables, and not a drop of the broth was wasted.

Soup remained the recourse of poor people, for it made a little food go a long way, and gave a comforting sense of fullness at the end of a long day. A widespread acceptance of the idea that the evening meal consisted primarily of broth shows in the fact that the Germanic words sip, sop, soup, and supper are all related.

As open fires gave way to fireplaces, cooks could hang kettles from cranes on the side. Soon they discovered that broth or stew kept at almost the simmering point resisted spoiling, and the *pot au feu* (pot at the fire) was born. Anything and everything went into it—bones, meat scraps, bits of vegetables; nothing was wasted, and when evening came supper was ready. Only at the beginning of Lent did the soup kettle get emptied. Then it had to be dumped and scrubbed, for no meat or fat could be used during the fast.

During the Middle Ages monasteries gave food and shelter to travelers. They, too, depended on great soup kettles. If there were many to be fed, water could be added, and if there were few, then some remained in the pot for another day.

The first accompaniment for soup was bread, and if it was

hard or dry at least it could be dipped into the broth and softened. The army biscuits and sea biscuits or hard tack supplied
as standard rations to soldiers and sailors were so hard as to be
inedible unless they were "dunked." In fact, the men complained
constantly that the biscuits were not porous enough.

Gradually these uninspiring prototypes evolved into flat, hard,
almost indestructible wafers that continued to be called biscuits
in England but came to be known as crackers in the American
colonies. The word is imitative of the "cracking" sound made
when the wafer is broken. In time these unleavened crackers came
to be called common crackers, though today they seem uncom-
mon enough to qualify as a specialty item requiring a search,
even in large supermarkets. Their place has been taken by the
soda cracker, introduced late in the nineteenth century.

Curiously, two other popular items in the present-day lexicon
of crisp and crunchy tidbits to accompany soup both recall the
same time and place, and even the same family. César Ritz, the
noted *hôtelier*, and Auguste Escoffier, the great chef, first became
partners at the Grand Hotel in Monte Carlo. Together they
moved to London in 1890 to take charge of the Savoy, then nine
years later they again moved together to the equally luxurious
Carlton Hotel.

Escoffier, alone in London (he never learned to speak English),
became a great friend of the Ritz family. One day Marie Louise,
César's young wife, complained to Escoffier that she could never
get a piece of toast that was crisp enough. Escoffier took a piece
of bread, toasted it, then split it and toasted the cut sides again.
Marie Louise was delighted; Escoffier smiled and said he would
name it Toast Marie in her honor. But Marie Louise was a true
hôtelier's wife. She would not hear of the idea, instead telling
Escoffier that he must wait and name it for someone famous.
Later Escoffier recommended it to Nellie Melba, the opera
singer for whom he had created Peach Melba, and named it
Melba Toast.

César Ritz, who already owned a small hotel in Paris, went on to build the Ritz Hotel in Piccadilly, which opened in 1906. Although his health failed a few years later, his wife and sons remained in the hotel business, opening a string of elite hotels in leading cities worldwide. The family name became a common noun "ritz," and a slangier adjective, "ritzy," both meaning sumptuous and elegant. The Nabisco Company, introducing a new cracker in 1934, named it the Ritz Cracker, even though it actually had nothing to do with the hotels.

But to return to the main subject of this chapter, soup of the evening, beautiful soup (to quote Lewis Carroll's Mock Turtle) is probably the most infinitely varied of the world's foods, since ingredients depend on what is at hand, and no two pots can ever be quite the same. All have in common, however, a liquid base, usually a stock made from water to which has been added vegetables, meat, poultry, or seafood, although milk, cream, and legumes can all substitute for or contribute to the basic stock components. The consistency can range from thin, clear broth or *bouillon* (from *bouillir*, to boil) to thick pottage (or *potage* in French); the texture can vary from strained or pureed to chunky, from clear broth swimming with noodles and bits of vegetables and meats to heavyweight legume soups, and combinations really more like stews; the serving temperature can be hot, room temperature, or cold, as in vichyssoise, gazpacho, or fruit soups.

Soup as a convenience item, too, has a surprisingly long history. In the first half of the eighteenth century a chef identified only as Lebas invented solidified and soluble bouillon. His only other claim to fame is an almost ludicrous cookbook in verse, but his "consommé in lozenges," as he called it, was the forerunner of all the dry and powdered soups of today.

The Campbell Soup Company, founded in Camden, New Jersey, in 1869 as the Joseph A. Campbell Preserve Company, began to produce double-strength condensed soups in 1897. They were the pet project of John Dorrance, a graduate of MIT who also had a doctorate from the University of Gottingen. Beefsteak Tomato, Consommé, Chicken, and Oxtail came first; Vegetable was added in 1898 and it was in that same year that the cans began to be wrapped in the familiar red and white labels, supposedly suggested by the striking new uniforms of the Cornell University football team. Today Campbell soups are available worldwide.

CONSOMMÉ MADRILÈNE
4–6 servings

The names of French dishes are often conventions derived from a specialty product associated with a particular town, geographic region, or famous individual. St. Germain stands for green peas because the best peas were said to be grown in Saint-Germain-en-Laye, a little village outside of Paris. Lyonnaise means in the manner of Lyonnais, the area around Lyon, where supposedly the best onions were grown. À la Crécy means with carrots, even though authorities do not even agree as to which town by that name reputedly grew the best carrots. St. Hubert indicates a dish made with game; legend has it that Hubert had been a profligate who went hunting on Good Friday but was converted by the miraculous appearance of a stag with a cross between its antlers. And Florentine denotes spinach because that vegetable was first introduced into France from Italy, presumably by the Florentine cooks who came in the wake of the Medici queens. Similarly, Madrilène, "in the manner of Madrid," always indicates a dish made with tomato juice.

The Madrilène convention, it must be noted, rests on firmer ground than some of the others. Spain was the first European country to use the tomato in cooking. The vegetable, really a fruit, probably originated in South America but was cultivated, more or less, by the Aztecs, who let the plants grow undisturbed in their fields of corn. The *conquistadores* brought tomatoes back to Spain in the first half of the sixteenth century, and from there they spread, very slowly, to other parts of Europe.

A consommé is a strongly flavored clear broth resulting from long, slow simmering of meat in water; served cold, consommé forms a jelly.

Note: *If preferred, omit gelatin and water and serve hot or chilled.*

3 envelopes unflavored gelatin
½ cup cold water
2 cups tomato juice
2 cups clear chicken bouillon (can be canned or made from bouillon powder)
2 tablespoons sherry
Lemon wedges

1. Soften gelatin in cold water. Heat tomato juice and bouillon. Pour over gelatin, stirring until gelatin is dissolved. Add sherry and chill consommé until firm.
2. Break up consommé with a fork before serving. Garnish with lemon wedges.

POTAGE CRÈME DU BARRY
8 servings

Marie-Jeanne Bécu, comtesse du Barry, was the last French-woman to have the role of *maîtresse en titre*, the acknowledged Mistress of the King, the king in this case being Louis XV. Some might say she was the most beautiful to occupy this semiofficial position that had been begun three hundred years earlier with Agnès Sorel, the paramour of Charles VII. In between there had been dozens. No doubt the pious peasants and respectable townsmen of each generation were scandalized, but the Royal Court grew increasingly blasé. Moreover, these women had great power, and power generally breeds respect. To the Royal chefs they were simply great ladies, and chefs have always liked to name new dishes for great ladies. Among the many conventions of French haute cuisine, du Barry's name has come to stand for any dish made with cauliflower. Whether the vegetable was actually a favorite of hers is not recorded. It is not the sort of thing biographers bother about.

Cauliflower cuisine is a strange tribute to a woman whose beauty has become proverbial, and whose life ended so tragically. After the death of Louis XV in 1774, du Barry was banished from the court. The new queen, Marie Antoinette, had never liked her, nor, for that matter, had any of the rest of the royal family. Du Barry retired to her country estate and lived quietly until all of France began to be convulsed by the first rumblings of the Revolution. Her kindness and generosity led her to make several trips to England to place her considerable fortune at the disposal of the fleeing *émigrés*. Had du Barry remained in England all would have been well, but something prompted her to return once more to France, and, as it turned out, to the guillotine.

Incidentally, the French *potage* comes directly from "pot," a word so old that it is found in almost identical forms in the Germanic, Romance, and Celtic languages. Cauliflower, actually a form of cabbage, takes its name from the Italian *cavoli a fiore*, cabbage flower.

1 head cauliflower (about 2 pounds)

2 cups water

1 tablespoon lemon juice

½ cup chopped onion

2 tablespoons butter or margarine

2 tablespoons all-purpose flour

2 cups chicken broth (can be canned or from bouillon powder)

1 cup half-and-half

Salt

Pepper

1. Separate cauliflower into flowerets. In a large saucepan heat water to boiling. Add cauliflower, lemon juice, and onion. Cover and boil until tender, about 10 minutes. Do not drain. Puree in blender or food processor.

2. In large saucepan heat butter till melted. Stir in flour. Cook, whisking constantly, until mixture is smooth and bubbly. Continue to stir, on and off heat, for several minutes to rid flour of raw taste. Stir in chicken broth. Heat to boiling, stirring constantly. Boil and stir 1 minute. Add cauliflower mixture and half-and-half. Taste and add salt and pepper as desired. Reheat, but do not allow to boil.

POTAGE PARMENTIER
6 servings

The potato was cultivated by the Indians of Chile and Peru long before the discovery of America by the Europeans. The *conquistadores* took it back to Spain. Precisely how potatoes were introduced into the British Isles is uncertain, but Sir Walter Raleigh is believed to have grown them on his estate in County Cork before 1590. Ireland was the first European country to wholeheartedly adopt the potato. The tiny island was terribly overcrowded, and potatoes not only grew well in the cool, moist climate, they provided more than twice the amount of food per acre than any grain crop, Two hundred years later a blight ruined the crops, causing the great Potato Famine of the 1840s. A million people died, and the Irish learned a terrible lesson on the danger of depending on only one source of food, but potatoes remain a major crop in Ireland today.

In the meantime, the potato gradually gained acceptance on the continent, in Italy, the Netherlands, Switzerland, and, most of all, in Germany. Not that the Germans, at first, were so fond of potatoes; rather, they saw that the potato could be a safeguard *against* famine. If the grain crops were good, the potatoes could be fed to livestock, but if the other crops failed, the potatoes would be there to subsist on.

Only the French held out against the potato; even as late as the eighteenth century the popular belief was that potatoes caused leprosy. Then Antoine Parmentier, a pharmacist in the French army, began his one-man campaign to get the French to grow potatoes. Like the Germans, he viewed the potato as a crop that could prevent famine. Moreover, he spoke from personal experience, having virtually lived on potatoes for months as a prisoner-of-war in Hanover during the Seven Years' War.

Parmentier was a clever man. Steadily advancing in the army, he managed to bring himself to the attention of Louis XVI, and eventually got permission to plant fifty acres of potatoes on some poor ground outside Paris. He cleverly had the field guarded by the soldiers of the *Garde Français* in the daytime and just as deliberately left it unguarded at night, so that greedy Parisians could steal the tubers. Despite the depredation of the thieves, the crop was a great success, and Parmentier presented the king with a bouquet of potato blossoms at a public reception. When the king plucked a blossom to wear as a boutonniere, the success of the potato in France was assured; by the early 1800s it had become a staple.

1 pound potatoes, peeled and cut up
2 leeks, washed and coarsely chopped
2 onions, peeled and sliced
1 celery stalk, cut up
2 ½ quarts water
Salt
¼ cup butter
½ cup half-and-half
Pepper
Chopped parsley

1. Place potatoes, leeks, onions, celery, water, and 2 teaspoons salt in a large kettle. Cover with a tight-fitting lid and cook over low heat for about 2 hours. Drain vegetables, reserving liquid. Puree vegetables using food mill, blender, or food processor.
2. Return mixture to liquid and add butter and half-and-half. Reheat and taste; add pepper and more salt if desired. Serve topped with parsley.

CLAM CHOWDER
6 servings

Unlikely as it sounds, chowder comes from a French word, *chaudière*, meaning a large copper pot. In the fishing villages of Brittany *faire la chaudière* meant to supply a cauldron in which to cook a mess of freshly caught fish with some savoury condiments, a hodge-podge to which each fisherman contributed and which all shared. The Breton fishermen probably carried the custom to Newfoundland, where men from a number of nations congregated each summer. Newfoundland was famous for its chowder even before New England adopted the dish, which in the beginning was as often made of fish as clams. Fat pork, onion, and crackers were considered essential right from the start; milk and potatoes came later.

Much has been made of the supposed war between Bostonians and New Yorkers over the relative merits of New England Clam Chowder and Manhattan Clam Chowder. The latter, always made with tomatoes instead of milk, may actually have originated in Rhode Island. It has obvious similarities to the many Mediterranean fish stews.

New England Clam Chowder:

¼ cup finely chopped salt pork or bacon
¼ cup finely minced onion
2 cans (6 ½ ounces) minced clams
2 cups finely diced potatoes

½ cup boiling water
2 cups milk
1 teaspoon salt
Pepper

1. In a kettle or large saucepan slowly fry pork or bacon until crisp; reserve. Add onion to remaining fat and sauté until transparent. Drain clams, reserving liquid.
2. Add liquid, potatoes, and boiling water to kettle. Cook until potatoes are tender, 10 minutes. Add clams, pork or bacon, milk, salt, and pepper as desired. Heat to boiling; serve at once.

Variation: *For Manhattan Clam Chowder, omit salt pork or bacon and cook onions in ¼ cup butter or margarine. Add ⅓ cup finely chopped celery and 1 cup chopped carrots with the potatoes. Use 2 cups canned tomatoes in place of milk, and add 2 teaspoons finely minced parsley just before serving.*

GUMBO
10–12 servings

Gumbo is an African word, one of only a handful to survive the rigors of slavery and enter the English language. It comes from the Bantu *gombo* or the Umbundu *ochinggombo*, both of which mean okra. The Africans brought the seeds of the okra with them, quite by accident, and when they saw the tall, distinctive plants growing on the edges of the cotton fields they used the immature fruits for food, as they had at home. Soon okra found its way into the big kitchens of the plantations, and the south had a new vegetable.

Eventually, however, gumbo came to be used not as a name for the vegetable (the word okra is derived from the west African *nkruma*) but rather for a soup or stew famed in Louisiana Creole cooking. Gumbo can be made from almost anything but the emphasis on seafood indicates that it had its beginnings as the French and Spanish colonists attempted to recreate bouillabaise, the famous fish stew made along the shores of the Mediterranean. Okra, which is very mucilaginous, was used to thicken the gumbo, or filé powder might be used instead.

The latter ingredient is as truly American as okra is African, for it was first made by the Choctaw Indians. The young leaves of the sassafras tree were dried and pounded to a powder, then sold, either in the French Market or by silent Indian women peddlers, who went with their wares from door to door. Its French name may have come from filet, meaning a small thread or string, for if boiled it did become decidedly stringy. Many Creole cooks avoided that hazard by adding the filé powder only after the gumbo had been removed from the heat, and then letting each diner add more filé powder at the table, to his or her own liking.

1 broiler-fryer chicken (about 2 ½ pounds),
  cut up

Salt

4 tablespoons vegetable oil

1 pound *andouille* (Creole sausage), sliced,
  or 1 pound Polish sausage, sliced

½ pound smoked ham, cut into ¼-inch dice

2 tablespoons finely minced garlic

1 ½ cups finely minced onion

1 ½ cups finely minced green onions, including 3 inches of dark green tops

1 cup finely minced green pepper

1 ½ cups finely minced celery

2 10-ounce packages frozen sliced okra

3 ½ cups canned tomatoes, broken up

2 bay leaves

1 teaspoon red pepper sauce

2 teaspoons Worcestershire sauce

¼ cup all-purpose flour

2 pounds raw shrimp, fresh or frozen,
  shelled and deveined

Pepper

Cooked rice

1. Place chicken (without giblets) in heavy kettle; add water just to cover and ¾ teaspoon salt. Heat to boiling; reduce heat. Cover tightly and simmer until thickest pieces of chicken are tender, about 1 hour. Refrigerate chicken in broth until cool. When cool, remove bones and skin, leaving chicken in fairly large pieces. Strain broth and measure 5 cups, adding water if necessary.

2. Heat 1 tablespoon vegetable oil in Dutch oven or large kettle with a heavy bottom and tight-fitting lid. Add sausage and cook, stirring often, until sausage is lightly browned. Stir in ham and cook for 1 minute. Remove meats and reserve.

3. Add the garlic, onion, green onion, green pepper, and celery to the pot and cook, stirring, till vegetables are wilted. Drain off fat and add okra. Cook until vegetables are fairly dry, about 5 minutes.

4. Stir in tomatoes, bay leaves, 4 cups of chicken broth, red pepper sauce, Worcestershire sauce, and reserved meats. Bring to a boil and simmer for 30 minutes.

5. Heat remaining 3 tablespoons of oil in small frying pan. Add flour and cook, stirring constantly, till flour is browned but not burned. Stir in remaining cup chicken broth with a wire whisk. Bring to a boil and stir mixture into vegetables and meat.

6. Add the shrimp and cook for 5 minutes. Add the reserved chicken and cook for another 5 minutes. Taste and add salt and pepper as desired. Serve in large soup bowls, with a mound of white rice in the center of each bowl.

Variation: *Use chicken broth made from bouillon powder or canned and in place of chicken use 1 ½ pounds lump crab meat.*

PHILADELPHIA PEPPER POT
6 servings

Pepper Pot, a Philadelphia specialty, was hawked in the streets in the nineteenth century and is still featured in many fine restaurants. The story has been told, over and over again, that it was first made at Valley Forge. According to most accounts, George Washington and his men were starving. The general's cook, desperate to provide a decent meal for the great man, took a piece of tripe, some spices, and very little else and created a masterpiece.

But the tale does not bear close scrutiny. In the first place it is an all too obvious imitation of the story of Napoleon and Marengo, food stories, like other stories, tending to repeat themselves. Besides, Washington was never starving. As a Virginia aristocrat, while he had a sincere concern for his men's welfare, he took for granted his own comfortable lifestyle as an officer and a gentleman. It is much more likely that the thrifty "Pennsylvania Dutch" brought the idea of tripe soup with them when they came from Germany. Moreover, there is a tripe and pepper soup well known in Poland even today, and the border between that country and Germany has changed so often as to have little meaning, at least where culinary customs are concerned.

1 pound soup bones

½ pound beef stew meat, cut into ½-inch cubes

1 pound tripe, cut into ½-inch cubes

6 whole black peppercorns

Salt

¼ cup butter or margarine

1 cup finely chopped onion

half a sweet red pepper, minced

half a sweet green pepper, minced

3 tablespoons flour

2 cups diced raw potatoes

Coarsely ground black pepper

Ground cayenne (hot red pepper)

1. In a large kettle combine bones, beef stew meat, and tripe. Add 2 quarts water or more if needed to cover meats by at least 2 inches. Bring to a boil over high heat, skimming as foam and scum rise to the surface. Add peppercorns and 1 teaspoon salt and reduce heat to low. Simmer partially covered for 2 hours or until tripe is tender.
2. With a slotted spoon remove bones, beef, and tripe. Reserve meat and discard bones. Strain broth and measure; add water if needed to make 6 cups.
3. Rinse out kettle and melt butter over low heat. Add onions and red and green pepper; cook till onions are soft but not brown. Add flour and mix well. Stirring constantly, pour in reserved broth. Cook over high heat until soup thickens, comes to a boil, and is smooth. Add potatoes, tripe, and beef. Reduce heat to low, cover partially, and simmer for 1 hour, stirring occasionally.
4. Taste for seasoning. Add more salt if needed and enough black pepper and cayenne to give soup a distinctly peppery flavor.

VICHYSSOISE
8 servings

Vichyssoise was created by Chef Louis Diat at the Ritz-Carlton Hotel in New York City, probably around 1917. Diat himself wrote in his first cookbook that

> One of my earliest food memories is of my mother's good Leek and Potato soup made with plump, tender leeks I pulled myself from the garden. . . . When I first came to this country I actually couldn't find any [leeks]. I finally persuaded one of my vegetable suppliers to find someone who would grow leeks for me.

Building on those fond memories of his mother's hot leek and potato soup, Diat made a cold soup, naming it for Vichy, the French city near his parents' home. Curiously, Diat does not mention his famous soup by name in his 1946 cookbook. By that time many French chefs in New York had tried to change the name to *crème gauloise* because of their hatred for the pro-Nazi government established at Vichy. After the war, however, the original name was restored, sometimes as Vichyssoise à la Ritz.

4 leeks

1 medium onion

¼ cup butter

5 medium potatoes

1 quart chicken broth (can be canned or made from bouillon powder)

1 ½ teaspoons salt

2 cups milk

2 cups half-and-half

1 cup whipping cream

Finely minced chives (optional)

1. Wash leeks and slice only the white parts. Peel onion and slice. In large, heavy kettle sauté leeks and onion gently in butter, but do not allow to brown. Peel potatoes and slice thinly. Add potatoes, chicken broth, and salt to kettle. Boil 35–40 minutes. Puree in food mill, blender, or food processor.
2. Return to heat and add milk and half-and-half. Bring just to a boil. Cool and rub puree again. Chill. Add remaining cream and chill again until ready to serve. Taste and add salt if desired. Sprinkle with finely chopped chives.

UNITED STATES SENATE BEAN SOUP
12 servings

United States Senate Bean Soup may be the only soup in the world named for a legislative body. It has been served for half a century in the United States Senate restaurant, which is operated for the senators and their guests.

1 pound dried white beans, washed and drained
1 large smoked ham hock
3 potatoes, cooked and mashed
3 medium onions, chopped
1 cup diced celery
2 garlic cloves, minced
Salt
Pepper

1. Cover beans with water, bring to boil, and boil for 2 minutes. Remove from heat, cover pan, and let stand for 1 hour.
2. Drain beans and measure liquid; add enough water to make 5 quarts. Bring again to boil and simmer, covered, for 2 hours or until beans begin to mush.
3. Add remaining ingredients except salt and pepper and simmer, covered, for 1 hour longer. Remove bone, cut up meat, and return meat to soup. Taste and add salt and pepper as desired.

CHAPTER 4

SALADS &
SALAD
DRESSINGS

Lettuce grew wild throughout the ancient Mediterranean world, and with the spread of farming, it was widely cultivated. The ancient Egyptians regarded lettuce as sacred to Min, god of the harvest. When the priests brought out Min's image at festival time and paraded it through the streets, the rejoicing crowds pelted the statue with lettuces!

Many other raw vegetables played an important part in the ancient Egyptian diet. Herodotus records that the laborers who built the Great Pyramid were paid in radishes, onions, and leeks, as well as bread, while the Israelites, wandering in the desert, mourned, among other things, the cucumbers and garlic they had relished in Egypt.

Almost all of these vegetables were enjoyed throughout the Fertile Crescent and in Greece, but it was in ancient Rome that the salad came into its own. Although the Romans were convinced that lettuce, watercress, and endive were hard to digest, they ate them anyway, preferring them dressed with vinegar and oil and sprinkled with salt at the table. They must have applied the salt liberally, as the English word salad and its equivalents in all the Romance languages come ultimately from the Latin *sal*, meaning salt.

Herbs were important, too. The Roman soldier-turned-farmer Columella, writing in the first century A.D., gives a basic recipe of "savory, mint, rue, coriander, parsley, chives or green onion, lettuce leaves, colewort, thyme or catnip and green flea-bane," a combination that sounds more appetizing if one takes into account the fact that early recipes never bothered with relative quantities. If the lettuce leaves formed the bulk of the salad and all the other ingredients were merely seasonings the combination was probably quite good.

Salads remained virtually unchanged for over a thousand years, an amazing observation in light of the revolutionary developments in other culinary fields. In the handwritten cookbook compiled around 1390 by the royal cooks who served England's Richard II, a recipe for "salat" reads:

> Take *parsel, sawge, garlec, chibollas, onyons, leeks, borage, myntes, fenel,* and ton *tressis, rew, rosemarye purslayne.* Lave, and waishe hem clene; pike hem, pluk hem small with thyn hande and myng hem wel with *rawe oile.* Lay one vynegar and salt, and serve it forth.
>
> Take *parsley, sage, garlic, small onions, onions, leeks, borage, mint, fennel, cress, rue, rosemary, purslain.* Rinse and wash them clean; pick them over, tear them with your hands and mix them well with *oil.* Add vinegar and salt, and serve it forth.
> [Purslain was a garden plant once used like lettuce; it has now sunk to the status of a weed in a number of countries.]
>
> (Aresty, *The Delectable Past*)

Gradually, salads began to include other ingredients besides fresh greens. A cookbook published in 1615, *The English Housewife* by Gervase Markham, gives a recipe for a "Compound Sallet" that includes sliced almonds, raisins, currants, oranges, and lemons and adds a small amount of sugar with the vinegar and oil. Forty years later, another cookbook included "The Queen's Chicken Sallet," supposedly a favorite of England's Henrietta Marie.

Salads were not of great importance in the American colonies. The early settlers seemed to prefer their greens boiled, often endlessly. The one notable exception was cole slaw, first made by the Dutch in New Amsterdam. The original name is in real danger of disappearing, as menus with increasing frequency offer it as "cold slaw." Occasionally one even hears of "hot slaw." But "cole slaw" has nothing to do etymologically with cold; the name comes directly from the Dutch *kool*, cabbage, and *sla*, a shortened form of *salaad*, salad. Nomenclature aside, cole slaw shows no sign of losing its popularity. Crisp, refreshing, and inexpensive, it is becoming a favorite all over the world, though it usually is thought of simply as an American salad.

Aside from the ever present cole slaw, however, Americans in the nineteenth century were not overly fond of salads. Good cooks learned to prepare potato salad, made with boiled dressing, but leaf lettuce (the only sort most people grew) was inevitably served wilted with hot vinegar and bacon fat, cucumbers were thought fit only for making pickles, and tomatoes were suspect in many parts of the country until the turn of the century. The fact that the tomato plant is related to the deadly nightshade gave rise to the notion that tomatoes were poisonous, and only gradually did the idea lose credibility.

Great advances in refrigeration in the early twentieth century made fresh fruits and vegetables available all year round. Salads benefited greatly, as they could now be served cold and crisp even on the hottest summer day.

Curiously, in the face of this abundance of fresh produce, cooks in the 1920s doted on strangely artificial salads constructed of edible ingredients in imitation of other objects, whether natural or manufactured. The most notorious was the candle salad, made of a short length of banana inserted into the center of a slice of canned pineapple. Dribbled mayonnaise represented the dripping wax, while a sliver of pimiento formed the flame. More entertaining, at least for children, was the bunny rabbit salad, a canned pear half placed cut side down on a lettuce leaf. The bottom of the pear formed the rear end of the bunny, while various edible garnishes became the tail, ears, and whiskers!

But, for the most part, salads were still geared to the ladies' luncheon. Served to the rest of the family at dinner, they were derisively termed "rabbit food," and were eaten more out of a sense of duty than with appreciation.

All of this began to change in the 1950s. A new emphasis on lighter, healthier eating made the salad an integral, important part of the meal, while salad bars, a restaurant innovation of the same decade, made them suddenly seem a treat.

WALDORF SALAD
4–6 servings

Waldorf Salad was created by Oscar Tschirky, better known as "Oscar of the Waldorf." Contrary to popular opinion, Tschirky never worked as a chef. Like so many in the restaurant business, he began as a busboy. By the time the Waldorf-Astoria opened in 1893, he was a well-known headwaiter. Eventually he became an executive, in charge of all the great dining rooms in the luxurious hotel and so highly regarded that he was listed in *Who's Who*.

Perhaps Oscar of the Waldorf's most influential invention, besides the famous salad, was the use of velvet-covered ropes to contain overflow crowds waiting to be seated. Despite predictions that the public would be insulted, Oscar's innovation only made dining at the Waldorf all the more popular.

4 red apples, cored and diced, but not peeled
2 tablespoons fresh lemon juice
2 cups chopped celery
½ cup coarsely chopped walnuts (optional)
1 cup mayonnaise or salad dressing (approximately)
Lettuce leaves, washed and dried

1. In medium bowl, toss apples with lemon juice. Add celery and walnuts.
2. Stir in enough mayonnaise to bind ingredients. Serve on lettuce leaves.

PERFECTION SALAD
4–6 servings

In 1905, Charles Knox, of gelatin fame, ran a cookery contest, with Fannie Merritt Farmer of the Boston Cooking-School as one of the judges. Third prize, a sewing machine worth a hundred dollars, was awarded to Mrs. John E. Cooke of New Castle, Pennsylvania, for a recipe she called Perfection Salad. Just *why* Mrs. Cooke thought a simple vegetable aspic deserved to be called "perfection" is impossible to determine, but the American public evidently agreed with her, for the recipe has become a classic.

Variation: *If preferred, Perfection Salad can be made with* one 3-ounce package of lemon-flavored gelatin, 1 ¾ cups boiling water, 1 teaspoon salt, *and 2* tablespoons lemon juice or vinegar. *Chill and add vegetables as directed.*

1 envelope unflavored gelatin

¼ cup sugar

½ teaspoon salt

1 ¼ cups water

½ cup vinegar

1 tablespoon lemon juice

½ cup shredded cabbage, red or green

1 cup chopped celery

2 tablespoons chopped pimiento,
   or 2 tablespoons chopped sweet red or green pepper

1. In small saucepan, thoroughly mix gelatin, sugar, and salt. Add ½ cup water. Place over low heat, stirring constantly until gelatin is dissolved. Remove from heat and stir in remaining ¾ cup water, vinegar, and lemon juice. Chill mixture to consistency of unbeaten egg whites.

2. Fold in shredded cabbage, celery, and pimiento or pepper. Turn mixture into 3-cup mold or individual molds and chill several hours or overnight, until firm. Unmold and serve with mayonnaise or salad dressing.

COBB SALAD
6–8 servings

Cobb Salad was invented in 1936 at the Brown Derby in Hollywood, California. According to most versions of the story, Robert Cobb, owner of the renowned restaurant, let himself in late one night after everyone else had gone home. Having had no dinner, he walked into one of the enormous restaurant refrigerators to see what interesting leftovers he might find. Putting them all together, he created the Cobb Salad and liked it so much that he added it to the menu.

Much of the salad's success depends on its presentation, with each ingredient attractively arranged and the mixing done at the table. It is also important to chop the ingredients rather finely, so that each forkful contains the same delicious mix of flavors.

¼ cup fresh lemon juice or vinegar

¾ cup salad oil

1 teaspoon salt

½ head iceberg lettuce

1 small head chicory

1 small bunch watercress

3 green onions, chopped,
    or 1 tablespoon finely minced yellow onion

2 medium tomatoes, peeled, seeded, and diced

3 hard-cooked eggs, coarsely chopped

6 slices bacon, cooked, drained, and crumbled

1 whole chicken breast, poached and chilled

3 ounces blue cheese, crumbled

1 large avocado, peeled, cut into ½-inch cubes, and tossed with
    juice of ½ fresh lemon

1. Combine oil, vinegar, and salt and whisk until well blended. Cover and place in refrigerator.
2. Dice lettuce and chicory by shredding and then cutting crosswise. Place in bottom of large salad bowl. Coarsely chop watercress; add with onions and toss. Arrange tomatoes in two rows at opposite sides of bowl.
3. Working toward center, make two similar rows of chopped eggs, then two rows of crumbled bacon.
4. Skin and bone chicken breast halves. Dice into ½-inch cubes. Make two rows of diced chicken inside rows of bacon. Make two rows of blue cheese and finally a center row of avocado pieces. Salad may be covered and chilled for two hours before serving.
5. To serve, drizzle salad with oil and vinegar dressing as desired and toss gently.

CAESAR SALAD
4–6 servings

Caesar Salad has nothing to do with Julius Caesar. It was first made during a hot Fourth of July weekend in 1924. The place was Tijuana, Mexico, and the inspired chef was an Italian immigrant, Caesar Cardini.

Caesar's Hotel was an elegant place for the little border town across from San Diego. Prohibition had dampened night life in California, and slipping across the border to Mexico for drinking, gambling, and dining in style was a popular pastime. Although *hôtelier* Cardini usually prepared the salad at the table, its success did not depend solely on showmanship—the blend of flavors was exciting, new, and delicious. Caesar Salad was quickly adopted by a number of well-known California restaurants and today it has worldwide recognition, though the arguments over the precise ingredients of the authentic Caesar Salad continue. According to Caesar Cardini's daughter Rosa, as quoted by Julia Child, the following recipe quite closely reproduces the original.

2 heads romaine lettuce

2 Grade A unbroken eggs

¾ cup garlic-flavored oil (see note)

½ teaspoon salt

½ teaspoon freshly ground pepper

1 large lemon, cut in half

½ teaspoon Worcestershire sauce

¼ cup freshly grated Parmesan cheese

1 cup garlic-flavored croutons

Note: *For garlic-flavored oil, slice 2 large cloves of garlic into a screw-top jar. Add ¾ cup olive oil or ½ cup olive oil and ¼ cup vegetable oil. Cover tightly and store 4–5 days in refrigerator.*

1. Wash and dry romaine, discarding outer leaves. Separate remaining leaves, wrap in clean cotton dish towel, and place in refrigerator. (Leaves may be torn into smaller pieces, if desired.)
2. Bring small pan of water to boil. Add eggs and remove pan from heat. After 1 minute, remove eggs from water. Set aside.

Please see "A Note about Eggs," p. 307.

3. Place romaine in large salad bowl and assemble all other ingredients on a tray. At the table, pour approximately ½ cup of oil over romaine. Toss gently, using a rolling motion. Add salt and pepper and briefly toss again. Squeeze lemon juice over salad and add Worcestershire sauce. Break eggs over salad, add remaining ¼ cup oil and cheese. Toss again until leaves are well coated. Add croutons and toss briefly. Serve at once on large salad plates.

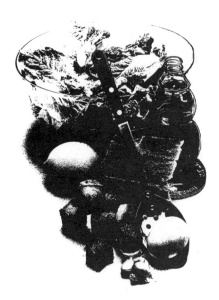

SALAD SIXTUS THE FIFTH
4 large servings

According to Italian legend, when Pope Sixtus V was still an obscure monk, he had as a great friend a certain wealthy lawyer. As the monk rose to the papacy, the lawyer fell steadily into poverty. Finally, the destitute lawyer undertook a journey to Rome to seek aid from his old friend the Pope, but fell sick by the wayside. He begged the kindly physician who was caring for him to let the Pope know of his sad state.

Receiving word of his friend's condition, Sixtus V said, "I will send him a salad," and he duly dispatched a basket of lettuces to the invalid. When the lettuces were opened, money was found in their hearts. From this comes the Italian expression regarding a man in need of money, "He wants one of Sixtus the Fifth's salads."

In the heyday of elaborate salads a Chicago chef created a Salad Sixtus the Fifth, included it in his own cookbook, and noted that it would be "appropriate for a dinner where dignitaries of the Catholic Church are being entertained"! Incidently, the only basis for the legend seems to be that Sixtus V, chosen pope in 1585, was an energetic reformer of the church administration, including its finances.

Lettuce

3 cups vegetables cut in coin shapes—any combination of cooked baby beets, cooked new potatoes, or raw cucumbers, radishes, carrots, plum tomatoes, or zucchini

4 hard-cooked eggs

¾ cup mayonnaise (see following recipe) or salad dressing

2 teaspoons prepared yellow mustard

1. Arrange lettuce cups on four large salad plates. Lightly toss vegetables and spoon over lettuce.

2. Remove yolks from hard-cooked eggs and set aside. In small bowl, coarsely chop egg whites and mix with mayonnaise and mustard. Thin with a few drops of water if desired, stirring to blend.

3. Spoon mayonnaise mixture over vegetables; grate or sieve egg yolks directly over mayonnaise. Serve at once.

MAYONNAISE
1 cup

Note: *Please see "A Note about Eggs," p. 307.*

Mayonnaise owes its name, even its very existence, to a battle. The year was 1756. The European powers had just blundered into the Seven Years' War but the French were not prepared to send an army into Germany. Instead they decided to take Minorca, one of the Balearic Islands away from Great Britain. The duc de Richelieu, marshal of France and grandnephew of the famous cardinal, was ordered to seize the port of Mahon. The British, who had held Minorca for almost fifty years, were in no hurry to surrender. Hoping for reinforcements that never came, they remained inside the walls of the old Spanish fortress of San Felipe and Richelieu had no choice but to lay seige.

In the meantime, his chef mingled with the native Minoreans, probably wandering in the marketplace and investigating the cook shops. Somewhere along the way he discovered *aioli*, the thick, emulsified sauce, redolent of garlic, that may have originated in Greece. Experimenting, he left out the garlic, and when San Felipe finally fell, he honored the occasion by serving the duc de Richelieu a new sauce, *mahonnaise*, named for the victory. Later *mahonnaise* came to be pronounced as mayonnaise.

Incidentally, Mahon takes its name from a Carthaginian general named Mago, not Hannibal's brother but an earlier general of the same name.

1 egg
2 tablespoons lemon juice,
   or 2 tablespoons vinegar
½ teaspoon dry mustard

¼ teaspoon salt
Dash of cayenne pepper
1 cup vegetable oil

1. Place egg, lemon juice or vinegar, mustard, salt, cayenne pepper, and ¼ cup of oil in blender container. Cover and blend on high speed 5 seconds. Stop blender.
2. Remove cover; blend on high speed, very gradually adding remaining oil and stopping blender occasionally to scrape sides of container. Refrigerate.

THOUSAND ISLAND DRESSING
1½ cups dressing

There are two distinct culinary traditions regarding the origin of Thousand Island Dressing. In the eastern United States, it is usually held that the dressing was introduced by George C. Boldt, original manager of the Waldorf-Astoria and owner of a summer home, Boldt Castle, on one of the Thousand Islands along the St. Lawrence River. Writers in the midwest, however, credit Chef Theodore Reums, who, they say, created the dressing for the opening of the Blackstone Hotel in Chicago and called it Blackstone Dressing, then changed the name to Thousand Island Dressing, presumably when he moved to the Drake Hotel.

There is probably a good bit of truth in both stories. Actually, Thousand Island Dressing was first made in Canada where, as early as 1916, it was being sold as a bottled dressing. Reums, like Boldt, liked to vacation in the Thousand Islands region; probably both men learned of the new dressing during their travels and then proceeded to introduce it in their respective cities. The name recalls the Thousand Islands in the St. Lawrence as well as indicating the numerous bits and pieces in the dressing.

Note: Thousand Island Dressing is rather heavy to offer with a mixed green salad, as many restaurants do today. It is really better served as it was in the 1930s, simply poured over a generous wedge of iceberg lettuce.

1 hard-cooked egg

1 cup mayonnaise or salad dressing

3 tablespoons chili sauce

1 tablespoon sweet pickle relish

1 teaspoon snipped chives

1 teaspoon chopped canned pimiento

½ teaspoon paprika

1. In a small bowl, finely chop egg. Combine all ingredients and mix well.
2. Cover and refrigerate until ready to serve.

CHIFFONADE DRESSING
1 cup dressing

Chiffon is a curious word. The French original simply meant "rags." Eventually the meaning was extended to scraps of lace and ribbon, pretty things that a lady might use in her needlework and store in her *chiffonière*, a small chest of drawers.

In the nineteenth century, on both sides of the English Channel, the word took on a quite different connotation. Chiffons were dress trimmings of every sort, all the frills and fripperies, fringes and bows, that loaded down Victorian gowns. Women didn't talk fashion, they talked chiffons!

As the turn of the century approached, the meaning of the word chiffon changed again; in England it began to be used as the name for a new fabric, filmy, gossamer, and usually woven of silk. The word never caught on in France as the name of a textile. To the French, who preferred *mousseline de soie* (silk muslin) for the fabric, *chiffon* still meant rags.

In the 1920s, silk chiffon became quite the rage in the United States, and eventually it gave its name to chiffon pie (see page 256) and chiffon cake (see page 253).

In the meantime, French chefs had begun to make *chiffonades*, vegetables shredded into fine strips or ribbons to resemble rags, then used to garnish consommé. The idea was picked up by American cooks but here chiffonade became a salad dressing containing little bits and pieces of vegetables cut to look like scraps or rags.

½ cup vegetable oil

2 tablespoons vinegar

2 tablespoons lemon juice

2 teaspoons sugar

½ teaspoon salt

½ teaspoon dry mustard

½ teaspoon paprika

1 hard-cooked egg, finely chopped

2 tablespoons finely slivered cooked beets

2 tablespoons finely slivered fresh green pepper

2 tablespoons chopped fresh parsley

2 teaspoons chopped chives or green onions,
    or 1 teaspoon chopped onion

1. In screw-top jar combine oil, vinegar, lemon juice, sugar, salt, dry mustard, and paprika. Cover and shake.
2. Add remaining ingredients. Mix, cover, and chill. Shake again just before serving,

GREEN GODDESS DRESSING
1 ½ cups dressing

Green Goddess Dressing was created at San Francisco's Palace Hotel (now the Sheraton-Palace) in the mid-1920s. A well-known actor, George Arliss, was staying at the hotel while appearing in William Archer's *The Green Goddess*, a play that was twice made into a motion picture. The plot involves an Asian potentate who holds a trio of British citizens captive in his tiny kingdom in the Himalayas. The green goddess is a great stone idol; the captives, imminently in danger of being sacrificed to her, are rescued at the last moment.

> 4–5 anchovy fillets
> ¼ cup finely chopped fresh parsley
> ¼ cup finely chopped fresh chives,
>   *or* ¼ cup finely chopped green onions with tops
> 1 ½ cups mayonnaise
> 2 tablespoons tarragon vinegar

1. In medium bowl, thoroughly mash anchovies. Add parsley, chives, and mayonnaise. Mix well.
2. Very gradually add vinegar, continuing to stir after each addition. Cover and chill several hours, until flavors blend.

ENTRÉES & EXTRAS

CHAPTER 5

SEAFOOD

Though it was the Hebrews who gave the sabbath its religious significance, the seven-day week had begun even earlier, with the Chaldeans of ancient Mesopotamia. They named the seven days for the sun, the moon, and the five known planets, believing them to be deities who ruled the destinies of men. The sixth day was named for Ishtar, the goddess of love and beauty.

After Alexander the Great's conquests the idea of a seven-day week was brought to the west, and the Greeks named the sixth day for their goddess of love, Aphrodite. The Romans, in turn, named it for Venus, and finally the Germans for Frigg, their beautiful mother goddess, patroness of marriage. Since fish was almost universally considered an aphrodisiac in ancient times, each of these peoples viewed fish as sacred to their goddess and to be eaten on her day. The early Christian missionaries, abhorring the goddesses and all they stood for, tried (at least at some times and in some places) to stamp out the custom, but to no avail. Eventually it came to be regarded as essentially harmless, and ignored.

In the meantime, the Christians had been forming their own traditions. As early as the second century they had begun to fast on Wednesday and Friday, partly to disassociate themselves from the Jews, who at that time fasted on Monday and Thursday, but also because Wednesday was the day on which Judas had betrayed Jesus and Friday was the day of the crucifixion.

There was, at this early date, no clear distinction between fasting (limiting the intake of food) and abstinence (abstaining from meat and meat products), but it was generally accepted that meat, eggs, cheese, and milk should all be banned on a fast day, though fish was permissible. Just why is unclear, but it is obvious that two very different traditions, one pagan and the other Christian, were converging. In the early Middle Ages the tradition of fasting would harden into canon law.

Spain was the first country to be relieved of the Friday obligation. Pope Innocent VIII greeted the news of the conquest of the Moors in Granada in 1492 with great rejoicing. A Te Deum was sung, and the Pope rewarded the Spaniards by granting them a permanent dispensation from Friday abstinence.

The Protestant reformers, in the following century, swept away any formal obligation to observe particular days of fast and abstinence, though it perhaps should be noted that they did not completely reject fasting as a private penance, or in times of great national catastrophe. Today, even for Roman Catholics, fasting and abstinence are mandatory only on Ash Wednesday and the Fridays in Lent.

But, of course, fish and shellfish have meant much more to mankind than mere religious custom. All of the Mediterranean peoples made good use of the bounty so easily obtained off their shores, as have the people of Western Europe. This harvest of the sea was dependable, rarely affected by catastrophes of climate, disease, or war, and it was worth traveling by sea long distances to find the richest catches.

When John Cabot discovered the Grand Banks of Newfoundland in 1497, Atlantic fishing changed almost at once. The banks are elevated areas of the ocean floor that are actually part of the continental shelf. They happen to be in the area where the cold Labrador current and the relatively warm Gulf stream meet, producing exceptionally favorable conditions for plankton and the start of a rich food chain that includes cod, haddock, herring, and mackerel. The English, the French, the Portuguese, and the

Basques all flocked to the area, using the island of Newfound-land itself as a summer base for salting and drying the fish. Fishing changed from a local occupation to an international industry, with a product that could be sold almost anywhere.

Four hundred years would pass before commercial fishing changed again, and then it changed more than it had in three thousand years. First steam and then diesel engines enabled fishing crews to travel faster and farther and in bigger ships, and then power equipment made it possible to handle bigger nets and take bigger catches. New methods of icing fish aboard ship increased the efficiency of the fishing fleets, while the development of factory or mother ships made it possible to fillet, freeze, or can the catch anywhere in the world.

Today the finest of seafood is available almost anywhere in the United States, and Americans are buying increasing quantities each year. Good cooks are finding new ways to enjoy seafood, but also are turning to the classic recipes developed all over the world.

COQUILLES SAINT-JACQUES À LA PARISIENNE
6 servings

Coquilles Saint-Jacques is a French phrase meaning scallops. A *coquille* is a shell; in English the word became "cockle" (although cockles are not in fact from the same family of bivalves as scallops), as in "cockles and mussels, alive, alive oh" or "cockle shells all in a row." The Saint-Jacques is Saint James the Apostle, whose great shrine was at Santiago de Compostela in Gallicia, northwestern Spain, near the Atlantic Ocean and in a region known for its veins of gold and tin.

As the age of metals began, early people moved along the coasts of western Europe in search of these precious commodities; with them came the cult of the great stone megaliths, of which Stonehenge is the best known example. Padron, one of the numerous small ports that focus on Santiago, still has two such megaliths. The tradition of the sanctity of the old stone monuments lingered for centuries and the legend arose that the body of St. James, after his martyrdom in Palestine, had been carried to Spain for burial and brought ashore at Padron.

The reputed discovery of the bones of St. James in the ninth century made Compostela a great shrine. Pilgrimages to Santiago de Compostela began in the Middle Ages. Each pilgrim received, as a badge of proof that he had made the journey, a scallop shell, symbol of St. James. Erasmus sarcastically suggested that perhaps the shell was chosen as a symbol because the beaches were full of them and they cost nothing. Another equally pragmatic explanation points out that since Gallicia was the only area of Europe harvesting scallops in a sizeable quantities, the scallop shell proved unequivocally that the pilgrim had actually made it to the site of the shrine to St. James. But since the site had held a pagan shrine before the Christian one, there may have been another, long-lost meaning to the scallop shell.

1 pound scallops

2 tablespoons finely minced onion

⅓ cup plus 2 tablespoons butter or margarine, divided

1 tablespoon lemon juice

Salt

¼ teaspoon paprika

¾ cup dry white wine

½ pound coarsely chopped mushrooms

3 tablespoons all-purpose flour

1 cup whipping cream

2 teaspoons finely minced fresh parsley

⅓ cup fine dry bread crumbs

6 individual baking shells, about 5 inches in diameter

1. If large sea scallops are used, cut each into 3 or 4 pieces. Wash scallops; remove any shell particles and drain.

2. In medium saucepan, melt 1 tablespoon butter. Add onion and cook, stirring, until tender. Add scallops, lemon juice, ½ teaspoon salt, paprika, and wine. Simmer 10 minutes. Add mushrooms; simmer 2 minutes longer. Drain liquid from scallop mixture and measure; add water to make ½ cup and set aside.

3. In a medium saucepan over low heat melt ⅓ cup butter. Blend in flour. Cook over low heat, stirring until mixture is smooth and bubbly. Continue to cook and stir, on and off heat, for several minutes to rid flour of raw taste. Stir in reserved liquid and cream. Heat to boiling, stirring constantly. Boil and stir 1 minute. Stir in parsley.

4. Melt 1 tablespoon butter in small skillet; add bread crumbs, stirring until brown. Set aside.

5. Reserving about ½ cup sauce in saucepan, pour remainder over scallop and mushroom mixture: heat through, stirring frequently, add salt if needed. Spoon scallop mixture into 6 individual baking shells; spread each with about 1 tablespoon reserved sauce.

6. Place shells on baking sheet. Broil shells 5 inches from heat 5–8 minutes or until sauce is bubbly and brown. Sprinkle with browned crumbs.

FINNAN HADDIE
6 servings

Finnan Haddie is smoked haddock, named for the little Scottish fishing village of Findorn, which became famous in the eighteenth century for its smoked fish. The fishermen's wives split the haddock, then salted them and smoked them slowly over green wood or peat fires.

Most of the fish sold as "finnan haddie" here in the United States is really smoked cod, but it, or other smoked fish, can be prepared in the traditional Finnan Haddie manner.

2 pounds smoked haddock
1 small onion, chopped
Juice of half a lemon
6 tablespoons butter or margarine
6 tablespoons all-purpose flour
3 cups milk
Salt
Pepper
2 tablespoons finely minced parsley
Hot buttered toast

1. Place fish in a large saucepan or skillet. Add onion, lemon juice, and water to barely cover. Cover with a close-fitting lid and poach, barely simmering, 15–20 minutes. Test for doneness by inserting a fork into thickest part; fish is done if it flakes easily.
2. Remove fish from liquor and skin and bone it; break up into fairly small pieces. Set aside, covered.
3. In a large saucepan over low heat, melt butter Stir in flour and cook over low heat, stirring constantly, until mixture is smooth and bubbly. Continue to stir, on and off heat, for several minutes to rid flour of raw taste. Whisk in milk. Heat to boiling, stirring constantly. Boil and stir 1 minute. Add fish and stir. Taste, adding salt and pepper if desired. Pour into warm serving dish and sprinkle with parsley. Serve with toast.

ANGELS ON HORSEBACK
26–32 appetizers

Angels on Horseback are oysters wrapped in bacon and broiled, served as an appetizer or hors d'oeuvre (literally, something outside of the work, in this case, outside the main courses of a meal). The name has a flippant, modern ring to it, but actually Angels on Horseback were created in Victorian England as a "savoury" to serve at the end of a meal. Just why angels would need to ride horseback is another mystery of nomenclature history. A companion recipe, prunes wrapped in bacon, is called Devils on Horseback.

Note: *For Devils on Horseback, use large, pitted, moisturized prunes in place of oysters.*

1 pint shucked oysters (see recipe for Oysters Rockefeller, next)
2 pounds sliced bacon
Toast squares, crusts removed (¼ slice bread per oyster)

1. Preheat oven to 450°F. Wrap a slice of bacon around each oyster (half slices may be used if oysters are small) and secure with a wooden cocktail pick.
2. Place wrapped oysters on a rack in a shallow baking pan and bake, turning once, until bacon is crisp on all sides, about 10 minutes. Remove picks and place each oyster on a square of toast.

OYSTERS ROCKEFELLER
4 servings

Oysters Rockefeller were first served at Antoine's, the elegant and venerable New Orleans restaurant celebrated for its cooking since 1840. Jules Alciatore, son of the original Antoine, conjured up the oyster preparation in 1899; tasting his creation, he decided that a dish so rich should be named for the richest man he could think of, John D. Rockefeller, Sr. It was actually an adaptation of *escargots à la bourguignonne* (snails simmered in a white wine broth and then served in their shells with herb butter). Bernard Gusto, the fifth generation of the family to manage the restaurant, explains simply that snails were unobtainable and oysters popular, so his great-grandfather thickened a Bourguignonne sauce and spread it on some oysters. Actually, there is a good bit more to it than that, and Antoine's has never divulged the restaurant's recipe, though many similar ones have been devised.

Rock salt

2 dozen medium oysters, in their shells

1 (10-ounce) package frozen chopped spinach

½ cup butter or margarine

1 bunch watercress, finely chopped

¼ cup minced parsley, preferably flat-leaf

6 green onions, including 3 inches of dark green tops, minced

½ teaspoon ground black pepper

1 teaspoon anchovy paste

½ cup whipping cream

Ground anise

Salt

Note: *The rock salt is only to hold the oyster shells upright. Crushed aluminum foil would do just as well, but would not look nearly as traditional.*

1. Preheat oven to 400°F. Spread rock salt to a depth of about ½ inch in four 9-inch pie pans. Arrange pans on baking sheets and set them in the oven to heat the salt while preparing oysters. Scrub oysters under running cold water. Break off thin end of shell with hammer. Force a table knife or shucking knife between halves of shell at broken end; pull apart. Cut oyster at muscle to separate from shell. Remove any bits of shell. Save bottom half of shells.

2. Cook spinach according to package directions. Drain, pressing till all moisture is removed, and set aside. In heavy skillet over medium heat melt butter. Add spinach, watercress, parsley, and green onions. Sauté until vegetables are slightly wilted, about 5 minutes. Puree in food mill or food processor if desired.

3. Return to skillet and add black pepper, anchovy paste, whipping cream, and dash of anise. Cook, stirring, until mixture is thick and creamy, about 5 minutes. Add salt if needed. Add few drops water if mixture is too thick to spread easily. Set aside.

4. Pat oysters dry on clean, dry dish towel. Place one oyster in each shell and nest shells in rock salt. Divide spinach mixture among oysters, spreading an even layer on top of each. Bake in oven until delicately browned, 10–15 minutes.

BISMARCK HERRING
3–4 servings

Bismarck Herring are named for Otto von Bismarck (1815–1898), the Prussian statesman who virtually founded the unified German Empire and became its first chancellor. Bismarck was a huge man, with an enormous appetite for both food and drink. German authorities agree that he was immensely fond of pickled herring and usually ate them for lunch.

4 fresh herring

1 cup water

1 teaspoon yellow mustard seeds

1 bay leaf

1 cup white-wine vinegar

1 large onion, cut in thin rings

1 mild onion, chopped

Half an apple, thinly sliced

1 tablespoon lemon juice

1 tablespoon finely chopped chives

1. Remove herring heads and tails. Fillet and wash each herring. In a small saucepan combine water, mustard seeds, and bay leaf. Bring to a boil. Remove from heat; cool slightly. Add vinegar and onion rings.
2. In a jar or earthenware pot, layer herring and vinegar mixture. Make sure fish are completely covered with liquid. Cover container and let stand in refrigerator for at least 48 hours or preferably a week. Drain before serving. Garnish with chopped onion, apple slices, lemon juice, and chives.

Note: *Fresh herring are not always available in the United States, but Bismarack Herring (sometimes under different names, such as "Homestyle Herring" or "Old-Fashioned Herring") can be purchased ready-made in most large supermarkets. Garnish as above. In Germany, Bismarck Herring are usually served as a supper dish with good bread or potatoes boiled in their skins.*

HANGTOWN FRY
4 servings

Hangtown Fry is a California dish, originating with the Forty-Niners. Hangtown, now known as Placerville, was a rough-and-ready mining camp, named for its rather numerous public hangings, but also the site of a number of good-sized strikes. When a lucky miner took a sack of gold to the Cary House restaurant and ordered the most expensive meal in the place, the chef suggested oysters and eggs, both high priced at the time. The concoction came to be known as Hangtown Fry. Bacon is the traditional accompaniment.

½ cup flour
Salt
Pepper
9 eggs
1 cup fine dry bread crumbs
12 slices bacon
12 oysters, shucked (see recipe for Oysters Rockefeller, page 80)
Butter or margarine

1. On a large plate mix flour with a sprinkle of salt and pepper; set aside. On a second large plate lightly beat 1 egg with 1 teaspoon water; set aside. Spread bread crumbs on a third plate. In a large bowl beat remaining 8 eggs.
2. In a large frying pan cook bacon and set aside.
3. Dredge each oyster in flour, then dip in beaten egg and roll in bread crumbs. Melt butter in a clean large frying pan over low heat. When butter is hot, add oysters and cook, turning, until golden brown.
4. Add beaten eggs and cook over medium heat until firm, lifting from bottom and sides of skillet to allow uncooked egg to flow under cooked mixture. Season with salt and pepper. Serve with bacon.

LOBSTER THERMIDOR
4 servings

Lobster Thermidor was introduced to the world on January 24, 1894, at Maire's, a well-known Paris restaurant located at the corner of the boulevards Strasbourg and Saint-Denis. On that evening Victorien Sardou's play *Thermidor* had its first performance at the Comédie-Français, and Maire decided to launch his new dish by giving it the name of the play.

Thermidor, one of three dramas by Sardou about events occurring during the French Revolution, in turn took the name of one of the summer months in the quickly forgotten revolutionary calendar. As a playwright, Sardou was a superb manipulator of tension, tears, terror, and laughter; his plays enjoyed immense popularity during his lifetime, but they lacked depth, and are seldom performed today. As someone has remarked, Lobster Thermidor has enjoyed a far longer run than the play for which it was named.

3 quarts water

3 tablespoons salt

2 live lobsters (about 1 pound each)

2 tablespoons butter or margarine

2 tablespoons chopped onion

1 can (3 ounces) sliced mushrooms

2 tablespoons flour

⅛ teaspoon paprika

½ cup half-and-half

½ cup chicken broth (canned or from bouillon powder or cubes)

½ teaspoon Worcestershire sauce

1 egg yolk, beaten

2 tablespoons sherry

Salt

Pepper

3 tablespoons dry bread crumbs

1 tablespoon grated Parmesan cheese

1. Heat water and salt to boiling in large kettle. Plunge lobsters headfirst into water. Cover; heat to boiling. Reduce heat; simmer about 5 minutes. Drain. Place lobster on its back. With a sharp knife cut lengthwise completely in half. Remove the stomach, which is just back of the head, and the intestinal vein, which runs from the stomach to the tip of the tail. Crack claws. Remove meat carefully (should be about 2 cups); reserve shells. Separate meat into small pieces.

2. Preheat oven to 450°F. In a large, heavy saucepan melt butter and add onion and mushrooms. Cook over moderately low heat until onion is tender. Stir in flour and paprika. Cook over low heat until mixture is bubbly. Continue to stir, on and off heat, for several minutes to rid flour of raw taste. Remove from heat. Whisk in half-and-half, chicken broth, and Worcestershire sauce. Heat to boiling, stirring constantly. Boil and stir 1 minute. Remove from heat. Quickly stir several tablespoons of the hot mixture into egg yolk. Blend egg mixture into remaining hot mixture. Stir in sherry and lobster meat; heat through. Taste; add salt and pepper if desired.

3. Place lobster shell halves in baking pan, 13 x 9 x 2 inches. Fill shells with lobster mixture. Mix bread crumbs and cheese; sprinkle over mixture. Bake 5–8 minutes.

Note: *The tradition that lobsters must be sold alive stems from the fact that lobster meat spoils so easily. If you find the idea of boiling a live lobster offensive, ask the fish market attendant to kill it for you by dispatching it quickly and humanely; then you can take it home and boil it at once. Or, have the market staff boil the lobsters for you and use the meat promptly.*

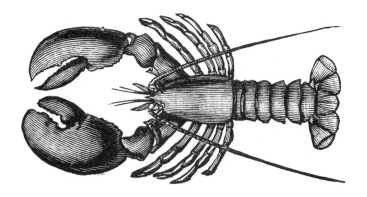

LOBSTER NEWBERG
4 servings

Ben Wenberg was a wealthy sea captain engaged in the fruit trade between Cuba and New York. When on shore he customarily ate at Delmonico's, the fine old restaurant in New York City. One day in 1876, home from a cruise, he entered the café (always less formal than the elegant dining rooms) and announced that he had brought back a new way to cook lobster. Calling for a chafing dish, he demonstrated his discovery by cooking the dish at the table and invited Charles Delmonico to taste it. Delmonico said, "Delicious!" and forthwith entered the dish on the restaurant menu, naming it in honor of its creator Lobster à la Wenberg. It caught the public fancy and became a standby of the aftertheater suppers then in vogue.

Then Wenberg and Delmonico had a falling out. The precise cause is a bit obscure, but it can be assumed that it involved a fist-fight at the restaurant. Such an occurrence, though hardly unusual in nineteenth-century society, even among gentlemen, was not something the dignified Delmonico's would countenance. Lobster à la Wenberg was taken off the menu at once. That did not stop patrons from continuing to call for it, so Delmonico was forced to compromise. By typographical sleight-of-hand he changed the spelling from "Wenberg" to "Newberg," and Lobster Newberg was born.

2 cups cooked lobster meat
¼ cup butter or margarine
¼ cup all-purpose flour
2 cups half-and-half
½ cup sherry
2 egg yolks, beaten
Salt
Pepper
4 baked puff pastry shells,
   or 4 pieces toast

Melt butter and sauté lobster meat briefly. (Butter should not brown.) Remove lobster meat and set aside. Add flour to butter and cook over low heat, stirring, until mixture is bubbly. Continue to stir, on and off heat, for several minutes to rid flour of raw taste. Add half-and-half, whisking, and bring to a boil. Boil and stir 1 minute. Add sherry and reheat. Quickly stir several tablespoons of the hot mixture into egg yolks, mixing well. Blend egg mixture into remaining hot mixture, stirring to blend. Hold over low heat for 2–3 minutes but do not boil. Add lobster meat and salt and pepper if desired. Serve in puff pastry shells or over toast.

DELMONICO'S

SHRIMP DE JONGHE
8 servings

Shrimp de Jonghe, created far from the ocean, is a Chicago specialty, named for a Belgian family who came to the city around 1890 and opened a restaurant called Jacque's on the South Side during the Columbian Exposition of 1893. Later the popular eating place moved downtown where it flourished until it was closed in the 1930s for violating Prohibition.

No one seems to know whether it was chef Emil Zehr or proprietor Henri de Jonghe who invented the magnificent casserole that now bears the owner's family name, but its fame has spread nationwide.

Note: *If preferred, 2 pounds of cooked, cleaned shrimp can be substituted for the 3 pounds of raw shrimp. Bake at 400°F 10–15 minutes, or just until crumbs are brown. (Overcooking toughens shrimp.)*

¾ cup butter

1 teaspoon salt

1 or 2 cloves garlic, finely minced

1 cup dry bread crumbs

2 tablespoons finely minced fresh parsley

½ cup sherry

⅛ teaspoon cayenne

¼ teaspoon paprika

3 pounds raw shrimp

1. Preheat oven to 375°F. In a large pot bring 2 quarts water to the simmering point.
2. Cream together butter, salt, and garlic. Mix in bread crumbs, parsley, sherry, cayenne, and paprika. Set aside.
3. Shell and devein shrimp, then add to simmering water. Cook only for a few minutes, until shrimp turn pink. Rinse with cold water and drain. Butter 8 individual ovenproof casserole dishes (about 5 inches in diameter). Divide shrimp among casserole dishes. Mound crumb mixture on top. Bake 20 minutes or until crumbs are golden brown and sizzling.

CHAPTER 6

MEATS & POULTRY

Although new breeds of domestic animals have been introduced throughout history, the actual species raised by humans for food have hardly changed since neolithic times. The first to be domesticated (with the possible exception of reindeer) were sheep and goats. Both were reasonably tractable and traveled together naturally in flocks, making them easy to herd. Almost certainly, in many parts of the world, wandering hunters had turned into wandering shepherds even before the development of agriculture.

The pig, on the other hand, was the meat animal of the early sedentary farmers. Notoriously difficult to drive, pigs could be domesticated only in a settled community, where they could be allowed to forage in the woods, or kept in pens. That pork has been thought unclean by a number of peoples perhaps derives from the age-old antipathy between the nomad and the farmer: the pig was first despised and then forbidden as the animal of the enemy.

The domestication of cattle aided both nomadic and sedentary societies. Certainly cattle could have been herded by primitive nomads to provide a reliable source of sustenance, as they are in some parts of Africa today; cows after all give even more milk than goats. That advantage also would have been obvious to early farmers, who prized cattle even more highly when they learned that oxen could be made to pull plows and later, carts.

Slaughtering time, in Europe at least, came in the early winter. Domestic animals could no longer be turned out to graze or forage and the scarcity of both hay and grain limited the number a farmer could feed through the barren months; the rest had to be killed. Besides, meat would keep longer during the cold weather. It was a natural time for early farmers to offer sacrifices to their gods, as well as to feast and rejoice. Both the Roman Saturnalia and the Germanic Yule turned into great winter festivals, a practice that in turn was quickly attached to the Christian celebration of Christ's birth.

The collapse of the Roman Empire plunged Europe into the Dark Ages, when feudalism imposed an insurmountable barrier between the social classes. Meat became a luxury almost unknown to the serfs who raised the animals because, inevitably, they went as taxes to the lord. The disparity between serf and master shows clearly in the English language: *ox* and *cow, boar* and *sow, sheep, calf,* and *deer* are all Anglo-Saxon, the language of the conquered, whereas *beef, pork, mutton, veal,* and *venison*—the names for the meat of those animals—all come from the language of the victors, the Norman-French. The poor could only hope for the scraps: calves' liver, pigs' feet, and oxtails.

Even after times got better, there was still the problem of storing meat in an era without refrigeration. Salting, smoking, and drying all played a role in meat preservation, but nothing made better use of every scrap of meat than sausages. And there were so *many* kinds of sausages! In time almost every region had its own specialty, and many of them made the crossing to the New World; wieners from Vienna (Wien in German), frankfurters from Frankfurt, bologna from the Italian city of the same name, thuringer from the Thuringian forest, and braunschweiger, a mild liver sausage, from the German duchy of Braunschweig, in English known as Brunswick and the ancestral home of the English Hanoverians.

The history of poultry is somewhat different. Ducks and

geese were kept in Egypt and Mesopotamia, but it seems that all of the chickens of the world are descended from the wild jungle fowl of India, which only gradually made their way to the west. Fowl required little feed compared to larger animals, and even some of the poorest households in any era could keep a rooster (to wake the family, making sure that everyone got up and got to work) and a few hens for eggs. Once in a while, surely, an aged hen or cock would find its way into the cooking pot. There the tough old bird would simmer for hours until it was finally tender enough to provide a welcome treat in a largely meatless world.

Larger and less commonplace birds were reserved for the nobility. Valued especially at the holidays, they were considered most appropriate gifts and thus found their way into the well-known carol, "The Twelve Days of Christmas." The "four calling birds" were originally "colly birds," that is, blackbirds, and the "five golden rings" were ring-necked pheasants, so all the gifts, up to the maids a-milking, were really birds for the table.

But the crowning glory of a fine medieval feast was neither swan nor goose but rather the lordly peacock. Native to India, the peafowl was semi-domesticated and, like the ordinary chicken, gradually introduced into the west. Cooks readying the bird for the table rarely plucked the gorgeous feathers; instead, after setting aside the head and feet, they carefully skinned the whole carcass, leaving the blue and green iridescent plumage intact. While the peacock roasted, the kitchen staff gilded the beak and feet and rubbed the skin with spices. Then, just before serving, they reassembled it all, including the great tail feathers. As a final fillip, a bit of rag soaked in some flammable liquid would be slipped into the open beak and lighted, so that the bird could be carried to the table apparently breathing fire. The whole effect elicited enthusiastic applause, and no one even minded that, in fact, the meat was tough, dry, and stringy.

Then, in the sixteenth century, the turkey began to replace

the peacock as the bird for festive occasions. A native of the Americas, it was domesticated by the Aztecs. Brought back to Europe by the returning *conquistadores*, the great birds received an appropriate name in French, *dinde*—which was originally *d'Indes* (from the Indies)—but a complete misnomer in English. The word "turkey" had first been applied to Guinea fowl, probably because they were introduced into England by merchants from the east, possibly only because "Turkey," like "Tartary," was applied indiscriminately to any distant, exotic place.

When the new birds from America began to appear in the markets, it was taken for granted that they and Guinea fowl must be related. The confusion, which makes little sense to the modern mind, existed in a number of countries. Even the great Swedish scientist, Linnaeus, used *Meleagris*, the classical name for the African fowl, as the scientific name for the American bird. Gradually the African bird came to be known as Guinea fowl when brought directly from West Africa by the Portuguese, while the older name turkey was retained for the much larger birds from the New World.

The following recipes represent a selection of meat and poultry dishes that all have fascinating and occasionally exotic origins, but call only for standard ingredients available at the supermarket and for simple techniques any cook can readily command. Gilding is strictly optional!

CHICKEN MARENGO
6 servings

Chicken Marengo takes its name from a battle fought on June 14, 1800. Napoleon Bonaparte had been made First Consul the previous November, and the war with Austria resumed in the spring. Planning a surprise attack, Napoleon took his army through the Alps even before the snows melted, and suddenly appeared behind the Austrians in Italy, where they were beseiging a small French force in Genoa. Napoleon, certain the Austrians were trying to escape, spent a few days maneuvering. He sent one division to the north to block any possible attempt to cross the Po River and another to the south to block the road back to Genoa. Early in the morning of June 14, the Austrians attacked. By 9 A.M., Napoleon was sending frantic messages to his missing divisions, urging them to return. By afternoon the French were all but defeated. Then a mud-spattered General Desaix rode up ahead of his men. The troops marching to the south had heard the sound of cannon and were returning even before they received the order to do so. Desaix looked the situation over and bluntly announced, "This battle is completely lost, but it is only two o'clock; there is time to win another." And win they did, though Desaix himself was killed in the attack. By six P.M. the Austrians were in full flight.

In the meantime, so the story goes, Napoleon's chef, a Swiss named Dunand, found himself in a predicament. In the confusion of the day the supply wagons had been lost. Nevertheless, he knew that the general would eventually appear for his dinner, exhausted and understandably famished, for Napoleon ate nothing on the day of a battle.

Hastily Dunand sent out men from the quartermaster's staff and ordnance corp in search of provisions. All they could obtain in the little nearby village of Marengo were three small eggs, four tomatoes, six crayfish, a small hen, a little garlic, and some oil. Quickly Dunand cleaned and cut up the chicken, browned it in oil, and then fried the eggs in the same oil with a few cloves of garlic and the tomatoes. Finally he added some water laced with brandy borrowed from Napoleon's flask, thickened the mixture with his own bread ration, and put the crayfish on top to cook in the steam.

The dish was served on a tin plate, the chicken surrounded by the fried eggs and crayfish, with the sauce poured over it. Bonaparte supposedly ate ravenously and told Dunand, "You must feed me like this after every battle."

The story is plausible. Napoleon did much to create the Napoleonic legend and often seemed to believe it himself. Marengo was not a great victory. It was a narrow escape from defeat and credit really should have gone to the loyal Desaix rather than to Bonaparte. But that was not the way the slight young Corsican chose to remember it. Marengo was his triumph, proof that Fate had smiled on him, proof of his destiny, a talisman. He chose Marengo as the name for his favorite horse and even on St. Helena, delirious at the end, he murmured incoherently of victory and Marengo. Finally he was buried in the grey overcoat he had worn on that fateful day.

But the dish? The dish is sheer legend. Louis Antoine Fauvelet de Bourrienne, Napoleon's private secretary, describing the evening after the famous battle in his memoirs, wrote simply, "Supper sent from the Convent del Bosco . . ." and, further, "in return for the abundance of good provisions and wine which they supplied . . . the holy fathers were allowed a guard to protect them against pillage."

The tale, so widely accepted, evidently started when an enterprising restaurateur decided to capitalize on the French devotion to Napoleon. He added bizarre garnishes to a standard dish, Chicken Provençal, contrived a believable story, and Chicken Marengo was created.

1 frying chicken, 2 ½–3 pounds, cut up

¼ cup flour

1 teaspoon salt

¼ teaspoon black pepper

½ cup olive oil or vegetable oil

1 clove garlic, finely minced

2 cups canned tomatoes

3 small eggs (optional)

Butter or margarine

3 slices bread, toasted (optional)

6 crayfish or 6 shrimp, cooked (optional)

Note: Crayfish are virtually impossible to obtain anywhere but Louisiana. Another possible substitute would be cooked lobster tails.

1. Remove skin from chicken and dust with flour, salt, and pepper. In a heavy skillet heat oil and brown chicken thoroughly. Pour off excess oil.

2. Add garlic and tomatoes and simmer 25–30 minutes or until chicken is tender. Stir occasionally and add a small amount of water if mixture becomes too dry.

3. Fry eggs individually in butter and place each on a circle of toast. Place chicken on large platter and pour over sauce. Garnish with eggs and crayfish or shrimp.

BEEF WELLINGTON
4 servings

Beef Wellington commemorates Arthur Wellesley, First Duke of Wellington, the man who crushed Napoleon at Waterloo. After Bonaparte's overwhelming defeat at Leipzig in 1813, the Duke served briefly as British ambassador to the court of the restored Louis XVIII; he then went on to represent Britain at the Congress of Vienna. It was here that he received the news that Napoleon had escaped from Elba. Confident that the French king could handle the situation, Wellington remained unperturbed, but as each French force sent out against Napoleon quickly and emotionally went over to the Emperor's side, Wellington's presence in Vienna proved invaluable. The allies quickly drew up plans for another campaign; Wellington and the old Prussian Field Marshall Blücher would invade France through Belgium while the Austrians and Russians came in from the east. In an emotional leave-taking Tsar Alexander I told Wellington that it was up to him to "save the world again."

The British and Prussian armies assembled first, and Wellington waited in Brussels, amusing himself at balls and cricket matches. His carefree demeanor almost certainly represented a deliberate ploy to raise morale.

Napoleon decided to strike at once. His *Armée du Nord* crossed the border into Belgium on June 15, 1815. The first French aim was to separate the British from the Prussians and in this they were successful. On the 16th the Prussian army was put to rout at Ligny, but was not destroyed. In a second battle fought the same day a different French force attacked Wellington, who had only a fraction of his men in the field. Had they commenced fighting early in the day, the French might have prevailed, but their inactivity allowed Wellington to send in thousands more men. On the 17th the French again wasted the whole morning while Wellington skillfully thinned out his forces and retired, assured that Blücher was moving toward him. By now a steady rain was falling. The muddy ground the next morning made it difficult to maneuver the huge French cannon. Again Napoleon put off an actual engagement until afternoon. It proved to be a fatal mistake, for it allowed the Prussians time to arrive in support of Wellington. Even after the battle began, Napoleon waited, reluctant to send in his best troops, the Imperial Guard; by the time they received their orders it was too late. Wellington and Blücher had united and all was lost for the French.

Volumes have been written about Wellington the soldier, but the dish that bears his name is surprisingly elusive. Almost certainly the pastry covering was at first a mere paste of flour and water, wrapped around the uncooked tenderloin so that it would roast without browning, a culinary fad of the era. In time the covering became puff pastry and an integral part of the dish. Then the chefs on the continent, with their oft-noted penchant for lily-gilding, inserted a layer of truffles and *pâté de foie gras*, today often simplified to mushrooms and chicken livers.

The Irish, too, claim the Duke, for he was born in Dublin in the days of the British ascendancy. In Ireland Beef Wellington, sometimes called Wellington Steak, remains a simple combination of excellent rare beef and flaky pastry. The dish is also known in France, where, not surprisingly, it is simply called *filet de boeuf en croûte*.

1 package (about 17 ounces) frozen puff pastry (2 sheets)

4 filets mignons, about 1 ½ inches thick,
   or 4 slices of rolled top sirloin roast

Salt

Pepper

1 egg, well beaten

1. Thaw puff pastry according to package directions.
2. Sprinkle filets mignons with salt and pepper and broil just until brown on both sides and very rare. Cool.
3. Preheat oven to 400°F.
4. Unfold thawed puff pastry sheets. With a sharp knife, trim two ½-inch strips from the longer side of each sheet, then cut both sheets in half. On a lightly floured board roll out the 4 sections to 8-inch squares.
5. Place 1 filet on each sheet of pastry. Wrap pastry around filet, enclosing it completely and sealing seams with water. Place seam side down on a baking sheet. With pastry brush, coat exposed pastry completely with beaten egg. Use reserved strips of pastry to form a lattice pattern trim. Gently brush lattice with egg.
6. Bake 20–25 minutes or until puffed and brown.

CHATEAUBRIAND
3–4 servings

In the final decade of the eighteenth century, François Chateaubriand (1768–1848) was living in London, a penniless emigré, after a brief adventure in America and a short stint in the French Royalist Army. He had fled his native France, where his brother had gone to the guillotine and his mother, sisters, and wife were all imprisoned. Twenty-five years later, with the Bourbons restored to the throne, Chateaubriand returned to London as the French ambassador, representing his country with great elegance at the Court of Saint James. In the intervening years he was an author, a philanderer, and a gourmet, not necessarily in that order.

As a writer Chateaubriand ushered in the age of French Romanticism. A devoted follower of Rousseau, he idealized the noble savage, despite the fact that he had met real Indians during his sojourn in the United States. His fashionable melancholy and delight in antiquities exactly suited the tastes of his generation.

Despite Chateaubriand's reputation as a talented writer, few read his works today. Instead he is remembered for a steak devised by his chef, Montmireil!

As originally conceived, Chateaubriand was a thick slice cut from the tenderloin of beef, then broiled sandwiched between two thin, inferior steaks. The outer steaks were discarded so that the Chateaubriand could be served in all its pink succulence. Chateaubriand Sauce accompanied the steak.

Few today would care to imitate Montmirail's carefully unbrowned meat, a fleeting fashion, and the original sauce might seem heavy and almost like gravy. But the cut remains a superb piece of meat, and, fortunately, a lighter version of the sauce has evolved that complements the steak perfectly.

½ cup dry white wine

½ cup canned consommé, undiluted

1 shallot, finely minced

1 tablespoon butter

1 teaspoon minced fresh tarragon *or* dried tarragon flakes

½ teaspoon fresh lemon juice

Dash cayenne

1 slice from middle of beef tenderloin, 1 ½–2 inches thick,
    1 ½–2 pounds in weight

1. In a small saucepan and over low heat, simmer wine, consommé, and shallot until reduced to ⅓ cup. Add remaining ingredients and reheat. If using dried tarragon, simmer for a few minutes until flakes no longer float. Set aside.

2. Broil or pan broil steak to desired doneness. Add pan juices to sauce if desired. Place steak on heated platter. Again bring sauce to a boil and pour over steak.

STEAK DIANE
6 servings

Steak Diane was originally a way of serving venison, and its sharp sauce was intended to complement the sweet flavor of deer meat. It was named for Diana, Roman goddess of the hunt, and since Diana was also the moon goddess, the small pieces of toast used to sop up the delicious juices are traditionally cut in crescent shapes.

Worcestershire sauce, a prime ingredient, has an interesting background of its own. As British involvement in India grew in the early nineteenth century, the flavors of the subcontinent found their way into British cookery. A number of English families began to produce piquant sauces for their own private use, always made from a secret recipe with Indian roots. The best-known survival is Worcestershire sauce, made, as the label on the original brand always says, "from the recipe of a nobleman in the country."

Note: *If preferred, Steak Diane may be prepared at the table, using an electric skillet or other table-top cooking device.*

6–9 slices white bread

Softened butter or margarine

½ cup butter or margarine

6 slices of beef filet, ½ inch thick, or other trimmed pieces of good-quality steak

3 tablespoons Worcestershire sauce

¼ cup ketchup (optional)

½ cup Burgundy wine

1 tablespoon minced garlic

2 tablespoons minced chives

½ cup sliced mushrooms

¼ cup Cognac or brandy, warmed

1. Lightly butter both sides of bread. Using a crescent-shaped cookie cutter, cut out 18 crescents. Grill in a heavy frying pan, a few at a time, till golden brown on both sides. Set aside.
2. Melt ½ cup butter in large heated sauté pan. Add slices of filet and cook, turning until done, about 3 minutes for medium rare.
3. Add Worcestershire sauce, catsup (if desired), wine, garlic, chives, and mushrooms. Cook until flavors are blended and mushrooms are almost tender, about 2 minutes. Gently pour Cognac over all and light carefully. Bring to the table and serve when flames die down, arranging three crescents of toast on each plate before adding steak and pan juices.

REFORM CUTLETS
6 servings

Reform Cutlets surely have one of the strangest names ever devised for a dish. No, they are not lamb chops out to change the world. They take their name from the Reform Club, one of London's oldest political clubs, founded by men who had backed the Reform Bill of 1832.

Alexis Soyer was the chef who invented the cutlet recipe. French by birth, he came to England as a young man and quickly distinguished himself. Taking charge of the Reform Club's modern kitchens, which he himself had designed, he virtually assured the success of the new gentlemen's club.

But Alexis Soyer was much more than a brilliant chef. Kindhearted and inventive, he was quick to offer his services to the British government, setting up soup kitchens in Ireland when the Potato Famine struck and accompanying Florence Nightingale to the Crimea, where he greatly improved the quality of the food served to the troops. He also invented a portable field stove that was used by the British army until well into the twentieth century and was the author of numerous books on food and cooking.

Variation: *If preferred, Reform Sauce may be served with plain broiled lamb chops, or with other cuts of meat.*

¼ cup butter or margarine

2 medium carrots, chopped

1 medium onion, chopped

1 clove garlic

4 ounces finely minced cooked ham, divided

5 cloves

¼ teaspoon mace

1 bayleaf

½ teaspoon thyme

1 tablespoon chopped fresh parsley,
    or 1 ½ teaspoons dry parsley flakes

1 cup red wine

1 ¾ cups beef stock,
    or 1 can (10 ½ ounces) consommé plus water to equal 1 ¾ cups

¼ cup currant jelly

2 tablespoons arrowroot

12 small lamb rib chops

2 eggs

2 cups dry breadcrumbs

Salt

Pepper

2 tablespoons oil

1. Melt butter in heavy saucepan and add vegetables, garlic, 2 ounces of ham, spices, and herbs. Sauté for a few minutes, then add the wine and stock or consommé. Bring mixture to a boil, cover tightly, and simmer for 30 minutes. Remove from heat and add currant jelly; allow to dissolve. Strain the liquid through a sieve, pressing down firmly on the vegetables with a spoon to extract all the juice. Discard vegetables.

2. Place arrowroot in top of double boiler and add a small amount of the strained stock. Add remainder of stock and place over low heat, stirring constantly until thickened. Place over hot water and keep warm over low heat.

3. Trim chops of any fat and set aside. Place eggs in small bowl and beat slightly. In another bowl mix remaining 2 ounces of ham with breadcrumbs. Season each chop with salt and pepper and dip first into eggs and then firmly into breadcrumb mixture, making sure each chop is well coated.

4. Heat oil in large frying pan and sauté the chops for approximately 12 minutes, turning frequently, until both sides are brown. Transfer to platter and serve with sauce passed separately.

BEEF STROGANOFF
4–6 servings

The Stroganovs (both spellings are common) were originally a Russian peasant family who succeeded in turning themselves into wealthy merchants. By the fifteenth century they were developing salt and iron mines and carrying on a lucrative trade in furs and timber. In a steady succession of moves to consolidate their power, the next generations of Stroganovs helped Ivan the Terrible annex western Siberia, backed Mikhail Romanov in his bid for the throne in 1615, and lent Peter the Great huge sums of money for his wars and innovations. In due time the Stroganovs were made barons and then counts.

Count Pavel Stroganov, a celebrity in turn-of-the-century St. Petersburg, was a noted gourmet as well as a friend of Alexander III. He is frequently credited with creating Beef Stroganoff or having a chef who did so, but in fact a recipe by that name appears in a cookbook published in 1871, well ahead of the heyday of the genial count. In all probability the dish had been in the family for some years and came to more general notice through Pavel's love of entertaining.

As an intriguing ethnographic note, Russian cooking, with its delight in sour cream, still shows the influence of the nomadic peoples of the steppes who lived mostly on what their herds could provide.

Note: *In Russia this dish is usually served with Russian fried potatoes, which are virtually identical to French fries. In the United States, however, it is often served with plain boiled noodles.*

½ pound mushrooms, sliced

6–10 tablespoons vegetable oil

2 medium onions, finely chopped

1 ½ pounds beef tenderloin or boneless sirloin steak

1 ½ cups beef broth (can be canned consommé or bouillon)

1 teaspoon salt

3 tablespoons instant-blending or all-purpose flour

1 teaspoon Dijon mustard

½ cup dairy sour cream

1. In heavy pan sauté mushrooms in small amount of oil; set aside. In same pan, sauté onions in small amount of oil; set aside. Wipe out pan.

2. Remove all fat from meat and cut across grain into thin strips about 2 inches by ½ inch. (To make cutting easier, meat can be partially frozen.) In same heavy pan, brown meat, a few strips at a time, in small amount of oil. Return all meat to pan. Reserve ⅓ cup broth and add remainder to meat; add salt. Heat to boiling; reduce heat. Cover tightly and simmer until beef is tender, about 10 minutes.

3. Mix reserved ⅓ cup broth with flour; gradually stir into beef mixture. Heat to boiling, stirring constantly. Boil and stir 1 minute. Stir in mushrooms, onion, mustard, and sour cream. Heat thoroughly but do not allow to boil.

HUNGARIAN GOULASH
6 servings

In Hungarian *gulyás* means "herdsman," and Goulash did originate as a shepherds' stew. When the Magyars began, in the ninth century, to move west from their homeland in the Russian steppes, they were a pastoral people, much more concerned with their flocks and herds than with settled farming. The silent men who continued the herding tradition, living outdoors for weeks at a time as they watched the sheep and cattle graze on Hungary's great plains, had to carry their sustenance with them. Before setting out with their herds, they cut meat into cubes, then stewed it with onions, slowly, until all liquid was gone. Drying the stewed chunks in the sun, they stored the dehydrated results in a bag made from a sheep's stomach. When they needed a meal, all that was required to reconstitute it was water, a kettle, and slow cooking until it became stew again.

Missing from this recipe, of course, were the tomatoes and paprika now considered essential ingredients, but unknown to the Hungarian herders, for both are native to the Americas. Brought to Spain by the returning *conquistadores*, both crops very gradually became known throughout Europe, but just when and why paprika became a national favorite in Hungary is unclear. Always mindful of their ancient enemy, the Hungarians are convinced that the Turks introduced the pepper in the course of their conquests, although in fact paprika did not become popular in Hungary until long after the Turks were gone.

3 large sweet onions, sliced

3 tablespoons shortening

2 pounds beef stew meat, cut into 1 ½-inch cubes

2 teaspoons salt

2 tablespoons paprika

1 can (8 ounces) tomato sauce

1 can (16 ounces) tomatoes

8 ounces egg noodles

2 tablespoons butter or margarine

1. In a large, heavy kettle sauté onions in shortening for 5 minutes. Remove onions and set aside.
2. Add meat and brown on all sides. Return onions to pan and add remaining ingredients. Cover and simmer over low heat for about 2 hours, or until meat is tender, adding water if mixture becomes too thick.
3. Cook noodles according to package directions. Toss with butter or margarine (to keep pieces separated) and serve with goulash.

SALISBURY STEAK
6 servings

Food faddists flourished in the nineteenth-century United States, partly because so little was known about human nutrition. While Sylvester Graham (see page 23) and the vegetarians railed against meat, Dr. James H. Salisbury (1823–1905) condemned "starches" as the cause of numerous diseases, and advocated a diet consisting mostly of lean beef, preferably ground. It would be easy to dismiss Salisbury as a simple crackpot, but he did in fact possess the scientific credentials to lend his claims some credibility.

A well-educated man with a background in chemistry and medicine, Salisbury all his life thought of himself as a research scientist as well as a physician. His early studies of fungi show that he was groping vaguely toward a germ theory of disease, sometimes approaching the solution to some of its mysteries but always falling short of realization. By the time germ causation of disease was established as scientific reality, Salisbury's interests lay elsewhere and he shared none of the honors for the discovery. It was then that he turned to "poor nutrition" as the source of mankind's ailments.

At any rate, Salisbury Steak survived as rather an elegant term for ground beef, its popularity no doubt reinforced during World War I, when the ubiquitous hamburger or Hamburg steak fell from favor as entirely too German.

Note: *Delicious with sautéed mushrooms or French-fried onions. Because ground beef can be used in so many ways, even good cooks tend to forget that it is beef and has the same good flavor as steak when cooked like steak.*

2 pounds lean beef, freshly ground
Salt
Worcestershire sauce

1. Divide the beef into six equal portions and shape into patties about ¾ inch thick.
2. Heat a heavy skillet and add a thin, even sprinkling of salt. Add the patties and, keeping heat high, brown thoroughly on each side. Continue cooking over moderate heat to desired degree of doneness.
3. Top each patty with a few drops of Worcestershire sauce and serve.

CHICKEN À LA KING
4–6 servings

Culinary writers frequently associate Chicken à la King with James R. Keene, American self-made millionaire who won, and lost, several fortunes during the last quarter of the nineteenth century. In one version of the story, the dish was created by the chef at Claridge's Hotel in London after Keene's horse won the 1881 Grand Prix. Others insist that it was Foxhall P. Keene, the son of the Wall Street broker, who originated the dish at Delmonico's restaurant in New York. In either case, of course, it must be presumed that Chicken à la Keene changed at some point into Chicken à la King.

A much better case can be made for E. Clark King Jr., proprietor of the old Brighton Beach Hotel, a fashionable summer resort outside of Manhattan. According to E. Clark King III, son of the restaurateur, it was in the early 1900s that Chicken à la King was first served to the public. One night the head chef at the Brighton, George Greenwald, sent word that he had concocted a new dish and would like to serve it to King and his wife. They enjoyed it immensely, and King readily agreed that it might be added to the menu, only remarking that "a fair price must be asked." The next day it appeared as Chicken à la King—$1.25 a portion.

¼ cup butter or margarine

2 tablespoons chopped green pepper

1 ½ tablespoons all-purpose flour

1 ½ cups light cream

½ teaspoon salt

2 tablespoons chopped pimiento

2 cups diced cooked chicken

⅔ cup canned sliced mushrooms, drained

2 egg yolks

2 tablespoons sherry (optional)

1. Melt butter in heavy saucepan. Add green peppers and sauté until tender. Remove from heat and stir in flour, blending well.
2. Gradually add light cream and blend. Stir over low heat until mixture is thick and smooth. Add salt, pimientos, chicken, and mushrooms and stir well. Continue cooking for 2 minutes, stirring constantly.
3. Beat egg yolks slightly; stir in some of the hot cream sauce and blend well. Pour egg mixture back into remaining cream sauce. Cook for 1 minute more, stirring constantly. Stir in sherry, if desired.
4. Serve over hot toast, patty shells, biscuits, or rice.

CHICKEN DIVAN
4 servings

Chicken Divan takes its name from a long-gone New York restaurant, the Divan Parisienne, but it is the word divan itself that is of interest. Originally Persian, it meant a sheaf of papers or a list, particularly of poems. Adopted by the Arabs, it came to have a connotation of material wealth or possessions. An early Muslim Caliph, flushed with success after a victory, called a list of his warriors and the spoils of war to which each was entitled a divan. To later Arab rulers, with more complicated ideas of government, it meant a state's financial transactions, and then the whole civil administration.

When the Ottoman Turks burst upon the scene in the 13th century they, too, adopted the word divan. To them at first it meant a court of law and later the whole imperial civil services headed by the grand vizier. In 1515 Selim I, also known as Selim the Grim, formed a new council, an advisory group made up of senior officials. It met four times a week, presided over by the viziers, who sat on cushioned benches while the Sultan listened, supposedly unnoticed, behind a latticed window. To the Turks this assembly also was a divan.

The Europeans, always nervously aware of the Muslim world on their borders, absorbed at least some of these varied meanings into their languages. Finally, in English, divan came to mean sofa, from the council chamber's benches, while in France it meant a meeting place or great hall. It was this last meaning that attracted the notice of the owners of the New York restaurant as they searched for a name that would imply continental elegance. Strange are the ways of words! In English, at least, all of these early meanings are slowly being lost. It may well be that to future generations divan will mean only chicken with broccoli in a flavorful sauce.

Incidentally, Hollandaise Sauce received its name only because Holland (the Netherlands) was noted for producing both butter and eggs of excellent quality.

Chicken and Broccoli:

2–2 ½ pounds chicken breasts and thighs

2 cups water

Salt and pepper

1 package (10 ounces) frozen broccoli spears

Hollandaise Sauce:

½ cup butter

3 egg yolks

2 tablespoons lemon juice

¼ teaspoon salt

White Sauce:

3 tablespoons butter or margarine

3 tablespoons all-purpose flour

Chicken broth (reserved from cooking chicken)

Milk

2 tablespoons sherry

Grated Parmesan cheese

1. Skin chicken and place in kettle or large saucepan. Add water and 1 teaspoon salt. Simmer, covered, for 45 minutes or until tender. Allow to cool in broth, then remove meat from bones in large pieces and cut into long strips. Reserve broth.

2. Preheat oven to 400°F. Cook broccoli according to package directions; drain and arrange in single layer in a shallow 7-inch by 11-inch casserole.

3. Make Hollandaise Sauce: Heat ½ cup butter to bubbling, but do not brown. Into warmed electric blender bowl put egg yolks, lemon juice, and ¼ teaspoon salt. Turn on low speed and add hot butter gradually. Blend about fifteen seconds or until sauce is thickened and smooth.

4. Make White Sauce: In a saucepan melt 3 tablespoons butter and stir in flour. Measure chicken broth and add enough milk to make 2 cups. Gradually stir into butter and flour. Cook over low heat, stirring constantly, until thickened and smooth.

5. Arrange chicken on the broccoli. Add ½ cup Hollandaise Sauce to the White Sauce; stir. Add sherry and stir. Season with salt and pepper if desired. Pour over chicken and broccoli. Sprinkle with Parmesan cheese. Bake 12–15 minutes, or until bubbly.

Variation: *If preferred, ½ cup mayonnaise may be substituted for the Hollandaise Sauce.*

CORONATION CHICKEN
6 servings

Coronation Chicken was first prepared for the festivities cele-brating the crowning of Queen Elizabeth II of England in 1953. The Cordon Bleu Cookery School in London, asked to serve a lun-cheon for the distinguished guests, confronted numerous dietary dilemmas in attempting to plan a menu. The dignitaries came from all over the Commonwealth; Muslims could not eat pork, while Hindus would be insulted if served beef. Moreover, the arrival time of the guests, depending on the speed of horse-drawn carriages, was unpredictable. The cooking facilities in Westminster Hall, a national monument dating back to 1097, were understandably lim-ited and the cooking was to be done by the students of the school. Chicken, served cold with an innovative sweet and spicy mayon-naise, proved a splendid choice and the dish has become a national favorite.

Chicken:

6 large chicken breast halves, skinned
1 onion, quartered
1 carrot, quartered
2 stalks celery, sliced
1 teaspoon peppercorns
¾ teaspoon salt

Curry mayonnaise:

1 tablespoon vegetable oil
1 small onion, finely chopped
1 tablespoon curry powder
6 tablespoons tomato juice
6 tablespoons red wine
3 tablespoons apricot jam
2 cups mayonnaise

Vinaigrette:

¼ cup lemon juice

½ cup vegetable oil

2 tablespoons chopped fresh oregano or tarragon (optional)

Salt

Pepper

To serve:

Paprika

1 ½ pounds Italian plum tomatoes, sliced

1. To poach chicken, place breasts in a heavy kettle and add onion, carrots, celery, peppercorns, and salt, plus enough water to cover. Bring to a boil, skimming surface occasionally. Reduce heat; cover; simmer until chicken is tender when tried with a fork, 45–60 minutes. Let chicken cool to tepid in liquid, then drain. Cover and refrigerate.

2. For curry mayonnaise, heat vegetable oil in saucepan. Sauté onion until soft but not brown. Add curry powder and cook gently 2 minutes. Add tomato juice and red wine and simmer until reduced by half. Stir in apricot jam and let mixture cool. Strain, pressing well to extract liquid. Stir liquid into mayonnaise. If necessary, add warm water a teaspoon at a time to thin mayonnaise until it just coats spoon.

3. For vinaigrette, whisk together lemon juice, vegetable oil, choice of herb, and salt and pepper to taste. Chicken, mayonnaise, and vinaigrette can be refrigerated separately up to 48 hours.

4. Not more than 30 minutes before serving, bone chicken and arrange down the side of a serving dish, coating each piece with mayonnaise. Sprinkle with paprika. Arrange tomatoes on other side of serving dish and spoon vinaigrette over. Chill dish until serving time.

COUNTRY CAPTAIN
6 servings

Country Captain is a dish that has long been popular in the southern states. According to an oft-repeated story, a sea-captain sailed into Charleston harbor with a shipload of spices from India. Entertained by the hostesses of a city noted for its graciousness, he repaid their kindness by teaching their capable cooks to make a delicious dish of chicken and curry. Alas for legend! A virtually identical dish is well known in England, where it goes by the very same name. The captain, if there ever was one, must have been a British officer stationed in the back country of India. An English writer has noted that "country captain" is also an Anglo-Indian term for the captain of a foreign ship, that is, a captain from a foreign country. Just how or if that fits into the puzzle would be difficult to say. Another suggestion is that Country Captain may be only a corruption of "country capon."

Variation: If desired, 1 ½–2 pounds other broiler-fryer parts, cut up and skinned, may be substituted for the chicken breasts.

2 medium onions, chopped

2 tablespoons butter or margarine

2 green peppers, chopped

1 tablespoon curry powder

1 can (16 ounces) whole tomatoes, broken up

½ cup chicken broth (can be made from bouillon)

1 tablespoon chopped fresh parsley, *or* 1 ½ teaspoons dry parsley flakes

½ teaspoon salt

¼ teaspoon black pepper

¼ teaspoon ground mace

1 clove garlic, finely chopped

¼ cup currants or raisins

6 chicken breast halves, boned and skinned

2 tablespoons all-purpose flour

2 tablespoons vegetable oil

1. In a large saucepan sauté onion in butter until lightly browned; add green pepper and cook 5 minutes. Stir in curry powder and cook 1 minute, stirring constantly. Add tomatoes (including liquid), chicken broth, parsley, salt, pepper, mace, and garlic. Bring to a boil, lower heat, and simmer, covered, 5 minutes.

2. Flour chicken breasts and shake off excess. Heat oil in large skillet and brown chicken thoroughly. Drain off excess oil and add tomato mixture. Cover and cook over low heat until tender, 20–30 minutes, stirring occasionally and adding water if mixture becomes too thick. Stir in currants or raisins and serve over hot rice.

BRUNSWICK STEW
4–6 servings

Brunswick Stew takes its name from Brunswick County, Virginia, which in turn was named for Brunswick (Braunschweig) in Germany, the ancestral home of the Hanoverians who had recently become kings of England. There is nothing German about the stew, however. It began as a squirrel stew created by one "Uncle" Jimmy Matthews. In 1828 Dr. Creed Haskins of Mount Donum, a member of the Virginia state legislature, wanted something special for a political rally he was sponsoring. He persuaded Matthews to part with his recipe, and the stew, with squirrel as the principal ingredient, remained for many years one of the main attractions at political rallies conducted by both the Whigs and the Democrats. Gradually more vegetables were added and, in most areas, chicken replaced squirrel as the major ingredient.

3 ½ pounds chicken parts, skinned

1 ½ teaspoons salt

¼ teaspoon coarse ground pepper

2 cans (16 ounces each) whole tomatoes, cut up

1 ½ cups fresh or frozen corn

1 ½ cups fresh or frozen lima beans

1 large potato, diced

1 medium onion, chopped

½ cup chopped celery, including tops

½ cup chopped fresh carrots

½ cup water

2 tablespoons instant-blending or all-purpose flour

1. Place chicken, salt, and pepper in heavy kettle or Dutch oven. Add water to cover and cook until chicken is tender and falls from the bone, about 1 hour. Pour off stock and reserve it, refrigerated. Remove bones and cut chicken into 1-inch chunks. Cover and refrigerate.
2. When stock is cold, remove all fat. Return stock and chicken to kettle and add vegetables. Cook uncovered until vegetables are soft. Stir flour and water together in a small bowl and stir into stew. Return stew to boiling and boil 1 minute, stirring constantly. Add more salt and pepper if needed.

KENTUCKY BURGOO
4 servings

Note: *By the time the vegetables are done, most of the broth will have cooked away and the mixture will be more like stew than soup. Like Brunswick Stew, Kentucky Burgoo is clearly a main dish, to be served in large bowls accompanied by good bread or rolls.*

Burgoo began as a sailor's term for gruel or porridge served with monotonous regularity aboard English sailing vessels in the eighteenth century. Originally it may have been a corruption of the Turkish *burghul* or bulgur, meaning "cracked wheat." In time burgoo became a name for any mixture of ingredients thrown together and cooked in a stew kettle, and it was in this sense that the word came to North America. Born of necessity and not always particularly appetizing, most of these "burgoos" have vanished. Only in Kentucky did burgoo survive to become an institution.

Clearly similar to the neighboring Brunswick Stew, Kentucky Burgoo is made in vast quantities and served to large crowds on the Fourth of July, Kentucky Derby Day, and similar events. Sometimes the festival or picnic itself is known as a burgoo.

2 tablespoons shortening

1 pound beef stew meat, cut into 1-inch cubes

2 ½ pounds chicken parts, skinned

1 teaspoon salt

1 bay leaf

Few peppercorns

2 medium onions, chopped

2 green peppers, chopped

1 cup fresh or frozen corn

1 cup fresh or frozen lima beans

3 large tomatoes, peeled and chopped, or 1 can (16 ounces) whole tomatoes, cut up

1 tablespoon Worcestershire sauce

Cayenne pepper (optional)

1. Heat shortening in large, heavy kettle. Add beef and brown well, stirring. Add chicken, water to cover, salt, bay leaf, and peppercorns. Cover and simmer 1 hour or until meat falls from bones. Pour off stock and refrigerate. Remove bay leaf, peppercorns, and bones and cut chicken into 1-inch chunks. Cover beef and chicken and refrigerate.

2. When stock is cold, remove all fat. Return to kettle with meat and vegetables. Cook uncovered for 20 minutes or until vegetables are soft. Add Worcestershire sauce and a dash of cayenne pepper, if desired.

CHICKEN TETRAZZINI
6 servings

Chicken Tetrazzini is named for the Italian opera singer, Luisa Tetrazzini, who was widely acclaimed and even idolized in the United States in the years preceding World War I. Presumably it was invented by an admiring chef or restaurateur, some say in San Francisco. It is one of the best-known of countless pasta dishes based on spaghetti (plural of the Italian word *spaghetto*, which in turn is a diminutive of *spago*, meaning cord or twine). Tetrazzini did not mention the dish in her autobiography, *My Life of Song*, published in 1921, and it is possible that she never heard of it. As someone has said, the singer is virtually forgotten while the dish becomes steadily more popular.

Variation: *For Turkey Tetrazzini, substitute cooked cubed turkey for the 2 ¼ cups chicken.*

¼ cup butter or margarine

¼ cup all-purpose flour

½ teaspoon salt

¼ teaspoon pepper

1 cup chicken broth (canned if preferred)

1 cup heavy cream

2 tablespoons sherry

1 4-ounce can mushrooms, drained

2 tablespoons chopped pimientos

2 ¼ cups cooked cubed chicken

7 ounces thin spaghetti, cooked and drained according to package directions

½ cup grated Parmesan cheese

1. Preheat oven to 350°F.
2. In a heavy saucepan melt the butter over moderately low heat. Stir in the flour and cook, stirring, for 3 minutes or until mixture is smooth and bubbly. Remove from heat and add salt, pepper, broth, and cream. Heat to boiling, stirring constantly. Boil and stir 1 minute. Stir in sherry, mushrooms, pimientos, chicken, and spaghetti.
3. Pour into ungreased 2-quart casserole. Sprinkle with grated cheese. Bake uncovered 30 minutes or until bubbly.

SPAGHETTI CARUSO
12 servings

Enrico Caruso, often called the greatest tenor of all time, was a contemporary of Luisa Tetrazzini, and it would be easy to dismiss Spaghetti Caruso as a mere companion piece to Chicken Tetrazzini, another dish created by an Italian-American chef to honor a great opera singer from his homeland. But there seems to be more to the story.

Biographers agree that Caruso, at least as a young man, loved to eat, loved to cook, and loved spaghetti. A flamboyant, exuberant man, he thought nothing of marching into the kitchens of a grand hotel and personally instructing the startled chefs as to just how he wanted the spaghetti he was ordering for his friends to be cooked. He was also inventive, garnishing the finished dish with any interesting little tidbits he happened to see lying about on the huge kitchen tables.

Carol Truax, whose father was both a justice on the New York Supreme Court and a noted gourmet, has written extensively if lightheartedly about New York society in the first decades of the twentieth century. She mentions Caruso as one of the many notables who regularly visited her parents' home and almost gleefully recalls how Caruso loved to go to the kitchen where he "clapped on the high chef's cap and created an enormous platter of his own very special spaghetti, with chicken livers."

At any rate, a number of Caruso Restaurants sprang up around the city and their menus always featured Spaghetti à la Caruso, served with both chicken livers and the assurances of the waiters that this was, indeed, the great tenor's favorite dish.

5 tablespoons olive oil, divided

½ cup chopped onions

1 large clove garlic, minced

2 cans (28 ounces each) Italian tomatoes

2 cans (6 ounces each) tomato paste

1 ¼ cups water

2 ¼ teaspoons salt, divided

1 teaspoon oregano

2 bay leaves

1 teaspoon sugar

¼ cup grated Parmesan cheese

1 pound chicken livers

1 cup sliced canned mushrooms, drained

1 ½ pounds uncooked thin spaghetti

3 tablespoons butter or margarine

1. Heat 3 tablespoons of the oil in a large heavy kettle. Add onions and garlic and sauté until tender. Add tomatoes, breaking up slightly with a fork. Add tomato paste, water, 1 ½ teaspoons salt, oregano, bay leaves, sugar, and cheese. Mix well. Simmer over low heat 1 ½ hours, stirring occasionally.

2. Sprinkle chicken livers with remaining ¾ teaspoon salt. Heat remaining 2 tablespoons oil in a large frying pan and sauté chicken livers. Add to sauce with mushrooms.

3. Cook and drain spaghetti according to package directions. Add butter and mix, tossing spaghetti lightly until butter is melted. Serve with hot sauce, and more grated Parmesan cheese if desired.

CHICKEN CORDON BLEU
8 servings

Chicken Cordon Bleu appears to have no connection whatsoever with the great cooking schools of Paris or London. Instead it is an American innovation of quite recent origin, but one that draws from two distinctly different European traditions.

The story begins with Chicken Kiev, an authentic Ukrainian dish named for the ancient city that stands high above the Dnieper River. Made of flattened chicken breasts wrapped securely around seasoned butter, breaded, and then fried, Chicken Kiev became popular in the United States in the 1960s, first as a specialty of fine restaurants and then with good cooks who wanted to duplicate the dish at home.

Variations inevitably proliferated. Someone, almost certainly a professional chef familiar with European cuisine, thought of the Veal Cordon Bleu of Switzerland and the almost identical Schnitzel Cordon Bleu of Austria. Both consist of flattened pieces of veal folded around thin slices of ham and Emmentaler or Gruyère cheese (both products of Switzerland), then breaded and fried. A combination of the concepts for Chicken Kiev and Veal Cordon Bleu resulted in Chicken Cordon Bleu.

Cordon Bleu or Blue Ribbon stands for best or first place in both French and English, probably because the heraldic insignia of the highest chivalric orders in both countries incorporated a blue sash. In France Cordon Bleu acquired a special association with cooking because the white aprons of female cooks were generally fastened with blue ribbons.

6 chicken breast halves, boned and skinned

Salt

8 small, thin slices of boiled ham

1 cup shredded Swiss or Gruyère cheese

2 eggs

Flour

2 cups fine, dry white bread crumbs

Vegetable oil for frying

1. Place each chicken breast half between pieces of plastic wrap or waxed paper. With a meat pounder or flat edge of a cleaver flatten each piece to ⅛-inch thickness. If holes appear in the meat, overlap the edges of the tear slightly, cover the patch with plastic or waxed paper, and pound gently until meat joins together.

2. Gently peel off plastic wrap or waxed paper and sprinkle chicken lightly with salt. Cut each slice of ham into ½-inch strips. Place on chicken breast with small amount of cheese. Using more plastic wrap or waxed paper, pound edges of chicken again, to paper thinness. Bring one of the wide ends of the breast up over the ham and cheese firmly and fold in the other two ends. Bring up the other wide end and press firmly.

3. In a small bowl beat eggs slightly. Spread flour and bread crumbs on two different plates. One at a time, dip each cutlet into the flour. Shake each one gently free of excess flour. Dip each cutlet into the eggs, making sure its entire surface is coated, and roll in bread crumbs, again making sure it is thoroughly coated. Place cutlets on platter or tray and refrigerate for two hours.

4. About 30 minutes before serving preheat oven to 200°F. Line a shallow baking pan with paper towels. Into a deep-fat fryer or heavy saucepan with frying basket pour oil to a depth of 3 or 4 inches. Place over high heat and heat to 360°F on a deep-fat thermometer. Fry cutlets four at a time for about 5 minutes or until golden brown, then transfer to baking dish and place in oven. Fry remaining cutlets. Place in oven if necessary, but cutlets should remain in oven for no longer than 10 minutes.

BUFFALO WINGS
48 pieces

Note: *For extra sauce, if desired, combine more melted butter or margarine and bottled hot sauce.*

Buffalo Chicken Wings were invented by Teressa Bellissimo of the Anchor Bar in Buffalo, New York. Late one night in 1964 her son Dom and some of his friends came into the tavern wanting something to eat. Bellissimo had nothing on hand except for some chicken wings she was saving for soup. Faced with hungry young men, she improvised with what she had, and the fiery Buffalo Chicken Wings were born. Served with blue cheese dressing and celery stalks to cool the tongue, they became an Anchor Bar attraction every Friday night. Their popularity spread, first in New York state and then across the nation; in most areas they are now known simply as Buffalo Wings.

24 chicken wings, rinsed and patted dry
⅓ cup butter or margarine
2–3 tablespoons bottled Louisiana-style hot sauce
Oil for deep frying
Celery sticks
Blue cheese dressing, commercially prepared

1. Split wings at joints; discard tips. Place wings in a large bowl.
2. Melt butter or margarine in a saucepan over low heat. Add hot sauce, stirring until well mixed. (Start with 2 tablespoons and taste; 3 tablespoons makes a very hot sauce.) Pour hot sauce over wings, stirring to make sure wings are coated. Let stand for 30 minutes, stirring occasionally.
3. Heat oil to 365°F. Fry wings 5–6 minutes, until crisp and golden. Drain on paper towels. Serve at once with celery and blue cheese dressing.

CHAPTER 7

SUPPER DISHES & SIDE DISHES

Supper dishes and side dishes need little introduction. Only rarely are they made by famous chefs or named for famous people. More often they were created by anonymous cooks who made do with what they had, laughed at adversity, and gave necessity a funny name.

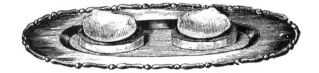

WELSH RABBIT (RAREBIT)
4 servings

The English, the Scots, and the Welsh do not always get along as well as most Americans might presume. The English traditionally scorned the Welsh as poor and not always trustworthy:

Taffy was a Welshman, Taffy was thief,
Taffy came to my house and stole a piece of beef.

When a new dish of melted cheese on toast was devised in the eighteenth century, it was jokingly called a Welsh Rabbit, meaning that a Welshman, too poor to have meat, would call his cheese a rabbit. The alternate spelling, Welsh Rarebit, developed later and is imitative. If a Welshman had some cheese, it would be a "rare bit" indeed.

¼ cup butter or margarine
¼ cup all-purpose flour
½ teaspoon salt
¼ teaspoon pepper
¼ teaspoon dry mustard
1 ½ cups milk
¼ teaspoon Worcestershire sauce
2 cups (8 ounces) shredded cheddar cheese
4 slices toast

1. In a large saucepan melt butter over low heat. Stir in flour, salt, pepper, and mustard. Cook over low heat, stirring constantly, until smooth and bubbly; continue to stir, on and off heat, for several minutes to rid flour of raw taste.
2. Whisk in milk. Heat to boiling, stirring constantly; boil and stir 1 minute. Stir in Worcestershire sauce and cheese. Continue stirring over low heat until cheese is melted. Serve over toast.

BLUSHING BUNNY
4 servings

American cooks are never slow to adopt a good dish, and never slow to change it around to suit themselves, either. In the 1930s the popular Welsh Rabbit inspired the even easier to make Blushing Bunny. Its other name is Rum Tum Tiddy.

2 cups (8 ounces) sharp cheddar cheese, shredded
1 can (10 ¾ ounces) condensed tomato soup
2 tablespoons ketchup
1 tablespoon finely minced onion
½ teaspoon Worcestershire sauce
¼ teaspoon dry mustard
1 egg, slightly beaten
4 slices toast

1. In a saucepan combine all ingredients except egg. Place over medium heat; stir until smooth. Stir small amount of hot mixture into egg; return to hot mixture, stirring quickly.
2. Cook, stirring constantly until thickened; do not boil. Serve over toast.

SCOTCH WOODCOCK
4 servings

Variation: *Traditionally there are two different ways of making this dish. Even in Britain some cooks prefer to dice hard-cooked eggs into a well-flavored white sauce. Add tuna or anchovies if desired, and serve over toast.*

The woodcock for centuries was the most prized game bird in Europe. In England the cocker spaniel was bred to aid in hunting this famed bird, while on the continent poets drifted into rhapsody as they wrote about the woodcock as a dish so fine it could be served at a "banquet of gods."

Just as the English laughed at the Welsh, they had scant respect for the Scots, who were deemed both poor and parsimonious. Jokes about the overly frugal Scotsman have gone around the world, but they began in England. It was almost inevitable, once Welsh Rabbit became well known, that someone would come up with a companion dish and name it Scotch Woodcock.

8 anchovy fillets, finely chopped
2 tablespoons butter or margarine, softened
4 slices toast
4 egg yolks
1 cup half-and-half
¼ teaspoon black pepper
1 tablespoon finely minced parsley

1. Combine anchovy fillets and butter and mash thoroughly. Spread lightly on slices of toast; set aside.
2. Beat egg yolks, cream, and pepper in top of double boiler. Cook over hot water, stirring constantly, until thick. Pour over toast and sprinkle with parsley.

WOODCHUCK
4 servings

There are woodcocks in North America, to be sure, but here, unlike in Europe, they are not particularly well known as game birds. This has in no way prevented good cooks in the United States from seeing the virtue in a quick, easy luncheon dish, nor has it kept them from recognizing Scotch Woodcock as a corollary to the better-known Welsh Rabbit. In any number of cities a combination of mushroom soup, hard-boiled eggs, and tuna is called, after a more familiar species of American wildlife, Woodchuck!

1 can (10¾ ounces) condensed cream of mushroom soup
½ cup milk
4 hard-cooked eggs, diced
1 small (3¼ ounces) can tuna
4 slices toast

1. In a saucepan combine cream of mushroom soup and milk. Add eggs and tuna and mix well.
2. Heat thoroughly, stirring occasionally; pour over toast.

TOAD-IN-THE-HOLE
4–6 servings

Toad-in-the-Hole is a homey little dish from England. Originally it was made with any leftover bits of meat, but today sausages are the usual "toads." The batter in which they are hiding is the same as that used for Yorkshire pudding.

1 pound pork sausage patties

1 cup all-purpose flour

1 cup milk

2 eggs

½ teaspoon salt

1. Preheat oven to 400°F. Cook sausage patties as directed on package; reserve drippings. Brush oblong baking dish, 11 x 7 x 1 inches, with sausage drippings. Place sausage patties in single layer in baking dish.

2. Combine flour, milk, eggs, and salt in blender jar. Blend at high speed for 2 or 3 seconds. Turn off blender, scrape down the sides of the jar, and blend again for 40 seconds. (Or, in large bowl, beat eggs and salt with an electric beater until frothy. Slowly add the flour, beating constantly. Then pour in the milk in a thin stream and beat until the mixture is smooth and creamy.)

3. Pour batter over sausages. Bake uncovered until puffed and golden brown, about 30 minutes. Cut into squares.

HEAVEN AND EARTH
4–6 servings

Heaven and Earth *(Himmel und Erde)* is a German dish. Apples are the "heaven" and potatoes the "earth." It is an old peasant recipe, usually served with sausages.

2 cups water
Salt
4 medium potatoes, peeled
2 tart cooking apples, peeled
2 teaspoons sugar
6 slices bacon, cut into 1-inch pieces
1 medium onion, peeled and sliced
1 teaspoon cider vinegar
Pepper

1. Cut potatoes into 1-inch cubes. Core and quarter apples, then cut each quarter again, crosswise.
2. In a large saucepan bring 2 cups water and 1 teaspoon salt to boiling. Add potatoes, apples, and sugar. Heat to boiling; reduce heat. Cover and cook until tender, 10–15 minutes. Drain.
3. While potatoes are cooking, fry bacon until crisp; drain. Separate onion slices into rings. Sauté in bacon fat until tender. Add vinegar to potatoes and apples and mix; taste and add salt and pepper as desired. Pour into serving bowl and top with bacon and onions.

QUICHE LORRAINE
1 9-inch quiche

The whole history of western Europe might have been different if Charlemagne's successor had been a strong king. Instead, his son, known as Louis the Pious, was a weak and ineffectual ruler, and when he died the empire was divided among Charlemagne's three grandsons. Few objected; most thought it obvious that the empire was too big for any one man to govern. The eastern third went to Louis the German and it became Germany. The western third went to Charles the Bald and it became France. The third son, Lothair, received a long, narrow strip of land in the middle, stretching from the North Sea to Rome. It never unified, never became a proper kingdom, and eventually broke apart, turning into the Netherlands and Belgium in the north and Switzerland and Italy in the south. In the middle were the provinces of Alsace and Lorraine, fought over by France and Germany for a thousand years. Only after World War II and the loss of eighteen thousand men who died fighting in the German armies on the eastern front, did Alsace-Lorraine finally decide to be unequivocally French.

This cultural confusion has always been apparent even in the cooking of the region. Though *quiche* may seem a typically French word, it is derived from the German *Kuchen*, meaning cake. Lorraine itself takes its name from Lothair, Charlemagne's grandson.

Variation: *This is the classic French version. To make the Quiche Lorraine better known in this country, add 1 cup (4 ounces) shredded Swiss cheese and ⅓ cup finely chopped onion with the crumbled bacon. To the French this would be* Quiche au Fromage.

1 unbaked 9-inch pie shell

12 slices bacon, cooked and crumbled

4 eggs

2 cups whipping cream,
  or 2 cups half-and-half

¾ teaspoon salt

¼ teaspoon pepper

1. Preheat oven to 425°F. Sprinkle bacon in pie shell. Beat eggs lightly; add cream, salt, and pepper and continue beating until well mixed.

2. Pour egg mixture over bacon. Bake uncovered 15 minutes. Reduce oven temperature to 300°F. Bake until knife inserted in center comes out clean, about 30 minutes longer. Let stand 10 minutes before serving.

POTATOES ANNA
6 servings

Potatoes Anna are named for Anna Deslions, a woman of fashion at the time of Napoleon III's Second Empire. The dish was created by Adolphe Duglérè, the chef at the Café Anglais in Paris. Duglérè, who had been a pupil of the great Antonin Carême (see page 194), was so proud of his creation that he invented a special round two-handled casserole with an interlocking lid to facilitate its preparation. When the potatoes are cut into thin strips instead of rounds, the dish is called Potatoes Annette, even though there never was an Annette to inspire the variation.

2 tablespoons butter or margarine
6 medium baking potatoes, peeled
1 teaspoon salt
Pepper
½ cup butter or margarine, melted

1. Preheat oven to 400°F. Slice potatoes in thin (⅛-inch) slices. Use two tablespoons butter to generously butter a 9- or 10-inch straight-sided casserole. Arrange a layer of potato slices in any desired pattern in bottom of casserole. Sprinkle with salt and pepper. Repeat until all potato slices have been added, sprinkling each layer with salt and pepper.
2. Pour melted butter over potatoes. Cover casserole and bake for 30 minutes. Loosen edge and bottom of potato cake with wide spatula. Place a flat plate over casserole, grasp firmly and invert. Slide potato cake back into casserole to brown other side. Cover and bake again for 30 minutes or until tender. Again loosen with spatula; place inverted dinner plate over casserole, grasp firmly and invert. Cut into wedges to serve.

Variation: *This is Duglérè's original version. To simplify, bake uncovered for 1 hour or until tender, then turn out onto dinner plate as directed.*

FRENCH TOAST/POOR KNIGHTS
1 serving

French Toast is definitely French in origin, and that may be the only simple statement a culinary historian can make about this very simple dish, which consists of bread dipped in egg and sautéed in butter. Here in the United States it has also been, at one time or another, known as Spanish Toast, German Toast, or Nun's Toast, while the Creole cooks of Louisiana, who have made a specialty of it, call it *pain perdu* (lost bread), presumably because it is made of day-old French bread that might otherwise be wasted.

In France today the usual name is also *pain perdu*, but in the past it has also been known as *pain crotté* (mud-spattered bread), *pain à la Romaine* (Roman bread), and *croûtes dorées* (gilded crusts). Probably older yet is the name *ameritte*, of uncertain origin, which gave rise to even more curious names in other languages. The Germans, hearing *ameritte*, turned it into *arme Ritter*, as did the Danes *(arme riddere)*, both of which mean Poor Knights.

The English usually use the name French Toast for slices of bread fried in butter (which tastes much better than it sounds), while the egg mixture, evidently learned from the Germans, became Poor Knights of Windsor. The last, which seems inexplicable to Americans, was actually almost inevitable, for there really are Poor Knights of Windsor in England. The military order of that name was created by Edward III in 1348 to care for aged and penniless knights. The order, later dignified as Military Knights, still exists. Its members are former army officers who receive pensions and live in rent-free apartments in Windsor Castle.

Incidentally, the Germans sometimes make this dish with wine instead of milk, in which case they call it Drunken Maidens.

ENTRÉES & EXTRAS

1 egg
1 tablespoon milk
1 teaspoon sugar
2 teaspoons butter or margarine
2 slices bread
Confectioners' sugar

1. On a flat dinner plate, lightly beat egg. Add milk and sugar and beat again until well mixed.
2. In a large frying pan melt butter or margarine over medium heat. Dip each slice of bread in egg mixture, turning once. Sauté in butter, again turning once. Serve with a dusting of confectioners' sugar.

SUCCOTASH
6 servings

Succotash is an authentic native American dish. Its name probably derives from the Narraganset *msickquatash*, meaning "ear of
corn." The Pilgrims learned to make this combination of corn and
beans; they frequently added meat, making it a sort of stew. Later
colonists followed their example, though for much of the year they
had to be content with "winter succotash," made of dried beans and
corn. Far better, though, is the delicious blend of fresh corn cut
from the cob and green lima beans, now available all year long in
frozen form.

> 1 package (10 ounces) frozen lima beans
> 1 package (10 ounces) frozen corn,
>   *or* 1 ½ cups fresh sweet corn, cut from the cob
> 1 tablespoon butter or margarine
> Salt
> Pepper

1. Cook lima beans and corn separately according to package directions; drain.
2. Combine vegetables with butter and mix gently. Add salt and
   pepper if desired.

BOSTON BAKED BEANS
12 servings

The Puritan sabbath was strict and stern. Beginning at sundown the night before, no work was allowed except tasks that could not possibly be avoided, such as milking the cows. Food could be served, but not actually prepared. Faced with these restrictions, Puritan women devised dishes that could be made well in advance and held for the sabbath meals. The most popular of these was baked beans. The big pot of beans set at the side of the fireplace could be prepared early Saturday morning, used for supper Saturday night, dished up again for Sunday breakfast, and even finished for Sunday dinner if need be. Long after the observance of the Sabbath had moderated, the tradition of baked beans and brown bread on Saturday night remained, earning Boston the nickname of "Bean Town."

2 pounds (4 cups) dried pea (navy) beans, rinsed and picked over

3 quarts water

4 teaspoons salt

¾ cup dark molasses

½ cup dark brown sugar

1 tablespoon dry mustard

1 teaspoon pepper

½-pound piece of salt pork

1 large onion, peeled and studded with 4 whole cloves

1. Place beans and water in a 4- or 5-quart Dutch oven. Bring to a boil; boil 2 minutes. Remove from heat, cover, and let stand 1 hour. Again heat to boiling, add salt, and reduce heat to low; cover and simmer 1 hour. Check from time to time and add more boiling water if necessary; beans should remain covered with water. Preheat oven to 250°F. Drain beans, reserving cooking liquid. Measure liquid and add water to make 2 quarts.

2. Return beans and liquid to Dutch oven. Add molasses, brown sugar, mustard, and pepper and mix well. Make 8–10 slashes in salt pork. Tuck onion into beans; sink salt pork so just the top shows. Cover; bake for 7 hours, adding more water if needed to keep beans moist, but not too wet. Before serving, find onion and remove cloves.

MOORS AND CHRISTIANS
6 servings

This Cuban dish recalls the seven hundred years of intermittent war between the Muslims and the Christians as they battled for control of the Spanish peninsula. The Muslims, called Moors in Spain because they crossed over from Morocco, invaded in the eighth century and soon held all but one tiny Christian kingdom in the north. They were not completely driven out until Granada fell to Ferdinand and Isabella in 1492. The black beans in this dish, of course, stand for the dark-skinned Moors, while the rice represents the Spaniards.

1 pound dried black beans, rinsed and picked over

6 cups water

1 cup chopped onion

1 green pepper, chopped

1 garlic clove, minced

½ cup olive oil, or ½ cup bacon fat, rendered

2 bay leaves

2 teaspoons salt

¼ teaspoon pepper

1 smoked ham bone (optional)

2 tablespoons vinegar

Cooked white rice

Chopped hard-cooked eggs (optional)

Minced green onions (optional)

Lemon wedges (optional)

1. In a large kettle or Dutch oven bring beans and water to a boil. Boil for 2 minutes. Cover pan and let stand for 1 hour. Remove from kettle, reserving liquid.

2. Dry kettle and add onion, green pepper, garlic, and olive oil or bacon fat. Sauté until onion is tender but not browned. Return beans to kettle with liquid and add bay leaves, salt, pepper, and ham bone (if desired). Bring to a boil and simmer, covered, for 2 hours, adding more water if necessary. Add vinegar, remove bay leaves, and serve with rice. Garnish with hard-cooked eggs, green onions, and lemon wedges, if desired.

HOPPIN' JOHN
6 servings

Any combination of beans and rice provides excellent nutrition, for the amino acids in each complement one another, providing the complete protein found in meat. Throughout the Caribbean, whole groups of people who know nothing of amino acids or protein nevertheless came to realize that beans and rice were good food for poor people.

The Cubans liked black beans and the Puerto Ricans grew pink beans, while in the islands owned by France the popular legume was the pigeon pea, in French *pois à pigeon*. Brought to the American South, where pigeon peas were unknown, the dish was made with yet another bean, the so-called black-eyed pea. Still, the unfamiliar French name hung on, till *à pigeon* slurred into Hoppin' John. Curiously, though Hoppin' John was an everyday staple, the idea that eating it on New Year's Day brought good luck was passed along through Spanish, French, and English.

1 pound (2 cups) dried black-eyed peas, rinsed and picked over
2 quarts water
¼ pound salt pork, diced
1 medium onion, chopped
Salt
Pepper
Cooked white rice

Note: *Black-eyed peas are also known as cowpeas or black-eyed beans.*

1. Place beans and water in large kettle. Bring to a boil and boil for 2 minutes; remove from heat, cover, and let stand for 1 hour.
2. In a large frying pan cook salt pork until almost crisp; add onion and cook until onion is tender.
3. Again bring beans to a boil; add salt pork, onion, and any remaining fat. Reduce heat to low; cover and simmer 1 ¼ hours or until beans are tender, stirring occasionally. Season to taste with salt and pepper. Serve with rice.

LIMPIN' SUSAN
6–8 servings

Variation: *In place of 2 cups of water and salt, use 2 cups of chicken broth (can be canned or made from bouillon powder).*

Limpin' Susan is a simple combination of okra and rice. Its name was bestowed by some anonymous cook, in imitation of the better-known Hoppin' John.

4 slices bacon, coarsely chopped

1 package (10 ounces) frozen okra, partially thawed

1 cup uncooked regular rice

2 cups water

1 teaspoon salt

⅛ teaspoon Tabasco sauce

1. In top of double boiler set over direct heat, fry bacon just until crisp; do not drain. Cut okra into rings and add to bacon. Cook until tender.

2. Add remaining ingredients and heat to boiling, stirring once or twice; reduce heat. Cover and simmer 14 minutes. (Do not lift cover or stir.) While rice is cooking, pour a small amount of water into bottom of double boiler and bring to a boil. Remove rice from heat, leave covered, and place over boiling water. Allow to steam for 10 or 15 minutes.

HUSH PUPPIES
20–25 pieces

Hush Puppies seem to have originated in the day-long hunting and fishing expeditions popular among Southern men a few generations ago. Cooking their catch over an open fire was part of their enjoyment of the day, along with being away from both their jobs and their womenfolk. As a side dish they fried little cornmeal cakes in the pan they had used for the fish, and when the meal was over the leftovers went to the tied-up, yelping dogs, presumably with the cry, "Hush, puppies!"

The name first appears in print in 1918, but probably was used much earlier. Today Hush Puppies are featured at many of the franchise restaurants serving fish, so they are almost as well known in the North as in the South.

¼ cup sugar

2 teaspoons baking powder

1 teaspoon salt

¼ teaspoon pepper

½ teaspoon garlic salt

⅔ cup chopped onion

1 egg, beaten

1 ¼ cups milk

Oil for frying

1 ½ cups yellow cornmeal

1 ½ cups all-purpose flour

1. In large bowl, mix sugar, baking powder, salt, pepper, and garlic salt. In a blender, mix onion, egg, and milk until the mixture is milkshake consistency. Pour over dry ingredients and whisk together. Let sit until bubbles begin to form, about 5 minutes.

2. In the meantime, heat oil in deep fryer or deep skillet to 375°F. Mix cornmeal and flour and gradually whisk into liquid mixture. Batter should be thick, like drop-cookie dough.

3. Drop hush puppies by heaping teaspoonful into hot oil. Fry only a few at a time. They will bounce to the surface in 2 minutes and be golden brown in 4–5 minutes. Remove from oil with slotted spoon and drain on paper towels.

HARVARD BEETS & YALE BEETS
4 servings

Harvard Beets get their name from the deep crimson color of their sauce, very much like the color of the Harvard football team's jerseys. Since Harvard and Yale are traditional rivals, it was perhaps inevitable that a Yale supporter would invent the competing Yale Beets.

Variation: *For Yale Beets, use ¾ cup orange juice in place of the beet liquid and 1 tablespoon lemon juice in place of the vinegar.*

1 can (16 ounces) sliced beets
1 tablespoon cornstarch
1 tablespoon sugar
¾ teaspoon salt
¼ cup vinegar

1. Drain beets, reserving liquid. Add enough water to beet liquid to measure ⅔ cup. In saucepan mix cornstarch, sugar, and salt. Gradually stir in beet liquid and vinegar.
2. Cook, stirring constantly, until mixture thickens and boils. Boil and stir 1 minute. Add beets; heat through.

FETTUCCINE ALFREDO
4–6 servings

Fettuccine Alfredo is an authentic Italian dish, but one of quite recent origin. Fettuccine itself, easily one of the most popular types of Italian pasta, is also among the most diminutive words in the culinary lexicon: meaning narrow ribbons, it is the plural of *fettuccina*, diminutive of *fettuccia*, a small slice or ribbon, which in turn is the diminutive of *fetta*, slice, probably an alteration of a Latin term for *offa* flour cake. Variant spellings of the word fettuccine include at least four possible combinations of t's, c's, and i's or e's. Fettuccine Alfredo, specifically, was created in Rome in 1920 by Alfredo di Lellio, a restaurant owner who first prepared the dish, so it is said, to restore the strength of his wife, who had just given birth to their son. The pasta, with its simple but rich sauce, was soon featured in Alfredo's restaurant on the Via della Scrofa. The dish became known to Americans when Hollywood actors Douglas Fairbanks and Mary Pickford came to Rome on their honeymoon in 1920 and dined at Alfredo's.

Di Lellio moved after World War II to the Piazza Augusto Imperatore, and his new restaurant became an attraction for visiting American tourists. His grandson has owned restaurants in the United States.

8 ounces fettuccine

½ cup butter or margarine

½ cup half-and-half

1 cup grated Parmesan cheese

Salt

Pepper

1. Cook fettuccine as directed on package. While fettuccine cooks, heat butter and cream in small saucepan over low heat until butter is melted. Stir in cheese and keep warm over low heat.
2. Drain fettuccine and add sauce. Stir gently until fettuccine is well coated. Add salt and pepper if desired.

JOE'S SPECIAL
4 servings

This dish originated in San Francisco, probably in one of the Italian restaurants in North Beach. The story is, as so often, one of necessity—a friend stopping by late at night and a chef faced with an almost empty larder. The problem is, a number of restaurants have claimed that the incident happened in *their* kitchens. Original Joe's, now in San Jose, has been serving the dish for over fifty years.

2 tablespoons olive oil or salad oil

1 ½ pounds ground beef

3 tablespoons chopped onions

1 package (10 ounces) frozen spinach, thawed

3 eggs

Salt

Pepper

1. Heat oil in a skillet over high heat. Add ground beef and stir until well browned. Push meat to one side and sauté onions until soft, about 3 minutes. Drain excess fat. Thoroughly drain spinach and add. Cook, stirring, another 3 minutes.
2. Lower the heat to medium, add the beaten eggs, and stir. Cook until set but not dry. Add salt and pepper to taste. Serve with French or Italian bread.

EGGS BENEDICT
6 servings

It is generally agreed that Eggs Benedict originated in New York City in the 1920s, but beyond that there is much controversy. According to one version of the tale, the dish is named for Harry Benedict, a prominent New Yorker who unfortunately tended to imbibe too much. Convinced that poached eggs were an unfailing remedy, he habitually ordered them when breakfasting at the Waldorf Astoria. Inevitably, embellishments were added and "Eggs for Mr. Benedict!" turned into Eggs Benedict.

Note: *Please see "A Note about Eggs," page 307.*

But another school of thought holds that the famed New York restaurant Delmonico's was the birthplace of Eggs Benedict, created when Mrs. LeGrand Benedict, a regular luncheon guest, complained that there was nothing new on the menu. Yet another possible namesake is Wall Street broker Lemuel Benedict.

Eggs and Bacon:

3 English muffins
6 slices Canadian-style bacon
6 eggs

Hollandaise Sauce:

½ cup butter
3 egg yolks
2 tablespoons lemon juice
½ teaspoon salt

1. Split English muffins and toast; keep warm. Cook Canadian-style bacon over medium heat until browned.
2. In a shallow pan heat water (1 ½–2 inches deep) to boiling; reduce to simmering. Break each egg into a custard cup or saucer; holding cup or saucer close to water's surface, slip 1 egg at a time into water. Cook to desired doneness, 3–5 minutes. Remove eggs from water with slotted spoon.
3. Heat ½ cup butter to bubbling, but do not brown. Into warmed electric blender jar put egg yolks, lemon juice, and salt. Turn on low speed and add hot butter gradually. Blend about 15 seconds or until sauce is thickened and smooth.
4. Place 1 slice bacon on split side of each muffin half; top with poached egg. Spoon warm sauce over eggs.

CHAPTER 8

SAUCES

The Romans went to the ends of their earth, searching for new, exotic meats, and then made them all taste the same by dousing them all with the same sauce. The sauce, known as *garum* or *liquamen*, was actually more of a condiment, to be added by diners as desired at the table.

The scale of the Romans' consumption of *garum* can perhaps be judged by the fact that they produced it in factories. Small fish such as anchovies and the offal of larger fish such as tuna were put into a large trough and thoroughly salted; sometimes shrimp or oysters were added. After twenty-four hours the concoction was transferred to an earthenware vessel and set in a sunny spot to ferment for two or three months. The resulting liquid was clear and golden in color, with a salty, mildly fishy, and somewhat cheesy flavor. It was sealed in small pots, much as mustard is today; one of these pots was found in the ruins of Pompeii, bearing the legend, "Best strained liquamen. From the factory of Umbricus Agathopus." Before serving, *garum* could be flavored by the addition of vinegar, oil, or pepper. Most popular was the pepper-flavored variation, called *garum nigrum*.

Certain cities around the Mediterranean became known for the manufacture of *garum* and shipped their wares throughout the empire. Perhaps precisely because it had been made commercially *garum* died out in the centuries following the fall of Rome. A faint recollection of its basic flavor lingers on in language; the French (and later English) word sauce and the Spanish salsa both come from the Latin *sal* for salt. The only surviving remnant of its fishiness seems to be the use of anchovy paste as a flavoring agent.

The sauces favored in the early Middle Ages were sharp and acidic, deliberately made so by the addition of vinegar or verjuice, the juice of sour crab apples or sour grapes. From these medieval dishes come our words "saucy" or "sassy" meaning sharp, pert, or impudent.

When exotic spices such as pepper, ginger, and cinnamon became obtainable in Europe, cooks applied them with a heavy hand, in sauces as well as in other types of dishes. This may have been, as has so often been suggested, to cover up the flavor of too-well-hung meat, but it could also represent an early example of conspicuous consumption. Cooks may have used the expensive imports with reckless abandon simply to prove that the household could afford the lavish gesture. Neither the roux made of flour and fat nor the thickening power of eggs had yet been discovered, so cooks relied on either ground almonds or bread crumbs to thicken sauces.

Cooking changed tremendously in the seventeenth century, especially in France. The transformation can be seen in the spate of new cookbooks published during that century. The most important, at least for tracing the history of sauces, is *Le Cuisinier français (The French Chef)* published in 1652. Its author was François Pierre de La Varenne, chef to the Marquis d'Uxelles. La Varenne avoided heavy use of spices, preferring to season his sauces with more subtle flavors. He favored truffles, while his mixture of mushrooms and onion became such a classic that it was later named for his employer and is now known as Duxelles. La Varenne understood the making of a roux of butter and flour and used the word, though since *roux* means reddish-brown in French, the roux at first must have been brown, not white. He even gave a recipe for a sauce that is very like modern hollandaise (see Chicken Divan, page 111). It may be the first recorded recipe for an egg-based emulsified sauce. With the publication of La

Varenne's book, French sauces began to come into their own; a century later one cookbook listed eighty different sauce recipes.

It was the great French chef Antonin Carême who first tried to bring order to this plenitude, early in the nineteenth century. His idea was to classify the sauces of the time into four families, each headed by a "mother" sauce (espagnole, velouté [velvety], allemande, and béchamel) from which numerous variations could be devised. It was a practical suggestion, aimed chiefly at restaurant chefs, who could keep each of the basic sauces on hand at all times. A century later, Auguste Escoffier followed the same sort of arrangement, but, quite sensibly, he omitted allemande, which is itself only a variation of velouté, and added hollandaise and tomato. All of the sauces mentioned so far are hot sauces, but sauces can be cold as well; of the basic cold sauces, the most versatile include mayonnaise (see page 66) and vinaigrette.

Today, however, the classic French sauces languish in a sort of limbo. Gourmet cooks take great pride in making them correctly, but young professional chefs of this generation are apt to shun them as "heavy." They prefer reduced stocks or natural pan juices, with little or no thickening of any sort. Whether this trend will continue is impossible to predict.

And, like it or not, busy cooks in present-day homes have created their own family of sauces, whose "mother" is the can of condensed soup. Purists may shudder, but traditions constantly change, whether the transformations be gradual and subtle, or sudden and drastic. A young woman who treasures the handwritten recipe for her mother's favorite sauce values it not one bit less for the fact that it begins, "Take a can of mushroom soup and . . ."

SAUCE ESPAGNOLE
2 cups sauce

Sauce Espagnole has puzzled many an inquisitive cook. *Espagnole* means Spanish but none of its ingredients are typically Spanish nor is it known in traditional Spanish cuisine. The name is presumed to stem from the brown color of the sauce and refer to the dark-complexioned Spaniards. The problem with this theory is that, all through the seventeenth and eighteenth centuries, Spain was a rival of France, and occasionally an enemy.

The recipe for the sauce first appears in print in Vincent La Chapelle's *Le Cuisinier moderne*, which was published in 1733. It may have been created earlier, and there seems to have been another, quite different, antique sauce bearing the same name. Louis XIII and Louis XIV both married Spanish princesses (in order to maintain an uneasy peace) and Louis XV was also betrothed to a young Spanish cousin, though the engagement was later broken. In all probability the name originated with one of these alliances; a dark sauce to honor an olive-skinned Spanish beauty would have seemed eminently suitable to an early French chef.

Sauce Espagnole was traditionally made with a roux of browned butter and flour and then was simmered and skimmed for hours to obtain, finally, a glossy, almost clear, finished product. According to *Larousse Gastronomique*, "Carême's recipe is considered to be the classic method of preparing an espagnole sauce. Nowadays," modern cooks will no doubt be interested to note, "partridge is not used in the stock." Escoffier himself suggested that it would be simpler to thicken a strong, well-flavored stock with arrowroot, and that is what most modern cooks prefer to do.

2 cups rich brown stock,
      or 2 cups undiluted canned beef bouillon
3 tablespoons finely minced lean cooked ham
3 tablespoons finely minced onions
3 tablespoons finely minced carrots
1 tablespoon finely minced celery
½ teaspoon dried parsley
½ small bay leaf
⅛ teaspoon thyme
2 tablespoons arrowroot or cornstarch
2 tablespoons cold water

1. Place stock, ham, vegetables, and herbs in a small saucepan. Bring to a boil and simmer over a low flame for 30 minutes. Strain through a fine sieve, pressing on solids to extract the juices. Discard solids.
2. In a small bowl or cup, blend the arrowroot or cornstarch with cold water. Blend into stock and simmer for 5 minutes, or until sauce is clear and lightly thickened. Serve with meat.

SAUCE ALLEMANDE
1 cup sauce

Sauce Allemande seems to have been named solely to contrast with Sauce Espagnole. Although *allemande* means German, the sauce has nothing to do with German cuisine. The velvety, pale yellow sauce was simply named for the blonde Germans. Escoffier, who had served in the Franco-Prussian War and had no love for Germany, suggested the alternative names *Sauce Blonde* or *Sauce Parisienne.*

Note: *For a simpler Sauce Allemande, use instant-blending flour according to package directions, adding other ingredients as directed in Step 3.*

2 tablespoons butter or margarine

2 tablespoons all-purpose flour

I cup chicken broth

1 egg yolk

2 tablespoons half-and-half

Salt

Pepper

1 teaspoon lemon juice

1. In a small saucepan heat butter over low heat until melted. Stir in flour and cook over low heat, stirring constantly, until mixture is smooth and bubbly. Continue to stir, on and off heat, for several minutes, to rid flour of raw taste, but do not allow the mixture to brown.
2. Stir in chicken broth. Heat to boiling, stirring constantly. Boil and stir 1 minute. Remove from heat.
3. In a small bowl, beat egg yolk. Add half-and-half and beat again. Add one or two tablespoons of sauce and stir rapidly. Return mixture to saucepan and, stirring constantly, bring to a boil. Boil and stir 1 minute. Taste and add salt and pepper if needed. Stir in lemon juice. Serve over poached or baked fish or poultry.

SAUCE BÉARNAISE
¾ cup sauce

Note: *Please see "A Note about Eggs," p. 307.*

Sauce Béarnaise is a nineteenth-century sauce named for a seventeenth-century king. It was created at a restaurant called Pavillon Henri IV, located in a part of a castle built by Henry himself in Saint-Germain-en-Laye, a suburb of Paris. The unknown chef who perfected it named it for the king, who was born in the little southern frontier province of Béarn and was often called "Le Grand Béarnais."

Henry, known as Henry of Navarre before his coronation, was a Protestant prince who became a Catholic king. He is best remembered for the cynical (and perhaps spurious) comment, "Paris is well worth a Mass." Actually, making the decision to convert caused him intense moral agony. He obviously coveted the throne but he also wanted to end the cruel and hideous religious wars that had all but ruined France. One of his first acts as king was to issue the Edict of Nantes, granting the French Protestants freedom of worship.

2 tablespoons white wine

1 tablespoon tarragon vinegar

2 teaspoons chopped fresh tarragon, *or* 1 teaspoon dried tarragon

½ teaspoon chopped fresh chervil, *or* ¼ teaspoon dried chervil

2 teaspoons chopped shallots or onions

½ cup butter

3 egg yolks (from Grade A, unbroken eggs)

2 tablespoons lemon juice

¼ teaspoon salt

1. In a very small saucepan combine wine, vinegar, tarragon, chervil, and shallots. Bring to a boil and simmer, briefly, till almost all of the liquid evaporates.
2. In a very small saucepan, heat the butter to bubbling, but do not brown. Meanwhile, immerse the jar of an electric blender in very hot water to warm. Dry and replace in blender.
3. Place egg yolks, lemon juice, and salt in blender jar. Cover jar and blend briefly. Remove the cover, turn blender to high speed, and gradually add the hot butter. Add the herb mixture, cover, and blend on high speed 4 seconds. Serve with broiled steak or fish.

SAUCE BÉCHAMEL
1 cup sauce

Sauce Béchamel, considered one of the fundamental sauces of French cuisine, is said to honor Louis de Béchameil, Marquis de Nointel, chief steward at the court of Louis XIV, the king who built Versailles. The "Sun King" had the largest and most elaborate court that Europeans had ever known, and Béchameil, a former financier, held an important post in it. He daily purchased food for between two thousand and five thousand persons and clearly he was not down in the kitchens creating sauces himself. But he was also a celebrated gourmet (perhaps that is why Louis chose him to be steward) and it has been presumed that some now anonymous chef created a new sauce and named it for his master.

Note: *For a simpler Sauce Béchamel, use instant-blending flour according to package directions, adding nutmeg or onion juice if desired.*

2 tablespoons butter or margarine

2 tablespoons all-purpose flour

1 cup milk

¼ teaspoon salt

⅛ teaspoon white pepper

⅛ teaspoon nutmeg or few drops onion juice (optional)

1. In a small saucepan melt butter over low heat. Stir in flour and cook over low heat, stirring constantly, until mixture is smooth and bubbly. Continue to stir, on and off heat, for several minutes, to rid flour of raw taste, but do not allow the mixture to brown.
2. Whisk in milk. Heat to boiling, whisking constantly. Boil and stir 1 minute. Add salt and pepper, and nutmeg or onion juice if desired.

SAUCE MORNAY
1 cup sauce

Sauce Mornay recalls the great French noble family of that name. It probably was named for Philip de Mornay, a prominent French Huguenot and Henry of Navarre's close friend and valued advisor. Both men fought in the French religious wars of the late sixteenth century, steadfastly on the Protestant side, and Mornay conducted, for Henry and the Huguenot cause, a series of important embassies to England and the Low Countries.

Mornay again helped Henry in his struggle for the throne, but the king's abjuration of his Calvinist faith on his succession in 1589 inevitably caused a great strain on the friendship. Mornay continued to write and speak for the Protestants and it soon became clear that he had lost Henry's favor. Mornay retired from public life and the two men never reconciled.

Note: *For a simpler Sauce Mornay, use instant-blending flour according to package directions, adding cheese as directed.*

2 tablespoons butter or margarine
2 tablespoons all-purpose flour
½ cup chicken broth
½ cup milk
½ cup grated Parmesan cheese or shredded Swiss cheese
Salt

1. In a small saucepan heat butter over low heat until melted. Whisk in flour and cook over low heat, stirring constantly, until mixture is smooth and bubbly. Continue to stir, on and off heat, for several minutes, to rid flour of raw taste, but do not allow mixture to brown.
2. Whisk in broth and milk. Heat to boiling, whisking constantly. Boil and stir 1 minute. Stir in grated Parmesan cheese or shredded Swiss cheese. Continue to stir, keeping mixture hot, but not boiling, until cheese is melted. Taste and add salt if needed.

ENTRÉES & EXTRAS

CUMBERLAND SAUCE
¾ cup sauce

Cumberland Sauce is named for a man the Scots still love to hate: William Augustus, Duke of Cumberland, younger son of King George II.

The year was 1745. Charles Edward Stuart, also known as Bonnie Prince Charlie or the Young Pretender, had landed in Scotland in July. He was the grandson of James II, the Catholic king who had been ignominiously chased off the throne by his Protestant son-in-law and daughter, William and Mary, fifty-seven years earlier. Now Charles had returned to a land he had never known to try to claim a throne securely in the hands of his German cousins, the Hanoverians. Few Englishmen really liked either George I or George II. They were dull, stodgy men who barely spoke English and made no secret of the fact that they much preferred Hanover to England. But they were indisputably Protestant and, perhaps even more important, they were content to let Parliament run the country. Only a few Englishmen still nursed a romantic loyalty to "the king over the water," and fewer still were prepared to do anything about it.

DUKE OF CUMBERLAND

The situation was quite different in the north. The Stuarts had been kings of Scotland long before they were kings of England, and the wild highlanders had no liking for the union of Scotland and England that had been forced through in 1707. If Charles hoped to raise an army, it would have to be in the highlands. And raise an army he did.

By September Charles had enlisted five thousand men and had taken Edinburgh. Two months later they marched south to invade England. Some towns resisted and were taken; others welcomed the Prince and even provided a few recruits. But the support promised by France did not materialize, and the level of English enthusiasm proved disappointing. At Derby Charles's officers insisted he turn back. Although Cumberland was in close pursuit, little happened over the next few months: eighteenth-century armies simply did not fight in the wintertime.

The two armies finally met the following spring, at Culloden Moor. Charles had forty-five hundred men, starving for want of supplies and exhausted from forced marches. Cumberland had nine thousand men, well fed and well trained, marching in ranks like tin soldiers and supported by merciless artillery. The battle amounted to little more than one desperate charge by the highlanders, who were slaughtered. It ended in a frenzy, as Cumberland's cavalry finished off the wounded where they lay.

Culloden marked the end of the highland way of life, as the fleeing rebels were hunted down and whole villages burned. The retaliatory destruction went on for months, but in England few cared. The country had been saved from disruption and dissent, and from a highly suspect Stuart prince. Cumberland suddenly became their darling and a number of dishes were created in his honor, the best known of which is Cumberland Sauce.

    1 large orange
    Half a lemon
    ½ cup red currant jelly
    ¼ cup port

1. With a vegetable peeler, remove colored zest from the orange in thin strips. Slicing diagonally, cut the peel into narrow strips, about ½ inch long and ⅛ inch wide. Drop into a small saucepan filled with boiling water and boil briskly for 5 minutes. Drain, chill quickly with cold water, and drain again.
2. Squeeze orange and lemon and strain juice into pan containing peel. Add jelly and port and gently heat until jelly is melted. Chill and serve with hot or cold ham, venison, or lamb.

KETCHUP
2 pints

Ketchup takes its name from either the Chinese *ke-tsiap* or the Malay *kechap*, both of which were essentially a brine made from pickled fish, not unlike the Roman *garum*. The Dutch may have been the first to bring the word to Europe, calling it *ketjap*, but it was the English who adopted it wholeheartedly, making "kitchup" or "ketchup" from oysters, walnuts, mushrooms (still a favorite), cucumbers, and even, occasionally, tomatoes.

Only in America did ketchup become standardized, and inseparable from the tomato. Recipes do appear, from time to time, for specialty items like grape ketchup or cranberry ketchup, but they have scant appeal except for the bona fide gourmet. For most families, though it be spelled ketchup, catchup, or catsup, it must be red, sweet, spicy, and indisputably tomato!

1 cup vinegar

1 ½ teaspoons whole cloves

1 ½ teaspoons coarsely broken cinnamon stick

1 teaspoon celery seed

8 pounds fully ripe tomatoes

¾ cup chopped onions

½ teaspoon red pepper (cayenne)

1 cup sugar

4 teaspoons salt

1. In a small saucepan combine vinegar, cloves, cinnamon stick, and celery seed. Bring to a boil and remove from heat.
2. Dip tomatoes in boiling water for 30 to 60 seconds or until skins split. Dip in cold water. Slip off skins and remove cores. Quarter tomatoes into a large kettle or Dutch oven. Add onions and red pepper. Bring to a boil and simmer 20 minutes, uncovered.
3. Put mixture through a food mill or sieve. Combine puree and sugar in kettle; cook, stirring frequently, for 45 minutes or until reduced by half. Strain vinegar mixture, discarding solids, and add with salt to tomato mixture. Continue cooking, stirring almost constantly, for 30 minutes or until thick.
4. Ladle into 4 hot sterilized ½-pint jars, and seal.

TARTAR SAUCE
1 cup sauce

Beef Tartare—finely minced lean raw beef—became fashionable in France in the nineteenth century. It was named for the Tartars (originally "Tatars") or Mongols who had terrorized eastern Europe in the days of Genghis Khan. They were said to have been such wild men that they did not even cook their meat, instead putting it under their saddles to let it warm by friction.

Beef Tartare was usually served as it is now, with a bevy of garnishes, including a piquant sauce with a mayonnaise base that came to be called Sauce Tartare or Tartar Sauce. Today, at least in the United States, it is more often served with fish.

¾ cup mayonnaise or salad dressing
3 tablespoons finely minced pickle (dill or sweet)
2 teaspoons finely minced onion
1 tablespoon lemon juice
1 teaspoon capers, finely minced (optional)

1. Combine all ingredients and mix well.
2. Cover and refrigerate for several hours or overnight to allow flavors to blend.

JEZEBEL SAUCE
2 ½ cups sauce

Even the good cooks of nineteenth-century America were not particularly noted for their sauces. The one fiery exception is Jezebel Sauce, long a favorite in the Old South.

It is named for the Jezebel of the Old Testament, a Phoenician princess who came to Israel to marry the king, Ahab. But Jezebel was no meek and timid maiden, content to accept her husband's God. She was a capable, strong-willed woman who brought with her a retinue of pagan priests and a determination to build, in the heart of Ahab's capital city, a great temple to her god, Baal Shamem.

Note: Jezebel Sauce was originally intended for cold roast meats, but it is equally good with cream cheese and crackers.

The ground swell of resentment that arose among the common people found voice in the prophet Elijah, and so Jezebel had an influence on world religion that she never dreamed of. For Elijah, in opposing Baal, gave a new dimension to Hebrew monotheism. There was no doubt in Elijah's mind. He did not view Baal as an enemy god, nor as a rival god, nor even as a demon. If Baal was not God, he was nothing, a non-entity. Only Yahweh, "He is God!"—and He was not to be found in the storm or the earthquake but rather in the "still, small voice" heard only in solitude.

Falling into the hands of an avenging king, Jezebel met her death without flinching. But whatever her possible virtues, her name has entered the English language as a word for a bold, wicked, abandoned woman.

1 jar (12 ounces) pineapple preserves
1 jar (12 ounces) apple jelly
6 tablespoons prepared horseradish
4 tablespoons dry mustard

1. Mix all ingredients together in a large bowl.
2. Place in tightly topped jars and store in the refrigerator. Will keep for several months.

SWEETS

CHAPTER 9

CANDY & COOKIES

The Egyptians and the Mesopotamians, the Greeks and the Romans, all enjoyed confections made of honey, dried fruits, nuts, and spices, but candy, in the modern sense of the word, was possible only after the art of sugar refining had been mastered. Sugarcane was cultivated in India as early as 3000 B.C. and a crude kind of sugar making was practiced, but it remained virtually unheard of in the west until the eighth century, when the Arabs spread the knowledge to all the lands from Persia to the Mediterranean. The Arabs, skilled chemists, improved the refining process, and equally talented Persian cooks began to use sugar in marzipan, probably the oldest candy that is still being made and enjoyed. Nasir-i Khusraw, a famous Persian traveler and historian of the eleventh century, describes a great feast at which the sultan's table was decorated with marzipan sweetmeats made of almonds and powdered sugar, and molded into the shapes of orange trees and statues.

For centuries after the returning crusaders introduced marzipan into Europe, it ranked with spices and silks as an imported luxury available only to the rich. Gradually a rising standard of living made it a treat affordable to the middle class as well, especially at holidays, and the German city of Lubeck made marzipan its specialty, forming it into the brilliantly colored fruits and vegetables so well known today. (For the recipe for marzipan, see Battenberg Cake, page 231.)

Though sugarcane had been grown, and sugar produced, in Arabic Spain and southern France as early as the eighth century, it was not until the fourteenth century that the Venetians introduced it to all of Europe. They imported it in quantity from Arabia, further improved the refining process, and sold it in conical loaves to the wealthy all across the continent.

Candy making in Europe began in the apothecaries' shops. Pharmacists of the late Middle Ages considered sugar one of their most valuable materials. Sugar syrups could mask the taste of other, often bitter, medicinal ingredients, and the first hard candies were almost certainly sold as cough drops.

The word candy, originally sugar-candy, goes back ultimately to the Sanskrit *khanda* (sugar in pieces); it was used in England for a time, an adaptation of the French *sucre candi*, but gradually the term was supplanted in both countries and remained in use only in the American colonies. The British usually spoke of sweetmeats, or more recently, sweets, while the French preferred *bonbons*. The *bonbon* got its name when little French children, tasting candy for the first time, cried, *"bon, bon!"* (good, good!). The word could have remained in the nursery but instead became the name for hard candies, and then for candies of all sorts. Much later the English-speaking world would discover French creams, *bonbons fondants*, and call them simply bonbons.

The Spaniards introduced sugarcane into the New World. As the plantations began to flourish, the price of sugar dropped drastically and commercial candy production began in earnest. By the late sixteenth century, confectioners' shops had sprung up everywhere. They made stick candy, and, at Christmas, shepherds' crooks that in America turned into the familiar candy canes. Crystallized fruit was popular, including the "sugarplums" that would also be forever associated with Christmas, at least in poetry, if not in fact. Nougat was another early favorite. First made in Italy, it later became a French specialty; it takes its name from *nucatum*, the late Latin word meaning nut.

Lollipops were being made in England by the end of the

eighteenth century. In the north of England, "lolly" was a slang word for tongue, and the "pop" presumably came from the sound made when the candy was, from time to time, extracted from the mouth! Taffy or toffee, for at first the words referred to the same candies, soon followed. Taffy was the preferred word in Scotland, Ireland, and North America, while the English always said toffee. Both words may be derived from "tafia," a cheap rum that apparently was used as flavoring in the original recipes.

Chocolate, as a candy rather than as a beverage, came into its own only in the nineteenth century. In 1828, C. J. van Houten of the Netherlands patented a process for obtaining "chocolate powder" (cocoa) by pressing the ground cocoa beans and removing much of the cocoa butter. His purpose was to produce a form of chocolate that would more easily dissolve in water, and in this he succeeded. "Breakfast cocoa" became a household staple. But as the new process caught on, uses were sought for the surplus cocoa butter, and in 1847, an English firm, Fry and Sons (later to combine with Cadbury's), introduced the first "eating chocolate," a combination of chocolate, extra cocoa butter, and sugar. In 1876, Daniel Peter and Henri Nestlé of Switzerland created milk chocolate by combining chocolate with the latter's newly invented sweetened, condensed milk, and a whole new era began for chocolate in Europe.

Chocolate manufacture in the United States commenced in 1765 when an Irish chocolate maker named John Hannon set up a mill in Dorchester, Massachusetts. Hannon's financial backer was Dr. James Baker, who took over the firm when Hannon was lost at sea on a voyage to the West Indies. In the mid-1800s an employee named German left Baker's and established his own firm; later the name and slightly different formula went back to the parent company, giving us Baker's German chocolate.

But both Baker and German were primarily concerned with chocolate as an ingredient for cooking. It was Milton S. Hershey who recognized that the manufacture of chocolate candy could become a major industry in the United States. Hershey, who owned a moderately successful caramel manufacturing plant in Lancaster, Pennsylvania, visited the World's Colombian Exposition in Chicago in 1893 and saw a marvelous display of chocolate-making machinery from Germany. Convinced that chocolate was the candy of the future, he brought out the Hershey Almond Bar and the Hershey Milk Chocolate Bar in 1894, and later moved his plant to Hershey, Pennsylvania. Hershey Kisses, introduced in 1907, were actually identical to Wilbur Buds, first made by the Wilbur Chocolate Company in 1894.

Hershey's predictions for the future of chocolate proved accurate, for today chocolate accounts for well over half the candy eaten in the United States.

Cookies are as old as the baker's art itself. The ancient Hebrews compared their providential manna to the "wafers made with honey" (Exodus 16:31) they had known in Egypt, while the Roman *dulcia*, served at the end of the meal, usually included small cakes. But the English have never accepted cookies—at least, not by that name: "biscuit" serves as their all-purpose word for both sweet and unsweetened wafers. The name for America's beloved cookie came over with the Dutch of old New Amsterdam, whose term *koekje* means "little cake."

Northern Europeans turned cookie making into a true art, especially at Christmas time. German Pfeffernüsse (pepper nuts), Zimsterne (cinnamon stars), Spitzbuben (rascals or naughty boys), and Berliner Kranser (Berlin wreaths); Swedish Kringle (pretzels) and Finskbrod (Finnish bread)—all are a legacy handed down by the countless thousands of immigrants who came to the United States in the nineteenth century. Among the tempting recipes contained in the following collection, the European holiday tradition provides two festive cookies from Germany, Springerle and Nürnbergers. In addition, there are treats here from all over Europe, cookies with origins in Africa, some distinctively New World recipes, and even representatives from the Pacific Rim.

PRALINES
1 ½ dozen candies

Pralines are named for the comte du Plessis-Praslin (César, later duc de Choiseul). Born in 1598, Marshal du Plessis-Praslin was a brilliant general who remained steadfastly loyal to the Queen Regent, Anne of Austria, mother of Louis XIV, as she struggled to quell the rebellion known in French history as the Fronde.

But even great men have their weaknesses, and the duc de Choiseul suffered from chronic indigestion. Someone, perhaps his physician, perhaps only a servant, suggested that he soothe his stomach with sugared almonds. The simple sweet caught on among the French elite, and, in time, the name came to be applied to several entirely different confections.

To the French, a *praline* is still an almond covered with a coating of cooked sugar (a specialty of the town of Montargis, where the duc de Choiseul's chef retired, founding the Maison de la Praline, which continues in business to this day), while *pralin* is an ingredient: almonds and sugar caramelized and then ground into a fine powder used to flavor cakes, ice cream, or custards. But it is in French Louisiana, where the Creole cooks replaced the almonds with native pecans, that the candies grew into the round, delicious patties so often associated with New Orleans.

> 1 cup sugar
> 1 cup firmly packed light brown sugar
> ½ cup light cream
> ¼ teaspoon salt
> 2 tablespoons butter or margarine
> 1 cup pecan halves

1. In large, *heavy* skillet or saucepan, combine sugars, cream, and salt. Cook over medium heat, stirring constantly, to 228°F on a candy thermometer (or until mixture spins a thread about 2 inches long when dropped from a spoon).

2. Stir in butter or margarine and pecans. Continue cooking, stirring constantly, to 236°F (or until small amount of mixture dropped into very cold water forms a soft ball that flattens when removed from water). Remove from heat and place pan in cold water 5 minutes to cool.

3. With large spoon, beat mixture until it is slightly thickened and coats pecans. Drop candy by large spoonfuls onto waxed paper.

4. Wrap pralines individually in plastic wrap or waxed paper and store tightly covered at room temperature.

FUDGE
2 ¼ pounds

Fudge, a homegrown American confection, became popular in the eastern women's colleges around the turn of the century. In a letter now in the archives of Vassar College in Poughkeepsie, New York, Emelyn B. Hartridge writes:

> Fudge, as I first knew it, was first made in Baltimore by a cousin of a schoolmate of mine. It was sold in 1886 in a grocery store . . . for 40¢ a pound. . . . From my schoolmate, Nannie Hagner . . . I secured the recipe and in my first year at Vassar, I made it there—and in 1888 I made 30 pounds for the Senior Auction, its real introduction to the college, I think.

Variations on Vassar Fudge soon appeared, including contributions from Vassar's sister schools—Smith Fudge and Wellesley Fudge.

The use of the word "fudge" to mean cheating or mild dishonesty is far older, leading many to suspect that the new candy was made after lights were supposed to be out, or in rooms where cooking was forbidden. An item in a 1905 newspaper about a fire that resulted from the "overturning of an alcohol lamp over which some girls were cooking fudge" serves to confirm the derivation. But these college girls must have been accomplished cooks, as the original recipes for fudge were quite tricky, even when made with proper equipment, and involved truly laborious beating. Newer recipes, made with marshmallow, are virtually indistinguishable and far more reliable.

Variation: *For Butterscotch Fudge, omit chocolate morsels and add 2 cups butterscotch morsels.*

1 jar (7 ½ ounces) marshmallow cream or fluff

1 ½ cups sugar

⅔ cup evaporated milk

¼ cup butter or margarine

¼ teaspoon salt

2 cups (12 ounces) semisweet chocolate morsels

½ cup chopped nuts

1 teaspoon vanilla extract

1. Grease 8-inch square pan and set aside.
2. In heavy saucepan, combine marshmallow cream, sugar, evaporated milk, butter or margarine, and salt. Bring to a full boil, stirring constantly, over moderate heat. Boil 5 minutes, continuing to stir carefully and constantly.
3. Remove from heat. Add chocolate morsels and stir until melted. Stir in nuts and vanilla. Pour into prepared pan. Chill until firm, then cut into squares.

MARSHMALLOW CRISPY TREATS
2 dozen squares

The marshmallow takes its name from an edible plant, the marsh mallow *(althaea officinalis)*, a close relative of the hollyhock. A jelly-like gum can be extracted from its roots; it was used first as a folk medicine and then as an ingredient in cough syrups. Later confectioners used it as a firming agent in soft, puffy "marshmallow candies," soon shortened to "marshmallows."

Today, confectioners use gum arabic or gelatin when making marshmallows, so the plant name has become a complete misnomer. Marshmallows can be made in the home kitchen, but there would seldom be any point in doing so. What *are* fun to make, however, especially for very young cooks, are the various no-bake cookies that can be made with marshmallows. One of the best of these recipes is for Marshmallow Treats, created in 1939 by Mary Barber, home economist for the W. K. Kellogg Company, and trademarked by the company. The original recipe began appearing on cereal boxes in 1941; there are many variations.

¼ cup butter or margarine
4 cups miniature marshmallows *or* 40 regular marshmallows
5 cups crisp rice breakfast cereal

1. Grease 13 x 9 x 2-inch baking pan and set aside.
2. In 3-quart saucepan, melt butter or margarine. Add marshmallows and cook over low heat, stirring constantly, until marshmallows are melted and mixture is syrupy. Remove from heat.
3. Add cereal and stir until well coated. Using greased spatula, press warm mixture evenly and firmly into prepared pan. Cool and cut into 2-inch squares.

HAMANTASCHEN
2 ½ dozen cookies

Purim, or the Feast of Lots, a Jewish holiday occurring in late February or early March, is a joyous occasion. It recalls the story of Queen Esther who, with the help of her uncle, Mordecai, saved her people from the wicked councilor, Haman. Envious of the success the Jews had achieved in Persia, Haman plotted to destroy them. At a great banquet Esther prepared for her husband, King Ahasuerus (Xerxes I), she successfully pleaded the cause of the Jews and exposed Haman's perfidy. Haman was sent to the very gallows he had ordered built for the Jews.

Traditionally, Jews go to the synagogue on the evening before the holiday, and the story of Esther is read from the scriptures. The children bring noisemakers and greet the reading of Haman's name each time with rattles, boos, and much stamping of feet, a bit of rowdiness not only allowed but encouraged. Later, relatives and friends exchange small gifts and extend their charity to the poor. A traditional Purim meal always includes Hamantaschen, small three-cornered pastries said to resemble Haman's purse, or sometimes his hat.

Filling:

1 pound dried prunes
1 orange
½ cup sugar
½ teaspoon ground cinnamon

Pastry:

2 cups all-purpose flour
⅓ cup sugar
¼ teaspoon salt
1 ½ teaspoons baking powder
¾ cup butter or margarine
2 eggs
Cold water (if necessary)

1. Prepare filling. In small saucepan, cook prunes in water to cover until soft. Drain, reserving liquid, and remove pits. Place prunes in container of blender or food processor and blend until smooth, adding only as much of reserved liquid as necessary. Return pureed prunes to pan and add juice and grated rind of orange. Cook over low heat, stirring constantly, until almost as thick as jam. Add sugar and cinnamon and continue cooking, stirring constantly, until the consistency of stiff jam. Set aside.

2. Prepare pastry. In large bowl, mix flour, sugar, salt, and baking powder. Using pastry blender or two knives, cut in butter or margarine until mixture resembles bread crumbs. Make a well and add eggs. Stir until mixture leaves sides of bowl and forms a ball. Add cold water, if necessary, by ¼ teaspoonful. Cover and chill several hours.

3. Lightly grease 2 baking sheets. Preheat oven to 350°F. On lightly floured surface, roll dough to a thickness of 3/16 inch. Cut into circles 2½ inches in diameter and place on prepared sheets. Drop a teaspoonful of prune filling onto center of each cookie. Bring edges together and pinch to seal, forming triangles but leaving a small space open for filling to show on top. Bake at 350°F for 20 minutes. Using spatula, immediately remove cookies from baking sheets and cool on racks.

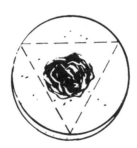
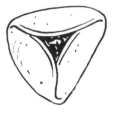

PETTICOAT TAILS
9 cookies

Petticoat Tails are a Scottish cookie whose unusual name has caused much speculation. The roughly triangular shapes into which they are traditionally cut do rather resemble old-fashioned petticoats, but it seems much more likely that "petticoat tails" resulted from a misunderstanding of *petits gatelles,* an old form of *petits gateaux,* French for little cakes. There was much contact between the two countries in the days of the "auld alliance"—after all, they always had England as a common enemy.

In one version of this story, the recipe was brought to Scotland by Mary, Queen of Scots, when she returned from France in 1561 to claim her throne, or, if not by Mary herself, then by one of the "four Maries," the young maids of honor who were her constant companions.

Though the name may well be French in origin, the cakes (as the Scots refer to what we call cookies) are obviously far older than their name and are also distinctively Scottish. The unusual pattern in which they are cut is clearly a crude representation of the sun, and this, plus the insistence that the cakes must be served in the same arrangement, as well as the unmistakable resemblance to the ancient Celtic hearth breads (see pages 4–6) make it almost certain that they predate both Victorian petticoats and Mary, Queen of Scots.

⅞ cup all-purpose flour

½ cup rice flour

½ cup butter, softened

¼ cup sugar

1. Preheat oven to 300°F.
2. In small bowl, combine flours and set aside.

Note: *The rice flour is neither essential nor really traditional, but modern Scottish cooks use it to enhance the crumbly texture so prized in this type of cookie. If preferred, 1 ⅜ cups all-purpose flour may be substituted for the ⅞ cup all-purpose flour and the ½ cup rice flour.*

3. In medium bowl, and with electric mixer, cream butter and sugar until light and fluffy. Gradually add flours, continuing to mix until dough resembles fine cornmeal. Using hands, form into a ball and knead lightly a few times, until smooth. Place on ungreased baking sheet and roll into a circle approximately 8 inches in diameter. Using a 3-inch round cutter, cut a circle in the middle, but do not remove. Cut outer ring into 8 segments. Using spatula, move each "petticoat" out from the center, so that cookies will bake evenly.

4. Bake at 300°F 20–30 minutes, until very pale golden, but not brown. Dust with additional granulated sugar and allow to cool slightly before removing from pan. Arrange on serving plate in the shape of the original design.

SPRINGERLE
2–3 dozen cookies

Springerle in German means little jumper. The suggestion has been made that the unusual name pertains to the embossed designs created by rolling or pressing the patterned Springerle mold into the dough, designs which, being raised, presumably "jump out" at the viewer. But in the south of Germany, the word was a nickname for a colt or young horse, and this derivation seems much more likely. Today the designs can be anything the carver of a Springerle mold fancies, but in the High Middle Ages, the cookies always featured saints. Peering farther back in the Dark Ages, which are indeed maddeningly "dark" for both folklorist and historian, it seems that saints were only the Christian missionaries' substitutes for a still earlier pagan symbol, the horse.

To the German tribes, the horse was sacred to Woden, the god who gave victory in battle, and horses were traditionally sacrificed at the great midwinter Yule festival. Those who could not afford to sacrifice a horse sacrificed a cake made in the shape of a horse, a substitution found acceptable in many pagan societies. (Similarly, the story of the runaway gingerbread man, which occurs in many of the languages of Europe, recalls dim memories of human sacrifice, the substitute pastry man becoming confused with a "victim" who was deliberately allowed to escape.)

Springerle molds can take the form of either rolling pins or flat blocks, deeply carved with rectangular images that leave an impression on the dough. Techniques and designs vary, but the cookies are always flavored with anise.

2 tablespoons butter or margarine, softened

1 cup anise seeds

2 eggs

1 ¼ cups sugar

1 teaspoon finely grated lemon peel

¼ teaspoon vanilla extract

Approximately 3 ½ cups all-purpose flour

1. Using 2 tablespoons butter or margarine, heavily coat 2 large cookie sheets. Sprinkle evenly with anise seeds and set aside.

2. In large bowl, beat eggs on low speed until thick. Gradually add sugar and continue beating until mixture is thick enough to fall back on itself in a slowly dissolving ribbon when beater is lifted from bowl. Beat in lemon peel and vanilla. Add 3 cups flour, 1 cup at a time, stirring well after each addition. Shape dough into a ball and place on lightly floured surface.

3. Knead dough approximately 10 minutes, adding flour if necessary, until smooth and pliable. Sprinkle board with flour again, and roll approximately half the dough into a rectangle ¼ inch thick. (Cover remaining dough with damp cloth to prevent drying.) Sprinkle a Springerle mold or Springerle rolling pin evenly with flour (2 tablespoons), then rap sharply on table to remove excess. Press the mold down or roll the pin firmly across dough, to print pattern on it as deeply and clearly as possible. With sharp knife, cut cookies apart and place 1 inch apart on prepared sheets, pressing them gently into anise seeds. Roll and cut remaining dough similarly, working quickly, as dough dries rapidly. Set cookies aside, uncovered, at room temperature, 24 hours.

4. Preheat oven to 250°F and bake cookies 20–30 minutes, until firm but not brown. With large spatula, transfer cookies to cake rack to cool. Set aside, uncovered, for a few days, to soften. Cookies may be stored several weeks in a tightly sealed metal canister.

NÜRNBERGER
about 5 dozen cookies

Many German cities have Christmas fairs, but none is as famous as that held at Nuremberg (Nürnberg), the old German city of toy-makers. Called the *Christkindlmarkt* (Christ Child market), it is tra-ditionally opened the first week of December by a young girl dressed as an angel, who welcomes the visitors. Vendors set up hundreds of booths in the marketplace and surrounding streets, selling only items pertaining to Christmas. Primarily, these are the hand-carved wooden toys for which the city is famous, the tradi-tional German hand-blown glass Christmas tree ornaments, and the cookies that are still one of the city's main industries. Every sort are sold, from hard, spicy Pfeffernüsse to delicate Spritz, but the favorites are Lebkuchen, the dark, molasses-sweetened ginger cakes so beloved by Germans, and Nürnberger, the lighter honey cakes named for the city itself.

Nuremberg's cookies are almost always lavishly decorated with almonds and cherries or with intricate frosting designs that some-times include tiny mirrors or sentimental embossed pictures of an-gels or St. Nicholas.

Cookies:

1 cup honey
¾ cup firmly packed light brown sugar
1 egg
2 ¼ cups all-purpose flour
¼ teaspoon ground cloves
½ teaspoon ground nutmeg
1 teaspoon ground cinnamon
½ teaspoon baking soda
½ cup finely chopped candied lemon peel
Candied cherries
Blanched almonds

Glaze:

1 cup sugar
½ cup water
¼ cup confectioners' sugar

1. In large saucepan, heat honey to boiling, then allow to cool. Stir in brown sugar and egg. In separate bowl, mix flour, spices, and baking soda. Add to honey mixture along with candied lemon peel and mix thoroughly. Cover and chill at least 8 hours.

2. Preheat oven to 400°F. Lightly grease 2 large baking sheets. On lightly floured surface, roll small amount of dough to ¼-inch thickness. (Keep remaining dough refrigerated.) Cut out rounds with a 2-inch cutter and place on prepared sheets. Place a candied cherry in center of each cookie and 5 blanched almonds around cherry. Repeat with remaining dough. Bake 10–12 minutes, or until no imprint remains when cookie is touched lightly.

3. Prepare glaze while cookies are baking. In small saucepan, mix granulated sugar and water. Cook over medium heat to 230°F on candy thermometer (or just until small amount of mixture spins a 2-inch thread). Remove from heat. Stir in confectioners' sugar. If glaze becomes sugary, reheat slightly, adding a few drops of water.

4. Using pastry brush, brush glaze lightly over cookies. Immediately remove from baking sheet. Cool on rack, then store in tightly covered metal canister with an apple slice. Cookies improve with several days' aging.

HUSSAR'S KISSES
2½ dozen cookies

Recipes, like inventions, can have more than one creator. The little Austrian cookies known as Hussar's Kisses are almost identical to our own "thumbprint" cookies, except that in the Austrian version, the end of a wooden spoon is used to make the indentations.

The Hussars were the dashing cavalrymen of eastern Europe. King Matthias Corvinus of Hungary raised the first corps of Hussars in 1458 to fight the Turks. At the time, the armies of central and western Europe lacked effective light cavalry. The fame of the Hussars spread rapidly and similar units formed in Austria, Prussia, and elsewhere. The brilliantly colored uniforms of the Hungarian Hussars also invited imitation: high cylindrical cloth hat, scarlet jacket with heavy braiding, and the heavier, fur-trimmed jacket traditionally worn hanging from the left shoulder.

Hussar, related to the Italian *corsair*, originally meant plunderer, and the original corps consisted of wild horsemen from the plains. Soon, however, the Hussars became an elite corps in the armies of an increasingly militaristic Europe, and to many a lovesick girl, a Hussar's kisses were sweet indeed.

½ cup butter or margarine, softened	1 cup all-purpose flour
¼ cup sugar	⅓ cup finely chopped almonds
1 egg, separated	Apricot jam or preserves

1. In small bowl, cream butter or margarine on low speed with sugar. Add egg yolk and mix well. Blend in flour. Chill dough 30 minutes.
2. Shape dough by teaspoonfuls into 1-inch balls. Beat egg white until foamy. Dip tops of balls into egg white, then into almonds. As balls are coated, set them aside on a plate. Make a depression in the center of each, using the end of a wooden cooking spoon. Refrigerate until firm.
3. Preheat oven to 350°F. Place cookies 1 inch apart on ungreased baking sheet. Bake 10–12 minutes, or until light brown. Immediately remove from baking sheet, allow to cool. Fill indentations with jam a few hours before serving.

MADELEINES
3 dozen cookies

In culinary lore, Madeleines are always associated with Marcel Proust, whose autobiographical novel, *Remembrance of Things Past*, begins as his mother serves him tea and "those short, plump little cakes called *'petites madeleines,'* which look as though they had been molded in the fluted scallop of a pilgrim's shell." The narrator dips a corner of a little cake into the tea and then is overwhelmed by memories; he realizes that the Madeleines bore "in the tiny and almost impalpable drop of their essence, the vast structure of recollection." As it turns out, it would take seven volumes for that recollection to unfold!

But Madeleines had existed long before Proust's boyhood. Numerous stories, none very convincing, attribute their invention to a host of different pastrycooks, each of whom supposedly named them for some particular young woman. Only three things are known for sure. One is that Madeleine is the French form of Magdalen (Mary Magdalen, a disciple of Jesus, is mentioned in all four gospels). Another is that Madeleines are always associated with the little French town of Commercy, whose bakers were said to have once, long ago, paid a "very large sum" for the recipe and sold the little cakes packed in oval boxes as a specialty of the area.

Finally, it is also known that nuns in eighteenth-century France frequently supported themselves and their schools by making and selling a particular sweet, just as the Christian Brothers still make wine. Evidently Commercy once had a convent dedicated to St. Mary Magdalen, and the nuns, probably when all the convents and monasteries of France were abolished during the French Revolution, sold their recipe to the bakers for an amount that grew larger with each telling.

1 cup butter or margarine, softened

2 ½ cups sifted confectioners' sugar

4 eggs

2 cups all-purpose flour

¼ teaspoon lemon extract

1. Preheat oven to 350°F. Generously butter molds in Madeleine pan and dust with flour, rapping on table to shake out excess. Set aside.
2. In medium bowl, and with electric mixer, beat butter or margarine until fluffy. Gradually add confectioners' sugar, continuing to beat. Add eggs, one at a time, beating at high speed after each addition. (If mixture starts to curdle, beat until smooth.) Add flour and lemon extract and mix thoroughly.
3. Fill each mold with approximately 1 ½ tablespoons batter. Bake at 350°F 20–25 minutes, or until cakes are lightly browned. Remove from oven and immediately turn Madeleines out of pan to cool. (If only one pan is available, batter can stand at room temperature while pan is washed, dried, buttered, and floured for reuse.)

BENNE SEED WAFERS
4 dozen cookies

Benne seeds, otherwise known as sesame seeds, were brought to the Old South by African slaves, almost certainly by accident. Scattered seeds took root, flourished in the rich soil and warm climate, and soon produced the tall, distinctive plants that were recognized at once by the slowly adjusting Africans, a poignant reminder of the home they had left behind. Black cooks, gradually developing a whole new cuisine in the kitchens of the great plantations, made use of the seeds on biscuits, in stews, and in the famed Benne Seed Wafers that eventually came to be linked to Charleston, South Carolina. The word *benne*, Malaysian in origin, was well known to both the Wolof and Mandingo peoples of West Africa; the seeds came to be thought of as a good luck symbol, probably because of their African origin.

Note: Benne Seed Wafers may be sweetened cookies (as prepared below) or unsweetened crackers. For an unsweetened wafer, add toasted sesame seeds to pie crust dough, cut into strips or circles, and bake on ungreased sheet at 400°F 10–15 minutes.

½ cup hulled sesame seeds
1 cup butter or margarine, softened
⅔ cup sugar
¼ teaspoon salt
1 tablespoon milk
1 ⅔ cups all-purpose flour

1. Preheat oven to 350°F.
2. Spread sesame seeds on cookie sheet and toast in oven 15 minutes, or until golden brown.
3. In medium bowl, cream butter or margarine, sugar, and salt on low speed until light and fluffy. Add milk, flour, and sesame seeds, mixing well. Chill. Shape into small balls and place on ungreased baking sheet 2–3 inches apart.
4. Bake at 350°F 15 minutes, or until lightly browned. Cool slightly before removing from sheet.

ANZACS
3 dozen cookies

Anzacs are a New Zealand cookie, or, as they would say, biscuit. The acronym ANZAC, standing for Australian and New Zealand Army Corps, was coined in World War I, when the troops from down under won renown for bravery in the ill-fated battle of Gallipoli. The "biscuits" also date from this time, the invention of women seeking a sturdy little sweet that would pack and travel well. Recipes varied, right from the start, but the name persisted.

Anzacs saw duty once again in World War II, sent to the troops stationed on Pacific islands where heat and humidity ruined most of the other treats from home. As one soldier later wrote, "even fruitcakes arrived seeming more like Plum Duff" (a sort of steamed pudding). But Anzacs proved reliable. One recipe that became a favorite was that given out by "Aunt Daisy," a radio personality whose morning show included recipes and handy hints. The cookies are still popular; sometimes sunflower seeds are used in place of nuts.

Note: *For a slightly less "sturdy" cookie, use only ½ cup whole wheat flour or finely crushed breakfast cereal.*

1 cup rolled oats
⅔ cup all-purpose flour
⅔ cup whole-wheat flour or finely crushed breakfast cereal
½ cup dried shredded coconut
¼ cup chopped nuts or sunflower seeds (optional)

¾ cup sugar
½ cup butter or margarine
1 tablespoon honey
½ teaspoon baking soda
3 tablespoons boiling water

1. Preheat oven to 350°F. Grease 2 large baking sheets and set aside.
2. Mix oats, flours, coconut, nuts or sunflower seeds (if desired), and sugar. Set aside. In large pan, melt butter or margarine. Add honey and stir. Mix baking soda in boiling water and quickly add to butter mixture. Add dry ingredients and mix well.
3. Drop by small teaspoonfuls on prepared sheets, allowing room for spreading. Bake at 350°F 10–15 minutes, or until golden brown. Immediately remove from baking sheets.

FILBERT FUDGE SLICES
4 dozen cookies

The filbert takes its name from St. Philibert, whose feast day, August 20, came as the nuts were ripe and ready to harvest. Philibert, an abbot in seventh-century France, was remembered not only for his personal sanctity, but also for the kindness and care he lavished on all who lived around the monasteries he governed.

The other common name for the filbert is hazelnut; the bushes, for they are seldom tall enough to be considered true trees, grow wild across Europe, Asia, and North America. The ease with which the nuts can be both picked and stored probably means that they were an important supply of food for winter for as long as humans have lived on any of these continents.

Because nuts make such a good addition to so many kinds of cookies and other baked goods, there is a tendency to look upon them as merely optional. Sometimes it pays to think the other way around. Here the filbert is set off by a rich chocolate sliced cookie that provides a perfect foil for the nut's pronounced flavor.

Incidentally, these sliced cookies, of the type often called refrigerator cookies, are much older than either refrigerators or ice boxes. They were known to generations of good cooks in Scandinavia, but could only be made in wintertime!

3 ½ squares (3 ½ ounces) unsweetened chocolate

⅔ cup butter or margarine, softened

2 cups sugar

1 egg

1 teaspoon vanilla extract

1 ¼ cups all-purpose flour

1 teaspoon baking powder

½ teaspoon salt

1 cup finely chopped filberts

1. Melt chocolate over boiling water. Combine in mixing bowl with butter or margarine, sugar, egg, and vanilla.
2. Mix flour with baking powder and salt; add to chocolate mixture along with filberts and blend. If necessary, place mixing bowl in refrigerator until dough is firm enough to form into rolls 1½ inches in diameter. Wrap rolls in waxed paper or aluminum foil and chill again until firm enough to slice, about 2 hours.
3. Preheat oven to 375°F. Cut rolls into slices 3/16 inch thick. Place on ungreased baking sheet and bake 6–8 minutes, or until firm. Cool slightly before removing from baking sheet.

MACADAMIA NUT SLICES
5 dozen cookies

The macadamia nut is the only cultivated food plant that Australia has given the world. In 1857, trees were discovered by two early Australian botanists, Ferdinand von Mueller and Walter Hill. Mueller named the tree for a friend, John Macadam, a Scottish physician and part-time scientist who was the secretary of the Philosophical Institute of the city of Victoria. According to legend, Macadam never tasted a macadamia nut, as he died shortly after the tree was named for him. Hill planted a seed in 1858, and the tree flourished and is still producing nuts today. Although Aborigines had always eaten macadamia nuts, the Australians of British descent valued the trees primarily as ornamentals—they are handsome, long-lived evergreens with dark shiny foliage and long racemes made up of hundreds of tiny white blossoms.

It remained for an American to see the culinary and commercial possibilities. William Herbert Purvis was the farsighted soul who gathered seeds near Mount Bauple in Queensland, Australia, and put in seedlings at Kukuihaele, Hawaii, about 1882. Again, one of the trees he planted is alive and still bearing.

The shell of the macadamia nut is extremely hard to crack, a problem that has been solved in Hawaii by modern machinery, and the macadamia industry is flourishing. Today the trees are also cultivated in California, Kenya, and South America, and even Australia has belatedly begun to grow the trees commercially.

Macadamia nuts remain quite expensive, both because tree crops are, by nature, slow to reach maturity, and because demand continues to exceed supply; nevertheless more and more Americans are discovering their delights. The following recipe sets off the macadamia's crunchy goodness and distinctive flavor by a simple background of crisp, rich cookie.

1 cup butter or margarine, softened

1 cup firmly packed light brown sugar

2 eggs

1 ½ teaspoons vanilla extract

3 cups all-purpose flour

1 teaspoon salt

1 jar (3 ½ ounces) unsalted macadamia nuts, finely chopped

1. In large bowl, and with electric mixer, thoroughly mix butter or margarine, brown sugar, eggs, and vanilla. Stir in flour, salt, and nuts.

2. Form into 2 rolls about 1 ½ inches in diameter. Wrap in waxed paper or aluminum foil and chill in refrigerator or freezer until firm enough to slice, about 2 hours.

3. Preheat oven to 400°F. Cut rolls into slices 3/16 inch thick. Place slices 1 inch apart on ungreased baking sheet. Bake 8–12 minutes, or until light brown. Immediately remove from baking sheet.

CHAPTER 10

THE DESSERT COURSE

By imperial Roman times the custom of ending a meal with a sweet was well established. All the peoples of the Mediterranean world appreciated and enjoyed fresh fruit and to these natural delicacies the Romans added little cakes, custards, cheesecakes, sweet omelets, fried cakes dipped in honey, and stuffed dried fruits.

Much less is known about sweets in the Middle Ages. Surely they existed, for honey was abundant. Peasants and manor houses alike kept beehives; the church used only beeswax candles for services, so honey was in effect almost a by-product. But the concept of a dessert course arose only sometime later. Cooks in the crude kitchens of the great stone castles sent all manner of dishes to the table at once. Even after "courses" became the norm, each consisted of a great jumble of unrelated foods, so that roasts, sweet dishes, and savory preparations were all served haphazardly together.

Still, at the end of the meal, the table was cleared and spiced wine served, with sweet wafers, raisins, nuts, and "comfits," as sugared caraway seeds and anise seeds were called. It is from these simple beginnings that our modern "dessert" stems, for the word comes from the French *desservir* and, ultimately, from the Latin *dis servir*, to remove what has been served, to clear (the table).

During the Renaissance, meals (like so many other things) took a more modern turn. Moreover, we have much wider knowledge of the recipes used, as cookbooks were among the earliest of the newly available printed books. A cookbook published in Italy in 1570 gives the menu for a banquet prepared for Pope Pius V and his guests. It lists four courses. The first, clearly corresponding to modern appetizers, was made up of cold dishes served from the credenza or sideboard, the next two were of hot main dishes served from the kitchen, and then came a last course, again served from the credenza, which included fresh fruit, assorted cheeses, little cakes, fruit tarts, and nuts, an array that would not be out of place on a modern dessert cart.

Inevitably, as the idea of true desserts spread, countries developed their own preferences. To Englishmen the only dessert that ever really counted was the pudding.

The English pudding came into its own only with the invention of the cloth pudding bag at the end of the sixteenth century, replacing the use of animal organs to encase the pudding mixture for the boiling process. Though now the pudding could be distinguished clearly from butchering and sausages, suet remained a prime ingredient, along with dried fruits and spices. Boiled puddings remained paramount but eventually both rice pudding and hasty pudding became popular, too. The latter took its name from the fact that, though constant stirring was required, it could be prepared much more quickly than the earlier boiled or steamed creations. Sometimes the hasty pudding was made of milk cooked with flour, sugar, and butter, a forerunner of the cornstarch pudding or even more modern instant pudding. Other times it simply meant the traditional stirred porridge, sweetened and served under a new name; only in America would the hasty pudding come to be made of cornmeal.

Dessert gelatins, too, eventually diverged from meat gelatins and aspics. To the gelatinous liquid obtained from boiling a calf's foot cooks added wine, sugar, spices, and isinglass; the latter was a form of gelatin made from the bladders of sturgeons and brought from Russia by Dutch traders. Eventually rosewater, lemon juice, or the juice of Seville oranges came to be popular additions, but the emphasis was more on color than on flavor. Ribbon-jellies enjoyed popularity; they featured stripes of red (using cochineal), green (spinach), yellow (saffron), and blue (syrup of violets).

While the English were learning to dote on puddings, the gourmets and gourmands of the continent were discovering pastries. And there was such a splendid choice of pastries! Short pastry could be used for a dazzling array of *flans* and *tartelettes*. Chou paste (the name comes from the French *chou*, meaning cabbage, which the finished product was said to resemble) could be used for cream puffs or the equally delicate éclairs. And, best of all, there was puff pastry.

Culinary experts believe that puff pastry was first created by the skilled bakers of ancient Persia. Gradually the technique of folding, folding, folding the dough spread to Turkey, to Greece, and to the various Balkan countries, where the pastries so created were known as baklava, phyllo, or strudel (the names tend to float from place to place, but not always with precisely the same meaning). Then the fascinating flaky pastry made its way to France, where the celebrated *pâtissiers*, the pastry chefs, named it *pâte feuilletée*, literally consisting of thin leaves.

Meanwhile, the folding technique had also come to the attention of the bakers of old Vienna. Although they hated the Turks with murderous ferocity, they also found themselves learning from their enemies. By adding yeast to the puff pastry, they created the *kipfel* or crescent; its very shape recalls the bitter wars with the Turks. Ironically, both the wars and the creativity of the Austrian bakers are largely forgotten, for the French adopted the buttery *kipfel* and today, in English-speaking countries at least, it is known only as the ever popular *croissant*. Austria gets due credit in other parts of the world, however. The Danes added just a bit of sugar to the dough, and much jam to the finished product, and created what Americans know as Danish pastries; happily, they are called Austrian pastries in their native Denmark.

In the meantime, Italian chefs were experimenting with frozen desserts. The first were probably ices and sherbets, but they had apparently evolved into true ice cream by 1560, when a writer described a "food from milk which is made of milk sweetened with honey and frozen. . . . Some call it the flower of milk, some call it cream."

Like so many other culinary innovations, ice cream soon traveled from Italy to France, where it became the delight of the nobility and then to England. In the early seventeenth century "creme ice" appeared regularly at the table of Charles I, and in the eighteenth century recipes began to appear in British cookbooks.

On the continent, ice cream first became available to the middle class by way of the coffeehouses. A Sicilian, Francesco Procopio dei Coltelli (Procope for short), in 1670 capped a long career as a successful Parisian *limonadier* (vendor of drinks, especially lemonade) by opening the Café Procope, a coffeehouse that also sold ice cream. The Caffe Florian in Venice sold the same combination of fashionable new treats, and may have been Procope's inspiration. Amazingly, both establishments are still in business.

The first known mention of ice cream in the American colonies comes in 1744, in a letter written by a guest of Governor William Bladen of Maryland. Later in the same century ice cream was being made and sold in major cities, and one confectioner's records show that George Washington ran up a bill for 5£/6s./2d. (about $200) for ice cream during the summer of 1790. Thomas Jefferson had a favorite, and elaborate, recipe for ice cream, but it was Dolley Madison who made it a glamorous specialty at state dinners in the White House.

Gradually, commercial ice cream production increased until the treat became available to all. And then the innovations began. The ice cream soda was invented in 1874, at the semicentennial celebration of the Franklin Institute in Philadelphia. Robert M. Green, a concessionaire at the exhibition, was selling a drink popular at the time, a mixture of sweet cream, syrup, and carbonated water (evidently a forerunner of the modern bottled "cream soda," which, of course, contains no cream). Early in the course of the celebration, however, he ran out of cream and began substituting vanilla ice cream. The new drink was such a success that Green's receipts jumped from $6 a day to over $600 a day; he went on to make a fortune as a manufacturer of soda fountains.

According to H. L. Mencken, writing in *The American Language, Supplement 1*, the ice cream sundae was invented in Two Rivers, Wisconsin, in the early 1890s. One night George Hallauer stopped in at an ice cream parlor kept by E. C. Berners and ordered a dish of ice cream. He spotted a bottle of chocolate syrup, used for making sodas, and asked Berners, "Why don't you put some of that chocolate on the ice cream?" Berners protested, "You don't want to ruin the flavor of the ice cream," but Hallauer answered, "I'll try anything once," and then found that the combination was delicious. News of the novelty spread, first in Two Rivers and then in neighboring towns. In nearby Manitowoc, George Giffy, who also operated an ice cream parlor, began to offer the new dish, but only on Sunday, presumably to bring the crowds in, and Sunday ice cream soon changed to "ice cream sundae." Soon the new concoction began to appear in college towns: Ann Arbor, Michigan; Ithaca, New York; and Evanston, Illinois.

But that is not the way the people of Evanston tell the story. According to them, Evanston was noted for its "blue laws," and the city fathers, annoyed that so many young people flocked to the soda fountains on Sunday (thus allegedly profaning the Sabbath), passed a law forbidding the sale of ice cream sodas on Sunday. An enterprising drugstore owner named Garwood began to serve the ice cream and syrup, minus the soda water, on Sunday and soon customers were ordering sundays every day of the week. In either version of the story, "sunday" was changed to "sundae" at the behest of those who still felt the sabbath was being profaned.

The Evanstonians have never come up with a shred of proof to document their claim, however, while Mencken, a scholar of some note, had the advantage of a newspaper column in which to solicit recollections and then sift through the replies. At any rate, if the argument must go on, it should be confined strictly to the *name* of the new treat, as a combination so simple and so obvious was probably "invented" over and over again in different communities. Indeed, a manual for new soda fountain owners published in 1901 quite solemnly assures its readers that sundae is the correct name, though the combination previously may have been known in their areas as a "throw-over," a "college ice," or a frappé.

By the turn of the century the float, the ice cream sandwich, and the banana split had joined the pantheon of ice cream delights, all of them invented by persons whose names may never be known, and the list seemed complete—except for the ice cream cone.

The cone first gained popularity at the St. Louis World's Fair of 1904, where it was known as the "World's Fair Cornucopia." Credit for its invention is usually given to Ernest A. Hamwi, a Syrian who was selling *zalabia*, a crisp, waferlike Persian pastry baked on a flat waffle iron. According to Hamwi's account, his stand was close to that of an ice cream concessionaire who ran out of serving dishes on an extremely busy day. The alert young Syrian rolled one of his wafers into a cornucopia, let it cool, and put a scoop of ice cream on it, and the ice cream cone was born. But, though there are eyewitness accounts to substantiate the story, so many other claimants have come forward that even the Missouri Historical Society has despaired of arriving at the definitive history. At any rate, the cornucopias were immensely popular and even before the World's Fair was over, foundries in St. Louis were turning out molds for the new cones, as they came to be called in other cities.

And so the parade of desserts continues. By now it might seem that the gamut has been run, and that every possible dish has been created. Almost certainly, it has not. Somewhere, sometime, an inspired chef will devise a totally new creation, and word of it will travel. Such discoveries are not monumental, perhaps, but they do make our meals a little more fun!

APPLE CHARLOTTE
6 servings

Numerous writers have tried to find a French origin for Apple Charlotte, but it seems to be thoroughly British. It is a simple, sturdy pudding made by packing slices of bread and sweetened stewed apples into a mold and baking. The name is first known to have appeared in print in 1796, in a verse by an American poet, Joel Barlow, clearly showing that the dish was already a familiar one on both sides of the Atlantic:

> The Charlotte brown, within whose crusty sides,
> A belly soft the pulpy apple hides; . . .

Apple Charlotte was almost certainly named for Charlotte of Mecklenburg-Strelitz, who married George III in 1761, or possibly for their daughter Princess Charlotte, who was born in 1766. The Charlotte, occasionally made with cherries, probably inspired the later British "summer puddings," which also combine bread and fruit and then allow the mixture to soak until it is one more or less homogenous mass.

8 tart cooking apples (about 2 pounds)
1 cup sugar
½ teaspoon cinnamon

Sliced bread
Butter or margarine, melted

1. Preheat oven to 400°F.
2. Peel, quarter, and core apples. Cook in small amount of water just until tender; drain. Mix cinnamon with sugar and add to apples, stirring well.
3. Cut bread slices into strips, leaving crusts on. Dip each strip into melted butter, then place, buttered side down, in 1 ½-quart ovenproof casserole. Continue until bottom and sides of dish are covered, cutting to fit and overlapping slightly where necessary. Place apples in dish and cover with more bread slices, buttered side up.
4. Bake at 400°F 30–45 minutes, or until bread is golden brown. Turn out or serve from casserole while still warm but not steaming hot.

Note: *Apple Charlotte may be served with* cream *or, though the practice is not traditional, with* vanilla ice cream.

CHARLOTTE RUSSE
8 servings

News of the delicious English Charlottes drifted across the channel and served as inspiration for a man who was perhaps the greatest genius ever to set foot in a kitchen. He was Marie-Antoine Carême.

Carême (who preferred to call himself Antonin) was born in 1784 into "one of the poorest families in France." One of twenty-five children (in all probability his father had married more than once), Carême was abandoned when he was twelve. In later life he recalled how his father took him to a cheap restaurant near the city gates, bought him a good meal, and then left him, saying, "Go, little one. In this world there are excellent callings. Leave us to languish; misery is our lot, and we must die of misery. This is the time of fine fortunes, it only needs wit to make one, and wit you have. Go, little one, and perhaps this evening or tomorrow some fine house will open its doors to you. Go with what God has given you."

Chance led the child to a humble cookshop, and by the time he was fifteen Carême had entered the service of Bailly, a celebrated *pâtissier*. Here he came to the attention of Talleyrand, a noted gourmet as well as one of Napoleon's chief ministers. Soon he was working in Talleyrand's own kitchens and then was made head chef. Carême taught himself to read and write; eventually he would write and illustrate seven books, five on cooking and two on architecture.

Carême was a restless man, and all of Europe vied for his services. Before retiring to complete his writings, he would supervise the huge kitchens of the Prince Regent of Great Britain (later George IV), Tsar Alexander I of Russia, the court of Vienna, the British embassy at Paris, and the Baron de Rothschild at his country estate. Yet few of Carême's dishes remain in the repertory today. Styles change, and his was a very elaborate, complicated cuisine. One exception is the Charlotte Russe.

Carême began by experimenting with English Charlottes, seeking ways, as he did with so many dishes, to make them more appealing. First he turned the Charlotte into a cold dish, a pastry shell filled with pureed applesauce; then he went on to create a totally new dessert, which he called *Charlotte à la parisienne*. The pastry shell had been replaced by sponge fingers, and the filling was now a rich Bavarian cream, a mixture of egg custard, gelatin, and whipped cream with varied flavorings. Carême served his new marvel to Louis XVIII, the reinstated Bourbon king, at a banquet for twelve hundred at the Louvre in 1815; for reasons now unclear the name was changed to Charlotte Russe during the Second Empire.

Carême's original *Charlotte à la parisienne* had a vanilla filling, but other chefs soon realized that the possibilities were endless. This Charlotte Russe is an appealingly tart lemon.

Note: *If desired, base of Charlotte can be garnished with a wreath of mint leaves, or with piped whipped cream.*

Please see "A Note about Eggs," p. 307.

1 envelope unflavored gelatin	¼ teaspoon salt
½ cup lemon juice	Grated rind of 1 lemon
4 eggs, separated	20–24 ladyfingers, split
1 cup sugar, divided	1 cup heavy cream

1. Sprinkle gelatin over lemon juice in small bowl. Let soften for 5 minutes.
2. In top of double boiler, and with electric mixer, beat egg yolks, ½ cup of sugar, and salt. Gradually beat in gelatin mixture. Cook over a small quantity of boiling water (do not allow top of double boiler to touch the water), stirring constantly, until mixture starts to thicken and gelatin is dissolved, about 6 minutes.
3. Pour into large bowl. Add lemon rind. Chill until mixture begins to mound, 15–20 minutes, stirring occasionally.
4. While lemon mixture is cooling, line bottom and sides of an 8-inch springform pan with ladyfingers, curved-side out.
5. Beat egg whites with electric mixer in large bowl until foamy. Gradually add remaining ½ cup sugar and beat until soft peaks form. In a separate large bowl, whip cream until soft peaks form. Fold beaten egg whites and whipped cream into the lemon mixture. Spoon into ladyfinger-lined pan. Cover and chill 4 hours or overnight. When ready to serve, carefully remove sides of springform pan.

MERINGUES
8 servings

Note: *Not all ovens can be set accurately at low temperatures. As an alternative: Put meringues into a preheated 450°F oven and immediately turn off the heat, letting the meringues stand several hours or overnight without opening the oven door.*

Although French chefs were already experimenting with the almost magical qualities of egg whites in the 1600s, meringues are believed to have taken their name from the Swiss village of Meiringen. According to standard culinary lore, they were first made by a young Swiss pastry chef named Gasparini, in 1720. The name may be correct, but the dates cannot be, for the word was already being used in English by 1706 and in French considerably earlier.

There are two quite different types of meringue. To European cooks a meringue is a firm, almost hard, sweet, that retains its pale color through long drying in a slow oven, while to American cooks the term has traditionally meant a soft, fluffy, browned topping used primarily on pies. The only real differences are in the proportion of sugar added to the beaten egg whites and in the method of baking. Hard meringues of the first sort are often made into shells or baskets by shaping the egg white mixture with a spoon or piping it from a pastry tube.

3 egg whites
¼ teaspoon cream of tartar

¾ cup sugar
½ teaspoon vanilla extract

1. Preheat oven to 250°F. Cover cookie sheet with heavy brown paper (can be cut from grocery bags).
2. In large bowl, and with electric mixer, beat egg whites and cream of tartar until foamy. Beat in sugar, 1 tablespoon at a time. Add vanilla and beat 5 minutes longer. Drop by spoonfuls into 8 equal mounds. With spoon, form each mound into a saucer, making a depression in middle and building up sides.
3. Bake 1 hour. Turn off oven; leave meringues in oven with door closed 1 ½ hours. Finish cooling meringues at room temperature. If difficult to remove from paper, place paper on top of a damp towel for a few seconds, and slide meringues off with a spatula.
4. Place on serving plates and fill with any combination of *ice cream, sweetened fresh fruits, dessert sauces*, and/or *whipped cream.*

NESSELRODE
8 servings

Nesselrode takes its name from Count Karl Nesselrode, a German by heritage who nevertheless served as foreign minister to the Russian czars for most of his career. An "iced pudding," it was created by Nesselrode's chef, one Monsieur Mouy, almost certainly during the Congress of Vienna in 1814–15, convened after Napoleon's first abdication.

The Congress of Vienna set out to redraw the map of Europe as if Napoleon had never existed. It could not be done, of course; the delegates might as well have tried to put Humpty Dumpty together again. But the foreign ministers of the leading European powers did manage to hammer out a whole string of treaties based on balance of power that gave Europe a hundred years of relative peace. While they did so, Vienna kept the crowned heads of Europe and all the aristocrats busy with balls and banquets. As it happened, these diversions, too, changed European life. The waltz became the rage; an almost scandalous innovation, it allowed men for the first time in social dancing to hold their partners in their arms. And the banquets made culinary history as hosts vied for the distinction of creating the most lavish array of foods. Nesselrode, a noted gourmet, certainly held his own in this atmosphere. A number of dishes in classic cuisine are named for him (soups, mostly) but few, if any, besides the elegant "pudding" still appear on menus today.

For many years, American cooks interpreted Nesselrode with the aid of a commercially prepared mix of candied fruit and nuts that could be used for pudding, pie, or ice cream. That product is no longer available, but a more authentic version of the dessert can be made with canned chestnuts. Raw chestnuts, sometimes available in the early fall, can be substituted if first boiled and peeled.

1 can chestnuts

3 egg yolks, beaten

½ cup sugar

1 cup milk

¼ teaspoon salt

2 cups chilled whipping cream

¼ teaspoon grated orange peel

2 tablespoons finely chopped maraschino cherries

2 tablespoons syrup from maraschino cherries

Variation: *For a simpler Nesselrode Ice Cream, slightly soften purchased vanilla ice cream and mix in chestnut puree, orange peel, and finely chopped maraschino cherries, to taste. Pack tightly into container, cover, and re-freeze.*

1. Puree chestnuts, including liquid in can, in blender or food processor or mash and put through sieve. Measure out ½ cup and set aside. (Remainder may be frozen for future use.)
2. Mix egg yolks, sugar, milk, and salt in 2-quart saucepan. Cook over medium heat, stirring constantly, just until bubbles appear around edge. Strain into a chilled bowl and refrigerate until at room temperature, 2–3 hours.
3. Add whipping cream, orange peel, cherries, syrup, and the ½ cup pureed chestnuts. Pour into ice cream freezer can and freeze according to manufacturer's directions.

STRAWBERRIES ROMANOFF
6 servings

According to one culinary tradition, the great chef Carême, during his brief stay in Russia, created Strawberries Romanoff as a tribute to Tsar Alexander I. That may well be true, but during the nineteenth century French chefs, as a sort of fad, often named new dishes for the great Russian noble families, Demidoff, Souvaroff, and so on. There is at least a good possibility that France is the origin of the elegant fruit dessert. All that can be said with certainty is that it commemorates the great Russian dynasty that ruled from 1613 to 1917.

1 quart strawberries
½ cup sugar
½ cup orange juice
½ cup curaçao
Sweetened whipped cream

1. Wash and hull strawberries. Place in a bowl, sprinkling each layer with sugar. Combine orange juice and curaçao. Pour over berries.
2. Chill, covered, for 1 hour or longer. Serve in sherbet glasses, garnished with sweetened whipped cream.

BISCUIT TORTONI
6–8 servings

Note: *Please see "A Note about Eggs," p. 307.*

"Biscuit" is a term that can lead a curious cook on a merry chase. To Americans a biscuit is a quick bread, probably derived from the Scottish scone, and always served hot. To the English it may be either a cracker or a cookie. To the French, from whom the English borrowed the word, it meant "twice-baked," and was at first a hard, dry, almost imperishable bread issued to sailors and to soldiers in the field. However, in French cuisine it has also acquired other, more appealing definitions, including crackers, cookies, little cakes, and even ice cream that is cut or formed into portions that look like biscuits.

Biscuit Tortoni goes a long way back in the annals of frozen desserts. In 1798 a new coffeehouse opened on the Boulevard des Italiens in Paris, named, for its Neapolitan proprietor, the Café Tortoni. It was a fashionable place; Talleyrand and Prince Metternich were among its regular patrons. Like most of the coffeehouses, it offered a frozen specialty, in this case Biscuit Tortoni, flavored with macaroons and rum, and traditionally served in small paper dishes. Much later it was introduced into the United States by way of the newly popular Italian restaurants that sprang up after World War II.

2 egg whites
2 cups chilled whipping cream
⅔ cup confectioners' sugar
1 teaspoon rum extract
1 cup crushed almond macaroons (recipe follows)

1. In a medium bowl beat egg whites on high speed until stiff peaks form.
2. In a large chilled bowl beat cream until soft peaks form when mixer blades are lifted upright.
3. Fold into whipped cream the macaroon crumbs, confectioners' sugar, beaten egg whites, and rum extract.

4. Pour mixture into a 9 by 5-inch loaf pan and place in freezer for 6–8 hours or until firm. When ready to serve, run table knife around sides of pan to loosen. Place loaf pan upside down on platter and surround with warm dish towels (heated in warm water and thoroughly wrung out) until frozen mixture slides from pan. Cut into ½-inch slices and, if desired, serve in paper cups.

Note: *Rectangular paper dessert cups are available at specialty shops that carry cake decorating supplies.*

Almond Macaroons (about 2 ½ dozen):

1 cup sugar
2 tablespoons flour
⅓ cup confectioners' sugar
1 can (8 ounces) almond paste
⅓ cup egg whites, unbeaten (2–3 eggs)

1. Preheat oven to 325°F. Cut brown wrapping paper to line baking sheet, but do not grease.
2. Mix sugar, flour, and confectioners' sugar in large mixing bowl. Add almond paste and cut in with two knives or pastry blender, then work with hands until almost no lumps are left. Add egg whites and continue to work until entirely smooth.
3. Drop teaspoonfuls of dough 2 inches apart on lined baking sheets. Bake until set and delicately browned, about 18–20 minutes. Remove from oven and set brown paper on a large, wet towel. Allow to remain for 1 or 2 minutes, until steam has loosened macaroons and they can easily be slipped off *with a spatula.*
4. Break up 12 macaroons and spread out on cookie sheet. *Turn off heat* and return these crumbs to oven to dry out for several hours. When thoroughly dry, crush coarsely to use in Biscuit Tortoni. Remaining macaroons may be served with the Tortoni.

NAPOLEONS
9 pastries

Napoleons are a delectable pastry; their widespread popularity is well deserved, but they have nothing to do with Bonaparte, the daring Corsican who almost managed to make himself master of Europe. The name is the result of a misunderstanding of the French *Napolitain*, which should have been translated as Neapolitan, pertaining to Naples. They are very like the French *mille-feuille* or the Italian *mille foglie*, both of which mean "a thousand leaves." Essentially, of course, all of these are puff pastry or *pâte feuilletée* combined with delicious fillings.

Variation: If desired, cherry pie filling can be substituted for the cream filling.

½ cup sugar

3 tablespoons cornstarch

¼ teaspoon salt

2 cups milk

3 egg yolks, slightly beaten

1 teaspoon vanilla

1 sheet frozen puff pastry (from 17 ¼-ounce package)

1 cup confectioners' sugar

1 tablespoon milk

2 ounces semisweet chocolate, melted

1. Combine sugar, cornstarch, and salt in a large saucepan. Gradually stir in milk, mixing well. Cook and stir over medium heat until thickened and bubbly. Cook 2 minutes more. Remove from heat. Stir small amount of hot mixture into egg yolks; immediately return to hot mixture. Cook and stir 2 minutes. Remove from heat, add vanilla, and allow to cool slightly at room temperature. Chill for several hours.

2. Preheat oven to 350°F. Set out frozen pastry sheet and thaw at room temperature for 20 minutes.

3. Unfold pastry sheet. Cut into 9 rectangles. Bake on ungreased baking sheet 18–20 minutes, or until puffed and golden brown. Set aside to cool.

4. Split cooled pastries in half vertically. Combine confectioners' sugar and milk and spread on top halves. Drizzle each with melted chocolate. Spread cream filling on bottom halves and top with frosted halves.

TIPSY PARSON OR TIPSY SQUIRE
4–6 servings

Tipsy Parson or Tipsy Squire comes from colonial Virginia. A dessert obviously very like the English trifle, its name is a double play on words. Since it contains sherry it could, conceivably, make one who overindulged a bit "tipsy," but it is equally true that a pudding made of cake and custard may wobble drunkenly if turned out of its mold.

12 ladyfingers (purchased)
¼ cup good-quality sweet sherry or Madeira
2 cups milk
3 eggs
¼ cup sugar
¼ teaspoon salt
½ cup raspberry jam

1. Line bottom and sides of a deep one-quart glass bowl, pudding mold, or serving dish with split ladyfingers, reserving some for middle layers to be added later. Sprinkle with sherry.
2. Heat milk in top of double boiler until it is scalded (tiny bubbles will form around the rim), but do not allow to boil. In medium mixing bowl, beat eggs on low speed, add sugar and salt, and beat well. Add hot milk, a little at a time, beating constantly. Return entire mixture to double-boiler top, place over double-boiler bottom containing hot but not boiling water, and cook, stirring constantly, for about 8 minutes, or until custard is thick enough to coat a spoon (165°F). Remove custard from heat and cool for about 5 minutes.
3. Pour about one-third of the custard over ladyfingers, add another layer of ladyfingers, sprinkle with more sherry and cover with half of jam. Add another third of custard and last of ladyfingers, sherry, and jam. Pour in the remainder of the custard. Chill for at least four hours. If desired, unmold before serving. Dessert may be garnished with sweetened whipped cream.

Variations: Leftover sponge cake or pound cake may be used in place of ladyfingers. If desired, eggs, sugar, and salt may be omitted and the milk combined with one package of egg-custard pudding mix, cooking according to directions on package and cooling custard 5 minutes before pouring onto ladyfingers.

ZUPPA INGLESE
8 servings

Zuppa Inglese is an Italian dessert. The name, translated literally, means "English Soup," but of course it is not a soup at all but another dessert clearly based on the English Trifle. It may have become part of the Italian repertoire in the period immediately after the Napoleonic wars, when the English were being hailed as the saviors of Europe, or in the decades following, when English tourists flocked to "sunny Italy."

Note: Please see "A Note about Eggs," p. 307.

½ cup sugar

3 tablespoons cornstarch

¼ teaspoon salt

2 cups milk

3 egg yolks, slightly beaten

1 teaspoon vanilla

3 8-inch sponge layers (recipe on page 245; or purchased)

¼ cup light rum

Sweetened whipped cream

Chopped candied fruit

1. Combine sugar, cornstarch, and salt in a large saucepan. Gradually stir in milk, mixing well. Cook and stir over medium heat until thickened and bubbly. Cook 2 minutes more. Remove from heat. Stir small amount of hot mixture into egg yolks; immediately return to hot mixture. Cook and stir 2 minutes. Remove from heat, add vanilla, and chill for several hours.
2. While cream filling is chilling, make sponge layers.
3. To assemble dessert, place one sponge layer on serving plate and sprinkle with 2 tablespoons rum. Cover with half of cream filling and then repeat with the second layer. Place remaining layer on top. Cover and chill for 4 hours or longer. Just before serving, cover with sweetened whipped cream and decorate as desired with chopped candied fruit.

MALAKOFF TORTE
8–10 servings

In the spring of 1854 several of the nations of Europe blundered into a totally useless war. Britain, France, and Turkey arrayed themselves against Russia, and, since most of the fighting occurred in the oddly shaped peninsula known as the Crimea, the conflict came to be called the Crimean War. Primarily in order to avoid campaigning in the interior of Russia, Britain and France decided to seize Sevastopol, a Russian port on the Black Sea. The British army was totally disorganized and the French hardly better.

Months passed with little action; the Russians at Sevastopol used the time to fortify six strong points around the southern approach to the city. One was a low hill called the Malakoff. The French armies finally took the Malakoff on September 8, 1855, in what has been called the one perfectly planned and executed operation of the war. To preserve secrecy, the assault commenced without a signal. Synchronization of watches (for the first time, perhaps, in military history) governed the move.

With the Malakoff taken, the Russian garrison evacuated Sevastopol, and all Paris rejoiced. The chefs, who felt that their skills must reflect public life, invented Malakoff Torte. Various versions of the dessert exist, some described as cakes and consisting of layers of nut meringues filled with mousse, others incorporating chou pastry, puff pastry, or sponge cake. This version is rather like a Charlotte Russe but with a richer filling. The flavorings can vary, but the combination of rum and coffee is traditional.

3 egg yolks	2 tablespoons hot water
1 cup superfine sugar	1 ½ cups heavy cream
1 cup butter or margarine, softened	20–24 ladyfingers, split
1 cup ground almonds	Sweetened whipped cream
½ cup dark rum, divided	Grated semisweet chocolate
2 tablespoons instant coffee	

1. Combine egg yolks and superfine sugar in top of double boiler, over hot water. Cook, stirring, 5 minutes or until sugar dissolves. Remove from heat; cool.
2. Place egg yolk mixture and butter in large mixing bowl. Beat on low speed until smooth and creamy. Stir in almonds and ¼ cup rum. Dissolve instant coffee in hot water. Cool and add to egg mixture.
3. Beat heavy cream until stiff. Add to egg mixture and combine.
4. Brush cut sides of ladyfingers with remaining ¼ cup rum. Use to line bottom and sides of an 8-inch springform pan, placing cut sides up. Fill pan with cream mixture and chill at least 6 hours or overnight.
5. When ready to serve, carefully remove sides of springform pan. Garnish as desired with sweetened whipped cream and sprinkle with semisweet chocolate.

RICE À L'IMPÉRATRICE
6 servings

Rice *à l'impératrice* takes its name from the Empress Eugénie (1826–1920), wife of Napoleon III. Many dishes were created in her honor, but this truly glorious rice pudding is the best known today.

Born a Spanish countess but with Scots ancestry, too, the auburn-haired, blue-eyed beauty first attracted the attention of Louis Napoleon while he was still president of France. The two were married with great pomp and ceremony at Notre Dame in 1853, just a few months after he had persuaded the French people to elect him emperor in imitation of his famed uncle.

Life was good for the young empress. The court was gay, even frivolous, and Paris was at its glittering best. Baron Haussmann's grand boulevards were under construction and every outing of the royal family was accompanied by such a clattering of horse guards that life seemed a succession of parades. The Empress Eugénie enjoyed the adulation of the people. When a son was born, ensuring the succession to the throne, life seemed complete.

But as the years went by, the Second Empire faltered. A series of mishaps and blunders at home and abroad made Frenchmen doubt the wisdom of Napoleon III and resent the influence of the empress, who was known to have strong views on the government. Then, in 1870, France entered into a needless and disastrous war with Germany. The emperor insisted on leading his troops himself even though he was so ill he could hardly stay upon his horse, and soon he and an entire army were captured by the Germans at the old French town of Sedan. In Paris the Third Republic was proclaimed and the empress barely escaped with her life, fleeing to England. There she was joined by her son, and, a few months later, the former emperor. Napoleon died in 1873 and six years later, the young Prince Imperial was killed in the Zulu War in South Africa, fighting for glory and his adopted country. Befriended by Queen Victoria, Eugénie lived in England another forty years alone.

3 cups boiling water

½ cup uncooked rice

2 cups milk, divided

1 envelope unflavored gelatin

2 tablespoons cold water

3 egg yolks

⅓ cup sugar

¼ teaspoon salt

1 teaspoon vanilla

⅔ cup finely chopped candied fruit

3 tablespoons kirsch, rum, or brandy

1 cup heavy cream

Sweetened whipped cream (optional)

Candied cherries (optional)

Angelica, cut into strips or fancy shapes (optional)

1. Pour boiling water over rice and let stand for 5 minutes. Drain. Put rice and 1 ¼ cups milk into top of double boiler. Bring just to a boil, then cover, place over simmering water, and cook until rice is tender. More milk may be added, if necessary, but any remaining after rice is done should be drained off.

2. Sprinkle gelatin over cold water and set aside to soften. In a small bowl, beat egg yolks with sugar and salt. Heat ¾ cup milk. Pour a little of hot milk into the egg mixture, then combine both mixtures and gelatin. Heat, stirring, till custard begins to thicken (165°F). Add vanilla and cooked rice and chill until the mixture begins to set.

3. Soak candied fruit in kirsch. When rice mixture starts to set, whip cream and add to rice with candied fruit. Pour into a 1 ½-quart mold. Chill until set. Unmold on serving plate and garnish, if desired, with sweetened whipped cream, candied cherries, and angelica.

MACÉDOINE OF FRUIT

The culinary term macédoine, meaning a mixture, usually of fruits but occasionally of vegetables, is taken from Macedonia, the lands just north of Greece. The term came into use in the late eighteenth and early nineteenth centuries, when it was first becoming apparent that Turkey was the "sick man of Europe" and the Balkans a very likely "powder keg." Macedonia encompassed a bewildering array of nationalities: Greeks, Serbs, Bulgars, Vlachs, Albanians, Armenians, and Sephardic Jews originally driven from Spain, all under the much-resented domination of the Turks. The goal of liberating Macedonia from the Turks unified all non-Muslim Macedonians, but beyond that they were almost ridiculously divided. To quote *Encyclopedia Britannica,*

> The Sofia nationalists argued that the Slavs of Macedonia spoke a dialect akin to Bulgarian and therefore should be regarded as Bulgars and that all Macedonia should be incorporated into Bulgaria. The Belgrade nationalists affirmed that, as the Macedonian Slavs retained the custom of *slava* (feast of ancestors), common to all Serbs but not occurring among the Bulgars, they could not be genuine Bulgars, but were at best superficially bulgarized Serbs whose land, it was argued, should be incorporated into a greater Serbia. The Greek nationalists maintained that the few hundred thousands of "Slavophones" whom they acknowledged to be in Macedonia were attracted by the superior Greek culture and considered themselves of Greek nationality. The Rumanians had no territorial claims in Macedonia but considered it useful to support the Vlachs, whom they called Arumanians.

Small wonder that a macédoine, in cooking, must contain at least six fruits or vegetables, finely diced, and in equal amounts!

½ cup sugar

⅔ cup water

1 tablespoon snipped mint leaves (optional),
  or ⅛ teaspoon almond extract (optional)

4 cups chilled fruit, made up of ⅔ cup each of any six of the following: raspberries or blueberries; melon balls; halved strawberries, sweet cherries, or grapes; peeled cubes of apples, nectarines, apricots, bananas, peaches, pears, pineapple, or oranges

1. In a small pan combine sugar and water and heat until sugar is dissolved. Add mint or almond extract if desired. Refrigerate until chilled, at least one hour.

2. Strain syrup if mint has been added. Pour over prepared fruit and serve at once. Garnish with mint leaves if desired.

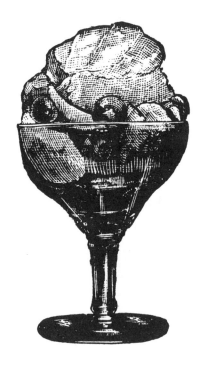

PEACH MELBA
4 servings

Georges-Auguste Escoffier (1846–1935) was the greatest chef of the nineteenth century, but his talents might have gone unnoticed had it not been for César Ritz. It was Ritz, a talented *hôtelier*, who persuaded Escoffier to leave his native France and take charge of the kitchens in the first of the luxury hotels, the fabulous Savoy in London, which opened in 1889.

Together Ritz and Escoffier revolutionized London's social life. Prior to this time, gentlewomen seldom dined in public, unless actually traveling. They gave private dinner parties, and their husbands frequently dined at their clubs, but dining out, in the modern sense, was left to actresses and other *demimondaines*. Actively campaigning to make hotel dining rooms fashionable, Escoffier delighted in creating light, lovely desserts, usually featuring fruit, and naming them for well-known beauties. Most of these are long forgotten, but Peach Melba has become a classic.

The fabled dessert was created in 1899 for Nellie Melba, the famed Australian opera singer. Melba, noted for her role in Richard Wagner's *Lohengrin*, was giving a small dinner party. The inventive Escoffier, anxious to please the great soprano, created a dessert of vanilla ice cream and peaches, served from a silver dish placed between the wings of a swan carved of ice (Lohengrin was the Swan Knight of German legend). Melba declared herself delighted with the dessert, though the familiar raspberry sauce was actually added later.

Escoffier was a truly great chef who cooked for kings and emperors and created many subtle and tantalizing dishes. Whether he minded that his name was forever linked to this one woman and this one simple combination of flavors is impossible to say.

2 large, ripe, freestone peaches

1 lemon

Sugar

1 (10-ounce) package frozen sweetened red raspberries

Vanilla ice cream

Variation: *For a simpler Peach Melba, surround scoops of vanilla ice cream with slices of freestone peaches, fresh or canned, then top with thawed frozen sweetened raspberries.*

1. Place peaches in boiling water, let stand for a few seconds, and then plunge into ice water. Peel, cut in half, and pit. Rub the peaches with a cut lemon to prevent browning, sprinkle with sugar, and put halves back together. Place in refrigerator tightly covered with plastic wrap.

2. Puree frozen raspberries in blender or food processor. Sieve to remove seeds. Chill.

3. Form a bed of vanilla ice cream in the bottom of each dessert dish. Place in freezer until ready to serve.

4. To assemble, place a peach half, cut side down, on each serving of ice cream. Cover with raspberry puree.

PEARS HÉLÈNE
4 servings

Pears Hélène were originally Poires Belle Hélène, named for Helen of Troy, but really meant to honor Hortense Schneider, the beautiful young woman who starred in Jacques Offenbach's operetta *La Belle Hélène*, which opened in 1865. As originally conceived the dessert was quite elaborate. The peeled pears were cored from underneath (so that the stems remained attached), poached, and, when cool, filled with a sweet buttercream made with powdered almonds. Each pear was then set upright on a bed of vanilla ice cream, and coated with melted chocolate. A marzipan leaf was placed near the stem.

Escoffier simplified the presentation, using pear halves and omitting the marzipan, but adding candied violets. He also changed the name to Pears Hélène. This last bit may have been a matter of diplomacy. Edward, Prince of Wales, had had an early and well-publicized romance with the lovely Hortense and Escoffier had no wish to offend Alexandra, the genuinely charming Danish princess who later married the genial Edward.

Note: *Candied violets are available in gourmet specialty shops.*

Chocolate sauce may be served warm, if desired.

1 can (16 ounces) pear halves	1 cup sugar
1 teaspoon vanilla	2 tablespoons butter
3 squares unsweetened chocolate	Vanilla ice cream
⅔ cup water	Candied violets (optional)

1. Drain pears. Heat syrup to boiling point; add vanilla and pour over pears in a small bowl. Cover and chill.
2. Combine chocolate and water in a small saucepan. Place over medium heat and stir until thickened. Add sugar, stirring until dissolved. Boil gently 4 minutes, stirring constantly. Remove from heat, stir in butter, and allow to cool to room temperature.
3. Form a bed of vanilla ice cream in the bottom of each dessert dish. Place in freezer until ready to serve.
4. To assemble, place a pear half, cut side down, on each serving of ice cream. Garnish with candied violets, if desired. Pass chocolate sauce separately.

STRAWBERRIES SARAH BERNHARDT
4 servings

Note: *Escoffier, in his original recipe, suggested tinting the whipped cream with strawberry puree so that, when placed on top of the pineapple, it would "give the illusion of a beautiful sunset."*

Strawberries Sarah Bernhardt were created by Escoffier to honor the famous actress, who was very fond of the ever popular berries. French by birth, "The Divine Sarah" made many appearances in London and frequently stayed at the Savoy. Magnetic, unpredictable, and enormously gifted, she fascinated two generations, dominating the stage for almost fifty years, until her death in 1923.

1 package (10 ounces) frozen sweetened strawberries, thawed
1 can (8 ¼ ounces) crushed pineapple in heavy syrup
Vanilla ice cream
Sweetened whipped cream

1. Place a large scoop of vanilla ice cream in each of four sherbet glasses. Surround scoops with strawberries.
2. Pour crushed pineapple over ice cream and top each serving with a generous dollop of sweetened whipped cream.

CHERRIES JUBILEE
4 servings

Cherries Jubilee were created in honor of Queen Victoria. Then, as now, the British public delighted in every detail of the royal family's life and everyone knew that cherries were the queen's favorite fruit.

Victoria had mellowed in old age and the sheer length of her reign captured the imagination of her subjects. The whole nation celebrated at her Golden Jubilee in 1887 and again at her Diamond Jubilee in 1897. It was during the earlier celebration that Cherries Jubilee first appeared.

Curiously, the original dish did not call for ice cream at all. Sweet cherries, poached in a simple syrup that was slightly thickened, were poured into fireproof dishes, then warmed brandy was added and set on flame at the moment of serving. Soon, however, Escoffier was serving vanilla ice cream *accompagnie de Cerises Jubilé* to many dignitaries, including the Prince of Wales, the future Edward VII.

Note: *Cherries Jubilee can also be made at the table in a chafing dish.*

1 can (16 ounces) dark sweet cherries
1 tablespoon sugar
1 tablespoon cornstarch
1 tablespoon lemon juice
1 cinnamon stick (optional)
¼ cup brandy (high-proof)
Vanilla ice cream

1. Drain cherries, reserving juice.
2. In a small saucepan mix sugar with cornstarch and add juice, a little at a time, stirring. Add lemon juice and cinnamon stick. Cook over medium heat, stirring constantly, until mixture is thickened. Remove cinnamon stick and add cherries. Place in a heated ovenproof or metal serving dish.
3. Heat brandy, pour over cherries, and ignite with a long match. Ladle flaming cherries over individual servings of ice cream.

CRÊPES SUZETTE
6 servings

Note: *Unless you have a seasoned crêpe pan, and are a seasoned crêpe maker, the first one or two crêpes may be crumpled disasters. Persevere! The rest should be fine, and this batter is a generous amount for the 12 crêpes needed for the recipe. Crêpes may be made in advance, cooled, and stored in the refrigerator for 2 to 3 days securely sealed in a plastic bag.*

In 1897 Suzanne Reichenberg, an actress who was known professionally by the simple name of Suzette, was appearing at the Comédie Française in the role of a maid. The plot of the play involved a meal at which she served crêpes. Monsieur Joseph, proprietor of the nearby Restaurant Marivaux, provided the crêpes for each performance. To attract the attention of the audience as well as to heat the crêpes for the actors who must eat them night after night, they were served flambé. Later Joseph moved on to the Savoy Hotel in London and served his now famous dessert to diners there.

The widely accepted claim of Henri Charpentier, French maître d'hôtel and later restaurant owner in the United States, that he invented the crêpes almost accidentally while serving Edward, Prince of Wales, is completely spurious. It is possible, though, that it was he who made them seem the essence of sophistication to many Americans during the 1930s.

Crêpes:

3 eggs
¾ cup flour
4 ½ teaspoons sugar
¾ cup milk
3 tablespoons water
2 teaspoons melted butter

1. In medium mixing bowl, beat eggs. Gradually add flour and sugar alternately with milk and water, beating with electric mixer until smooth. Beat in melted butter.

or

Combine ingredients in blender jar; blend for about 1 minute. Scrape down sides with rubber spatula and blend for another 15 seconds or until smooth.

2. Refrigerate batter for at least 1 hour.

3. Brush crêpe pan or small (6-inch), heavy frying pan with butter or oil. Heat pan over moderate heat until drops of water sprinkled onto cooking surface bounce and sizzle. With one hand, pour in 2–3 tablespoons of batter (a ¼-cup measuring cup makes a handy scoop). At the same time, lift the pan above the heating unit and tilt pan in all directions, swirling batter so that it covers the bottom of the pan in a very thin layer.
4. Cook crêpe until bottom is browned, then carefully turn with a spatula. Brown other side for a few seconds. Remove from pan with spatula; stack on plate or tray.

Sauce:

6 small sugar cubes
2 large oranges
⅔ cup butter, softened
3 tablespoons granulated sugar
⅓ cup orange liqueur
⅓ cup brandy (high-proof)

1. Rub sugar cubes on surface of whole unpeeled oranges, turning each cube to coat it on all sides; set aside.
2. Squeeze oranges and strain juice to make ⅔ cup. Add sugar cubes and mash and stir until dissolved. Cream butter with remaining sugar.

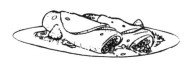

3. When ready to serve, warm butter in chafing dish. Add orange juice and boil, stirring, for 1 minute. Reduce heat.
4. Place orange liqueur and brandy in small saucepan and warm over low heat; do not overheat (overheating burns off the alcohol needed to ignite sauce).
5. While liqueur and brandy are warming, place cooked crêpes in the orange sauce in chafing dish, one at a time. With a fork and spoon fold each crêpe in half and then into quarters. Arrange, overlapping, around the rim of the dish.
6. Carefully pour warmed (not hot) liqueur and brandy into center of pan. Ignite with a long match. Spoon sauce over crêpes until flames die out. Serve at once.

Note: *The folding and overlapping of the crêpes is tricky (it did, after all, originate as a bit of "stage business"!) and must be practiced before being attempted in front of guests.*

CANTALOUPE LILLIAN RUSSELL
4 servings

Culinary history was made at the Waldorf-Astoria Hotel in New York one evening in the 1890s when Lillian Russell came in with her constant escort, financier Diamond Jim Brady. The lovely but slightly spoiled actress could not decide upon her dessert. First she chose ice cream and then she chose cantaloupe and then at the suggestion of the indulgent Brady she said she would take both. With typical Waldorf aplomb the waiter disappeared and soon returned with a beautiful melon neatly scooped out and a mound of luscious vanilla ice-cream nestled in the hollow. Diamond Jim's pet was delighted. Oscar Tschirky, the maître d'hôtel (better known as Oscar of the Waldorf), was impressed with the instant success of the impromptu dessert. He named it Cantaloupe Lillian Russell and so it remained through the 1920s and '30s. Then gradually the name began to be forgotten. It was partly, no doubt, because it was long enough to be unwieldy and partly because Russell herself was no longer in the public eye. But the combination remains, and has been called one of the most typically American of desserts.

Cantaloupe itself is an interesting word, for it comes from the little Italian village of Cantalupo, once the site of the pope's summer residence, and the place in Europe where this type of melon was first grown.

1 ripe cantaloupe
Vanilla ice cream

1. Quarter cantaloupe. Scoop out and discard seeds.
2. Place melon skin side down on serving dish. Place scoop of ice cream in hollow.

BAKED ALASKA
10–12 servings

In 1867, at the urging of Secretary of State William H. Seward, the United States purchased Alaska from the Russians. Americans everywhere suddenly became aware of their new territory. In New York, Delmonico's, the elegant and already venerable restaurant that set culinary style for almost a century, celebrated with a new dessert. It was spectacular: cake, topped with solidly frozen ice cream, the whole enveloped in meringue, then browned and served still warm from the oven. The inspiration of Delmonico's head chef, Charles Ranhofer, it was at first called Alaska-Florida, a name soon changed to Baked Alaska.

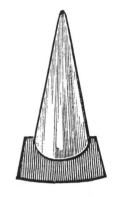

ALASKA–FLORIDA MOLD

But Ranhofer was not the first to discover the possibilities of ice cream and meringue. A virtually identical dessert had been created years earlier by a brilliant but erratic physicist named Benjamin Thompson, Count Rumford. Thompson crowded a vast quantity of experiences and accomplishments into his life. An American Loyalist in the Revolution, he spied for General Thomas Gage, went to London when Boston was evacuated in March of 1776, and became an undersecretary of state. Resigning his position, he returned to the colonies as a British officer, serving until the end of the war; he was knighted by George III in 1784.

Leaving Britain to serve the elector of Bavaria, he reorganized the Bavarian army, established workhouses for the poor, became minister of police, and laid out an attractive park in Munich that is still known as the English Gardens.

ALASKA–FLORIDA

Along the way he made a number of serious and important discoveries as to the nature of heat, and this interest led inevitably to an interest in cooking. He invented a fire-grate, a double-boiler, an oil lamp, a coffee percolator (he greatly favored coffee over tea), the kitchen range (as opposed to cooking at an open fireplace), and, as a result of his interest in the insulating qualities of egg whites, a dessert that he called "omelette surprise," virtually identical to Ranhofer's later Baked Alaska.

And, almost thirty years after the introduction of the novelty at Delmonico's, Chef Jean Giroix of the Hôtel de Paris in Monte Carlo began to feature an *Omelette à la Norvégienne*, again almost identical to the Baked Alaska. Just how these three desserts are related remains a question. Ranhofer may have known of Thompson's work; but he was a clever, innovative chef who may have made the same discovery on his own. Giroix, at Monte Carlo, may have known of the Delmonico's specialty or may have heard of Thompson (the similarity of names for the two "omelettes" would seem to indicate that he had), but apparently neither speculation can be substantiated. What can be said with certainty, however, is that the dessert remains a favorite.

1 layer cake, any flavor

1 quart ice cream, any flavor, cut from a rectangular half-gallon brick

5 egg whites

⅔ cup sugar

1. Bake layer cake in a 9 x 13-inch pan. (Cake must be at least 1 inch thick.) Remove from pan and allow to cool thoroughly.

2. Measure carton of ice cream and cut cake 1 inch larger on all sides. Place on wooden cutting board. Cut brick of ice cream horizontally and center one half on cake. (Return remaining half to freezer for another use.) Put board, cake, and ice cream in large plastic bag and seal tightly. Place in coldest part of freezer for several hours.

3. When ready to serve, preheat oven to 500°F. With an electric mixer beat egg whites until stiff. Gradually add sugar and continue beating until very stiff peaks form when beater is lifted. Remove cake and ice cream from freezer. Leave on wooden board and spread quickly with meringue. Meringue must be thick and must *completely* cover both cake and ice cream, to seal out the heat. Place in oven 3–4 minutes or just until meringue starts to brown. Serve immediately.

Note: *If you do not wish to serve directly from wooden cutting board, you can place a piece of heavy brown paper between the board and the cake. Use the paper to slide or lift the completed dessert from the board and to the serving plate, then gently pull out the paper.*

A round Baked Alaska can be made by baking a layer of cake at least 1 inch thick in a spring-form pan and packing 1 quart of ice cream into a suitably sized round bowl; refreeze ice cream for several hours and then proceed as above.

AMBROSIA
4–6 servings

Ambrosia, a dessert long favored in the southern states, takes its name from Greek mythology. Ambrosia was the food of the gods on Mount Olympus as nectar was their drink. Ambrosia means "immortal"; nectar, of unknown origin, has lent its name to the nectarine, a naturally occurring sport of the peach.

Ambrosia is made by layering sections of fresh oranges with coconut. Other fruits, such as bananas or pineapple, may be added if desired.

¼ cup sugar
¼ cup water
2 cups orange sections
1 cup pineapple chunks, fresh or canned
¾ cup flaked coconut

1. In a small pan combine sugar and water and heat until sugar is dissolved. Cool to room temperature.
2. Layer orange sections, pineapple chunks, and coconut in individual dessert dishes or sherbet glasses, reserving a small amount of coconut for garnish. Pour syrup over fruit and garnish with remaining coconut. Chill.

Note: *If canned pineapple is used, ⅓ cup pineapple syrup can be substituted for the sugar and water. To prepare orange sections easily, cut oranges in half and cut around each section with a serrated knife, exactly as if preparing grapefruit for the table. Remove orange sections with a small, pointed teaspoon.*

BANANAS FOSTER
4 servings

Bananas Foster, created in the restaurant Brennan's in the old French Quarter of New Orleans, resulted from a promotion the restaurant began to run in the 1950s, Breakfast at Brennan's; the "breakfasts," of course, were elegant brunches that ended with splendid desserts. Robert Foster, for whom this dish was named, was a New Orleans businessman, close friend of the Brennan family, and enthusiastic patron of the restaurant. The combination of rum and bananas was a happy one, and the fame of the dish has spread far beyond New Orleans.

Variation: *In place of ¼ cup banana liqueur and ½ cup rum, use ¾ cup rum.*

¼ cup butter
½ cup light brown sugar
4 firm ripe bananas, peeled
¼ teaspoon ground cinnamon
¼ cup banana liqueur
½ cup rum
Vanilla ice cream

1. Light flame under chafing dish. Cut bananas lengthwise into halves. Place a scoop of vanilla ice cream on each of four dessert plates and hold in freezer. Arrange other ingredients conveniently around the chafing dish.
2. Combine butter and brown sugar in the chafing dish and stir until the mixture becomes a smooth syrup. Add the bananas and baste with syrup just until hot. Sprinkle with cinnamon. Add rum and banana liqueur; allow to warm slightly and then ignite with a long match. Continue basting with sauce until flames burn out. Place two banana halves around each scoop of ice cream and spoon sauce over all. Serve at once.

PAVLOVA
6 servings

Pavlova, fast gaining a reputation as the national dessert of Australia, is named for the famous Russian ballerina, Anna Pavlova. In 1929 Pavlova toured Australia for the second time and created a sensation in Perth, in Western Australia, where she stayed at the Esplanade Hotel. The chef at the time was Bert Sachse.

Several years later, in 1935, Sachse was asked by the hotel's owners to develop something new for afternoon tea. The chef began experimenting with meringue. He wanted something crisp on the outside, but gooey and marshmallow-like inside. After a couple of months he came up with the secret: adding cornstarch and vinegar to the beaten egg whites. The dessert got its name when it was presented to the owners for approval. The hotel manager said, "It is as light as Pavlova."

Pavlova is usually served with whipped cream and one or more fresh fruits, sliced and sweetened. Strawberries, peaches, and kiwifruit are all favorites; the last is probably most appropriate, for kiwis, like the dessert, come from the lands "down under."

Seeds of a small berry known in China as mihoutao or monkey peach were brought to New Zealand early in this century. By the 1930s experiments had yielded a larger, more flavorful fruit called the Chinese gooseberry. Exported to Europe in the 1950s, it was strongly promoted in the United States for the first time in 1962 by Los Angeles produce marketer Frieda Caplan, who specializes in new, little-known fruits and vegetables. Realizing that Chinese gooseberry was not a name that would particularly attract American customers, she and the New Zealanders agreed that in the United States it would be known as kiwifruit, a particularly apt name since its fuzzy brown skin does make it resemble New Zealand's flightless kiwi bird. The woody vines planted some years ago in California are now in full production; since the California crop matures in October and the New Zealand harvest begins in May, kiwifruit is available all year.

4 egg whites

¼ teaspoon salt

¼ teaspoon cream of tartar

1 cup sugar

2 teaspoons cornstarch

2 teaspoons white wine vinegar or distilled white vinegar

1 teaspoon vanilla

Fresh fruit, sweetened to taste

Sweetened whipped cream

1. Preheat oven to 250°F. Butter a cookie sheet and line it with foil, then butter and flour the foil. Using a round dinner plate, trace a circle in the butter and flour as a guide for the meringue.
2. In a large bowl and with electric mixer, beat egg whites and salt and cream of tartar until stiff. Gradually add sugar, beating constantly. Beat until stiff peaks are formed when mixer blades are lifted. Beat in cornstarch and, when dissolved, mix in vinegar and vanilla.
3. Spoon three-quarters of mixture into evenly spaced mounds on outside of circle; the mounds should touch. Use remaining meringue to spread within circle to form bottom of "bowl" for fruit. Bake in 250°F oven for 1 hour and 30 minutes. Turn off oven and leave meringue in oven for another 30 minutes. Take out of oven and allow to cool on cake rack for 30 minutes. Peel off foil, and put meringue on serving dish. When cold, fill with whipped cream and fruit and serve at once.

CHAPTER 11

CAKES

The tall, lovely cakes that mark the milestones in our lives—christenings, birthdays, weddings, and anniversaries—are relative newcomers on the culinary scene. The earliest examples were sponge cakes, leavened only with the air laboriously beaten into them. Sponge cakes probably originated in Italy, gradual enlargements of simple ladyfingers, once known as Naples biscuits. Other early cakes, the pound cakes and fruit cakes, also were raised only by vigorous mixing. Some recipes called upon the cook to "beat for one hour!" The only alternative was to use yeast, but these yeast-raised cakes now seem, for the most part, to be the forerunners of sweet breads and coffee cakes, and not true cakes at all.

Experiments with chemical leavening agents proceeded slowly. Bakers in the United States began to use pearlash made from wood ashes in the late 1700s, and it became popular in Europe, too, despite the fact that its soapy taste limited its use to spicy mixtures like gingerbread. Pearlash gave way to saleratus, a crude bicarbonate of potash noted chiefly for its bitterness. In the British Isles, some cooks relied on hartshorn (carbonate of ammonia, originally made from the antlers of deer) even though it left the kitchen reeking of ammonia.

Gradually all of these leavening agents were superseded by baking soda, which worked well, if a little unpredictably, as long as the batter contained sour milk or some other acid.

True baking powder, sodium bicarbonate plus an acid, usually tartaric, began to be produced commercially in the United States in the 1850s, and cake-makers quickly saw the possibilities. Butter cakes, rich, fine-grained, and usually served as gloriously frosted layer cakes, had almost eclipsed the long-favored sponge when it suddenly got a new lease on life in another form.

White sponge cakes, made only with the whites of eggs, became popular in the 1870s; when someone aptly named them angel cakes or angel food cakes their success was assured. A contrasting demon cake quickly appeared in response to the heavenly angels, but it was a spice cake, dark with molasses, and did not catch on. Spice cakes, after all, were neither new nor particularly dazzling. A genuine innovation was the devil's food cake created around the turn of the century. It was the first true chocolate cake to be widely made in the United States. Earlier "chocolate cakes" had consisted of yellow cakes merely filled and frosted with chocolate or yellow cakes with a small amount of grated chocolate added to the batter, much the way finely chopped nuts or coconut might be added. The name of the new dark and luscious chocolate layers scandalized some pious members of society in a time more outwardly religious than our own, but objections were futile. Both the cake and the name were here to stay.

The only really new cake added in the twentieth century is the chiffon cake, introduced in the late 1940s. It combines the richness of a butter cake with the lightness of a sponge, and has remained a favorite, both here and abroad, where, along with angel food and devil's food, it is quite properly referred to as an "American dessert."

VICTORIA SPONGE
1 7-inch cake

Victoria became queen in 1837 and remained on the throne until 1901. Her long reign, the longest in English history, completely changed the character of the British monarchy. Her predecessors, the hard-drinking and often unappealing Hanoverians, were largely ignored by the British public, although they played a small but useful role in British government. By the end of Victoria's reign that kernel of political power had vanished, but in return the monarchy had gained the respect and affection of the entire nation.

Victoria, a young woman when she came to the throne, married her German cousin, Albert, and the royal wedding was the beginning of England's love affair with its queen. Enthusiasm never wavered as the royal family grew to a total of nine children, and Prince Albert's untimely death in 1861 was mourned by the entire nation. Inevitably, everything was named for the queen (including more places on the face of the earth than for any other single person) and this even included cakes.

In the eighteenth century an English sponge cake contained a great many eggs, sometimes as many as ten in one cake, but, being a true sponge cake, no butter at all. By Victoria's day, however, butter had become an acceptable ingredient, and the resulting cake, not too different from the French *génoise* (a light, versatile sponge cake named for the city of Genoa), became known as Victoria Sponge.

1 cup flour
1 teaspoon baking powder
⅛ teaspoon salt
½ cup butter or margarine
3 eggs, at room temperature
⅔ cup sugar
1 tablespoon milk
Strawberry or raspberry jam
Confectioners' sugar

Note: *English tea cakes are usually quite small. If 7-inch pans are unavailable, cake may be baked in a 7 x 11 pan. After it has cooled, trim edges and cut the cake in two. Put halves together with jam and dust with confectioners' sugar.*

1. Preheat oven to 375°F. Grease and flour 2 7-inch cake pans.

2. Mix flour, baking powder, and salt together and set aside. Melt butter or margarine over *very* low heat and set aside. Beat eggs in small bowl with electric mixer (high speed) for 5 minutes, until very thick and light in color. Gradually beat in sugar. Beat in milk. Gradually add dry ingredients, beating just until batter is smooth. Quickly stir in melted butter.

3. Pour into prepared pans and bake 12–25 minutes or until cake is golden and tests done with a wooden pick. Remove from oven and cool for at least 10 minutes before turning onto a rack. When cake is cool, put layers together with jam. Dust the top with confectioners' sugar.

VICTORIA CAKE
1 8-inch cake

Besides Victoria Sponge, there was also Victoria Cake, really a raisin-less fruitcake, filled with cherries, the queen's favorite fruit.

¾ cup butter or margarine

½ cup brown sugar

¾ cup ground almonds

3 eggs

1 ½ cups flour

½ teaspoon baking powder

½ teaspoon cinnamon

2 tablespoons brandy

½ cup chopped candied lemon peel

½ cup chopped candied orange peel

½ cup chopped citron

1 ½ cups chopped candied cherries

1. Preheat oven to 325°F. Line an 8-inch springform pan with aluminum foil, cutting an 8-inch circle plus a band 18 inches long and 1 inch wider than the height of the pan to line the walls (the extra inch of foil, folded over the top rim of the pan, holds the band in place). Grease foil.
2. Cream the butter and then add sugar gradually, beating at low speed until the mixture is light and fluffy. Add the ground almonds. Add the eggs, one at a time, beating at low speed after each addition.
3. Mix the dry ingredients and gradually add to batter, beating only enough to mix. Add the brandy and mix, then the fruit and mix again. Spoon the batter into the lined pan and smooth the top, making a slight depression in the middle, so that the cake will be level when baked.
4. Bake 55–75 minutes or until cake tests done with a wooden pick. Allow to cool in its pan for 30 minutes, then turn out onto a cake rack and cool completely. Wrap in aluminum foil and put in a metal container with a tight-fitting lid to age in the refrigerator for several weeks before serving.

Note: *This cake, like all English fruit cakes, is very rich. Slice in thin slices and serve small portions. If stored in a tightly sealed container, it will keep for several months in the refrigerator.*

BATTENBERG CAKE
1 8-inch cake

Victoria was also said to be very fond of Battenberg cake. The Battenbergs were royal in-laws, for in 1884 Prince Louis Alexander of Battenberg married Princess Victoria of Hesse-Darmstadt, a granddaughter of the queen, and the following year his younger brother, Prince Henry, married Princess Beatrice, the queen's youngest daughter. In 1917, at the request of King George V, the family changed its name to Mountbatten. Battenberg was entirely too German a name to use as World War I was raging. The cake, however, continued to be spoken of in the old way. It is a colorful and elaborate concoction, quite typical of Victorian desserts. Perhaps it should be noted that the fate of the Battenbergs and the Windsors continued to intertwine, for Philip, Duke of Edinburgh, the husband of the present queen, is the grandson of Louis Alexander.

Cake:

1 ¼ cups flour	⅓ cup hydrogenated shortening
1 cup sugar	1 egg
1 ½ teaspoons baking powder	1 teaspoon vanilla
½ teaspoon salt	Red food coloring
¾ cup milk	Apricot jam

1. Have all ingredients at room temperature. Preheat oven to 350°F. Prepare baking pan. Tear off a piece of aluminum foil 28 inches long. Cut to 8 inches in width. Fold crosswise in the middle, then turn down the crease two inches and then another two inches. Fit foil into an 8-inch square baking pan, with the folded bit upright in the middle, so that it forms a divider, and the ends folded over the sides of the pan, to hold the foil in place. Grease foil.

2. Measure all ingredients, except for food coloring and jam, into a large mixing bowl. Blend ½ minute on low speed, scraping bowl constantly. Beat 3 minutes on high speed, scraping bowl

occasionally. Divide mixture in half. Add 5–6 drops of red food coloring to one half to tint it pink. (Color deepens during baking.) With spatula, smooth batters into divided pan, yellow on one side and pink on the other. Use spatula to push batter toward the corners of pan (not the divider), so that top of cake will be flat.

3. Bake 35–40 minutes or until cake tests done with a wooden pick. Cool 10 minutes in pan, then turn out and complete cooling on cake rack.

4. When cakes are cool, slice each cake lengthwise down the center. Trim away crusts remaining on tops and sides. Warm apricot jam and strain it. Placing a yellow cake strip next to a pink strip, use a pastry brush to spread apricot jam generously to join the two strips. Repeat with the remaining two strips. Spread the top of one joined cake with jam and place the second joined cake on top, placing pink on yellow and vice versa. Wrap cake tightly in aluminum foil and put in refrigerator for several hours.

Marzipan topping:

1 8-ounce can almond paste
¼ cup light corn syrup
2–3 cups confectioners' sugar
Red food coloring

1. Break up almond paste in large mixing bowl and add corn syrup. Add 2 cups confectioners' sugar and mix, first with a spoon and then by hand. Add a few drops of food coloring and continue to knead, adding confectioners' sugar until mixture is no longer sticky.

2. Roll out marzipan to approximately 3/16 inch thick, making sure that it is large enough to cover the cake on all six sides. Coat bottom of cake with rewarmed apricot jam and place on marzipan. Coat sides and top of cake with jam and wrap in marzipan, pressing it firmly in place. Trim marzipan where it meets and on both ends. Refrigerate till serving time. (Leftover marzipan can be used to make candies.)

POUND CAKE
1 loaf cake

Another English tea time favorite was the pound cake, which dates from the early eighteenth century. It takes its name from the old recipes that called for a pound of butter, a pound of sugar, a pound of eggs, and a pound of flour. It may have been an adaptation of a similar French cake, the *quatre-quarts*.

1 ⅞ cups flour

¼ teaspoon baking powder

¼ teaspoon mace

1 cup butter or margarine, softened

1 cup sugar

¼ teaspoon grated lemon rind

½ teaspoon vanilla

4 eggs (1 cup), at room temperature

1. Preheat oven to 300°F. Grease and flour a 9 x 5 x 3-inch loaf pan.
2. Mix flour, baking powder, and mace together and set aside. Cream butter or margarine for 1 minute with electric mixer. Add sugar *gradually*, beating for another 10 minutes in all. Beat in lemon rind and vanilla. Add eggs one at a time, beating 1 ½ minutes for each. Add dry ingredients all at once and beat just until smooth.
3. Pour into pan and bake 75–90 minutes or until cake tests done with a wooden pick. Turn out on a cooling rack. Cool thoroughly. Best if kept in an airtight container for 24 hours before serving.

SIMNEL CAKE
1 8-inch cake

The Simnel Cake has roots that go back far into British history. The name comes from *simila*, the Latin word for fine white flour, and it is mentioned by English writers throughout the Middle Ages. Simnel Cakes were sometimes associated with Palm Sunday or Easter in the western Church calendar, but much more often they were made for Mid-Lent or Mothering Sunday, the fourth Sunday in Lent, a day that by tradition allowed for a relaxation of the strict observance of the Lenten fast.

Life was harsh in medieval England. Children left home even before they reached their teens to serve apprenticeships or to become servants in the great houses of the gentry. Days off were almost nonexistent, but Mothering Sunday was an exception. All young persons were allowed to go home to see their mothers, perhaps taking her flowers or trinkets, but according to tradition by always bringing a Simnel Cake. Robert Herrick, the seventeenth-century poet, wrote

> I'll to thee a Simnell bring
> 'Gainst thou go'st a-mothering
> So that when she blesseth thee,
> Half that blessing thou'lt give me.

It was, for some, the only time in the whole year that the entire family would be together. A fine meal would be served, and the mother was often referred to as the "Queen of the Feast." A visit to the local parish, too, was customary, with a gift for "Mother church."

Just what the Simnel Cake consisted of varied greatly over the centuries. In the beginning it was probably just what the name implied, a loaf made of fine white flour, which would have been a treat indeed for a family whose usual fare was oatmeal, barley bread, cabbage, and turnips. Later, it might contain dried fruit or saffron or spices, when those were the luxuries currently sought after, and then almond paste became its crowning glory.

Pleasant as the Mothering Sunday customs were, they cannot be explained on the grounds of sentiment alone. The observation of Mothering Sunday in fact appears to have Roman roots. Conventional wisdom among historians holds that Roman Britain was totally destroyed by the invasion of the Angles and the Saxons in the sixth century, its people either killed or driven to the north or west. Folklorists are not so sure. The Romans had a festival, the *Matronalia*, held each year on March 1 in honor of Juno, patroness of women. Roman women made offerings at her temple, entertained their female slaves, and received presents from their husbands.

The resemblance between Mothering Sunday and Matronalia is unmistakable. Even tiny details fit the picture. In Lancashire and Yorkshire the emphasis was all on figs, a fruit sacred to Juno, and in Shrewsbury and a number of other areas the Simnel Cake, whatever its ingredients, must be topped with twelve balls, just like the cake traditionally made for Matronalia. Precisely what the balls signified is impossible to say. The Romans, famous borrowers, may simply have been copying a Greek festival cake that is known to have been decorated in a similar way. In Christian times the balls were said to represent the twelve apostles.

Simnel Cakes are still made in England, usually for the modern Mother's Day or for Easter. They almost always consist of a plain fruit cake layered with marzipan. Strangely enough, the twelve balls are gradually turning into Easter eggs!

Marzipan:

Make marzipan as for Battenberg Cake (recipe on page 231), omitting food coloring. Set aside one-fourth for balls and then divide remainder into two equal portions. Roll out one of these ⅜ portions into an 8-inch circle and set aside. Wrap other portions of marzipan in plastic wrap and store in an airtight container in refrigerator.

Cake:

1 ½ cups flour

¾ teaspoon baking powder

¼ teaspoon salt

½ teaspoon cinnamon

½ cup butter or margarine

½ cup sugar

2 eggs

⅓ cup milk

¾ cup dark raisins, chopped

¾ cup light raisins, chopped

½ cup dried currants

¼ cup diced citron, finely chopped

¼ cup diced candied orange peel, finely chopped

Apricot jam

1. Preheat oven to 325°F. Prepare 8-inch springform pan as for Victoria Cake (recipe on page 229).
2. Mix flour, baking powder, salt, and cinnamon together and set aside. Cream butter thoroughly and gradually add sugar, beating until light and fluffy. Add eggs one at a time, beating thoroughly after each.
3. Add flour mixture and milk alternately to the butter mixture, stirring after each addition only until well mixed. Fold in the raisins, currants, citron, and orange peel. Pour one-half the batter into prepared pan. Drop circle of marzipan in on top and cover with the rest of the batter, making sure all fruits are submerged. Make a slight depression in middle so that cake will be level when baked.
4. Bake 55–75 minutes or until cake has begun to shrink from sides of the pan and tests done with wooden pick. Cool 15 minutes before removing from the pan. When completely cool, wrap in aluminum foil and allow to age in refrigerator for at least a week before using.
5. When ready to assemble, roll out larger portion of reserved marzipan into an 8-inch circle. Warm and strain apricot jam. Use a pastry brush to coat top of cake. Press circle of marzipan firmly onto cake and divide remaining marzipan into 12 equal balls. Place in a circle around top edge of cake.

BABAS AU RHUM
6–12 servings

France, too, has its distinctive cakes, though the story of one of its most famous, Baba au Rhum, began in Poland. *Baba* in Polish means old woman; *babka* means grandmother and the Poles for centuries have made a rich holiday bread called *Babka Wielkanocna*, Grandmother's Easter Bread. It was always filled with raisins and usually finished with an icing flavored with rum.

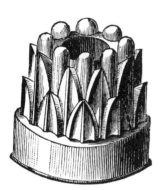

Babka was brought to France by Stanislaus Leszczynski, a deposed king of Poland whose daughter had married the French king, Louis XV. Leszczynski, a scholarly man who spent the rest of his life studying philosophy, accepted Louis's offer of the dukedom of Lorraine and set up a modest court at Luneville. He was, it seems, fond of the Babka of his homeland and either he or, more likely, his chef gradually increased the rum-flavored icing until something resembling the modern Baba au Rhum had been created. The cake was introduced in Paris by a pastry-cook named Sthorer, who had apparently seen it made in Luneville. Originally it was baked in a tall mold; today individual Babas are more often made. The modern Baba mold is a tapered cylinder about two inches high.

Dough:

1 ½ cups flour

¼ teaspoon salt

2 tablespoons sugar

1 package active dry yeast

¼ cup warm water (105–115°F)

3 eggs, slightly beaten

½ cup butter or margarine, softened

½ cup raisins

1. Dissolve yeast in warm water. Mix flour, sugar, and salt in a large mixing bowl. Make a well in the center of the flour mixture and add yeast, butter, and eggs. Blend, then beat on low speed for 5 minutes until dough is very smooth and elastic. Cover bowl and let rise in a warm place until double, 45–60 minutes.
2. Preheat oven to 400°F and thoroughly butter molds. (If baba molds are not available, custard cups can be used, or deep muffin tins). Mix raisins into dough and spoon into molds, filling no more than ½ to ⅔ full. Cover and let rise in a warm place 15–25 minutes or until dough almost reaches the top of molds. Bake 15–20 minutes or until they test done with a wooden pick. While babas are baking, prepare syrup.

Syrup:

1 cup sugar
1 cup water
¼–½ cup rum

1. Bring sugar and water to a boil in heavy saucepan and boil for 5 minutes or until a drop of syrup tested between finger and thumb is sticky. Add rum.
2. Turn babas out of pans while still warm and place in a dish 2 inches deep. Prick tops in several places with skewer or trussing needle. Spoon warm syrup over babas. Keep basting the babas until they are saturated. Serve at once.

SAVARIN
1 9-inch cake

Sometime later another Parisian pastry chef, one Julienne, tried omitting the raisins from the Baba dough, baking it in a ring mold, and using a different syrup, thereby creating a cake he called Brillat-Savarin, later shortened to Savarin.

It is named, of course, for Anthelme Brillat-Savarin, the noted gourmet, or, as he would have said, gastronome. Brillat-Savarin was a lucky man. A lawyer and a moderate, he was elected to the Estates-General that began the French Revolution but managed to escape the Reign of Terror a few years later. He spent three years as a refugee in the United States, giving French lessons, playing the violin in a theater orchestra, and appreciating the abundance and good quality of American food, if not its sophistication.

Brillat-Savarin returned to France and became an eminent jurist, but his name would long since have been forgotten if he had not written *The Physiology of Taste or Meditations on Transcendental Gastronomy*, a work considered one of the best of its type in existence. It consists mostly of essays, but begins with twenty aphorisms, including the often paraphrased, "Tell me what you eat; I will tell you what you are."

Make dough as for Babas au Rhum (p. 236), omitting the raisins. After the first rising, pour into a well-buttered 9-inch ring mold. Cover and let rise in a warm place until dough rises to the top of the mold. Bake at 400°F or until savarin is brown and begins to shrink from the sides of the pan. Make syrup and baste as for Babas, but substitute kirsch for rum. If desired, the center of the cake may be filled with *sweetened whipped cream.*

SACHERTORTE
1 9-inch cake

Cake, to the Austrians, can be either *kuchen* or *torten* but the two are hardly to be uttered in the same breath. A kuchen is a simple thing, stirred up quickly for the family, while a torte is an elaborate creation, a work of art.

The best known of all tortes is the Sachertorte, named for Franz Sacher, chef to Prince Metternich (1773–1859), for whom he created it in 1832. It was one of the earliest of chocolate cakes, made apparently only to please a demanding and somewhat irascible nobleman who was always requesting new desserts. For Metternich by this time was an old man, no longer the dashing, youthful prince who had dazzled all of Europe at the Congress of Vienna in 1814–15. But the city has always stood for grandeur and the Sachertorte has become almost a symbol of Vienna and its talent for good living.

Edouard Sacher, grandson of Franz, allowed the recipe to be published and also gave a famous Viennese pastry shop, Demel's, the right to call their version the Genuine Sachertorte. Inevitably, Demel's rivals protested. The Hotel Sacher, run by a distant cousin, sued, and much to the amusement of the Viennese, it took the courts seven years to decide in favor of the hotel. The only difference between the two versions was one extra layer of apricot jam, and not all of Vienna's chefs agreed with the courts.

Cake:

½ cup butter or margarine, softened

1 cup sugar, divided

6 egg yolks

6 ounces semisweet chocolate, melted and cooled

¾ cup sifted flour (sift flour, then measure)

¼ cup ground almonds

8 egg whites

¼ teaspoon cream of tartar

1. Have all ingredients at room temperature. Preheat oven to 350°F. Grease a 9-inch spring-form cake pan, line with a circle of wax paper and grease and flour.
2. Cream butter and ½ cup sugar on medium speed until very fluffy. Add egg yolks one at a time, beating well after each addition. Add chocolate and blend well.
3. Combine flour and almonds and set aside.
4. In a large bowl, with clean, dry beaters, beat egg whites and cream of tartar until soft peaks form. Add remaining ½ cup sugar and beat until very stiff. Fold a third of the flour-almond mixture into the butter-egg yolk mixture, then fold in a third of the egg whites. Repeat, folding very lightly, until all are combined.
5. Pour batter into prepared pan and bake 45–55 minutes or until cake tests done with a wooden pick. Cool 10 minutes, then remove side of pan. Allow to cool thoroughly, then remove bottom of pan and wax paper.

Note: This makes the Demel's version of the cake. For the Hotel Sacher's version, split the cooled cake into two layers, then put the layers together with warmed, strained apricot jam. Continue with Glaze, steps 2 and 3. Sachertorte is traditionally served with a generous dollop of sweetened whipped cream beside (not on) each piece of cake.

Glaze:

Apricot jam
⅓ cup light corn syrup
2 tablespoons butter or margarine
1 tablespoon water
6 ounces semisweet chocolate, broken up or chips

1. Coat top and sides of cake with a thin layer of warmed, strained apricot jam and set aside.
2. In a small pan combine corn syrup, butter, and water. Bring to a boil over moderate heat, stirring constantly. Remove from heat and add chocolate. Stir until melted and smooth. Chill until of desired spreading consistency.
3. Place cake on cake rack. Frost sides, then pour remaining glaze on top of cake.

LINZERTORTE
1 9-inch cake

Another well-known Austrian pastry, the Linzertorte, takes its name from the medieval city of Linz, which, like Vienna, stands beside the Danube and prospered as a trading center. The Linzertorte itself is a raspberry-filled delight that has become increasingly popular here in the United States. It has inspired miniature Linzer Tarts, and, more recently, Linzer Hearts, filled cookies that allow just a bit of raspberry jam to peek through a heart-shaped opening in the center.

1 ½ cups all-purpose flour
⅛ teaspoon ground cloves (optional)
¼ teaspoon cinnamon
½ cup sugar
1 cup finely ground almonds
1 teaspoon grated lemon peel
2 hard-cooked egg yolks, thoroughly mashed
1 cup butter or margarine, softened
2 lightly beaten raw egg yolks
1 teaspoon vanilla
1 ½ cups thick raspberry jam
Confectioners' sugar

1. Lightly but thoroughly grease a 9-inch springform pan. Mix dry ingredients in a large mixing bowl. Add almonds, lemon peel, and mashed egg yolks. Mix in butter, raw egg yolks, and vanilla. Continue to beat with heavy spoon until the mixture is smooth. Form the dough into a ball, wrap in plastic wrap, and chill for at least an hour or until firm.

2. Remove about three-quarters of the dough and return remainder to the refrigerator. Put into the greased pan and with fingers press and push it out so that it covers the bottom and extends up the side of the pan almost to the rim. (If *too* firm, let it

soften slightly.) Spread the raspberry jam evenly over the bottom of the pastry shell. Roll out the rest of the dough ¼ inch thick. With a scalloped pastry wheel (or with a sharp knife) cut the dough into narrow strips. Lay strips across the cake and then rotate the pan about one-quarter of the way to the left and repeat the pattern with remaining strips. (They should be laid at an angle, so that a pattern of x's and diamonds are formed.) Run a sharp knife around the top of the pan to loosen the bottom dough that extends above the strips. Press it down into a border ¼-inch wide. Refrigerate for 30 minutes.

3. Preheat oven to 350°F. Bake torte 45–50 minutes or until lightly browned. Let cool for 10 minutes, then slip off the rim of the pan and sprinkle with confectioners' sugar. Serve at room temperature.

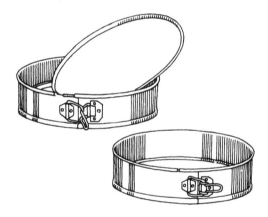

HARTFORD ELECTION CAKE
1 large cake

The first American cookbook was written by Amelia Simmons and published in Hartford, Connecticut, in 1796. Little is known about Simmons—she styled herself on the title page as "an American orphan"—but she was the first to give directions in print for such typically American dishes as pumpkin pie, cranberry sauce, and Indian pudding. *American Cookery* was such a success that a second edition was brought out in the same year and in it Simmons gives recipes for three brand-new American cakes. Here the very young republic shows its pride and patriotic fervor, for they bear the almost smile-provoking names of Independence Cake, Federal Cake, and Election Cake. The last, which had been known in colonial days, is the only one to survive. Often called Hartford Election Cake, it was, in fact, a favorite throughout New England, baked to celebrate both the right to vote and the fact of voting. Yeast-raised, it would seem more like a coffee cake than a true dessert to us.

2 packages active dry yeast

½ cup warm water (105–115°F)

½ cup lukewarm milk (scalded, then cooled)

1 ½ cups flour *and* 1 ¾ cups flour

1 teaspoon salt

1 ½ teaspoons cinnamon

½ teaspoon mace

½ teaspoon nutmeg

¼ teaspoon cloves

1 cup raisins

½ cup chopped pecans

½ cup butter or margarine, softened

¾ cup sugar

3 eggs

1 cup confectioners' sugar

¼ teaspoon vanilla

Extra milk or cream

1. Dissolve yeast in warm water. Stir in milk. Add 1 ½ cups flour gradually, beating well at low speed after each addition. Beat until mixture is smooth. Cover and let rise in warm place until very light and bubbly, 30–45 minutes.

2. Mix together 1 ¾ cups flour, salt, and spices and set aside. Chop raisins, mix with nuts, and set aside. Cream butter or margarine with sugar until light and fluffy. Add eggs one at a time, beating after each addition. Blend in yeast mixture. Gradually add dry ingredients, beating until smooth after each addition. Add raisins and pecans and mix well. Thoroughly grease and flour a 9-inch tube pan or a large (12-cup) bundt pan. Pour mixture into prepared pan.

3. Cover and let rise in a warm place until pan is almost full, 1 ½–2 hours. Bake at 350°F 40–50 minutes or until golden brown and edges begin to draw away from the pan. Cool 10 minutes in pan, then cut around tube with a knife to loosen cake. Turn out on a cake rack and cool completely. Glaze, if desired, with a mixture of confectioners' sugar, vanilla, and enough milk or cream to give a spreading consistency. Glaze should cover top of cake and drizzle down the sides.

ROBERT E. LEE CAKE
1 8-inch cake

American cakes would not for long remain simple treats, appreciated mostly for the spices and dried fruits they contained. They were destined to soar to new heights as layers were piled upon layers, with fillings and frostings to both dazzle and delight. These new, more lavish cakes were especially favored in the south and one in particular, the Robert E. Lee Cake, was immensely popular.

The name of this cake seems to be authentic—the recipe was supplied by the General's wife, Mary Custis Lee (Martha Washington's great-granddaughter)—but it must be noted that the South had many other cakes that merely bore dedications to famous men. Before the custom died out there were cakes named for George Washington, James Madison, James Polk, Stonewall Jackson, Sam Houston, and even John Nance Garner, F.D.R.'s vice president!

Cake:

1. 1 ⅛ cups cake flour
1 ½ teaspoons baking powder
½ teaspoon salt
6 eggs, separated
1 ⅛ cups sugar
3 tablespoons water

Preheat oven to 350°F. Grease bottoms of 3 8-inch round cake pans, line with circles of wax paper and grease and flour.

2. Mix together flour, baking powder, and salt and set aside. Beat egg whites until stiff, adding half the sugar gradually. Place the egg yolks in a small bowl and beat until thick. Add the remaining sugar gradually. Continue beating until very thick and cream-colored. Add the water gradually while continuing to beat. Pour slowly over egg whites and fold gently. Dust about one-third of the flour mixture at a time over the top and fold in.

3. Divide batter evenly among the three pans and bake 15–20 minutes or until tops are golden brown and centers spring back when lightly touched with finger tips. Cool in pans on cake racks 10 minutes; loosen edges with knife and turn out. Remove paper and finish cooling on racks. Fill and frost with the filling and frosting recipes on the next page.

Filling:

1 ½ cups sugar

6 tablespoons cornstarch

½ teaspoon salt

1 ½ cups water

3 tablespoons grated lemon rind

¾ cup lemon juice

3 tablespoons butter or margarine

1. Combine sugar, cornstarch, and salt in a large saucepan. Add other ingredients and mix well.
2. Bring to a rolling boil and boil 1 minute, stirring constantly. Chill before using.

Frosting:

4 cups confectioners' sugar

⅓ cup butter or margarine, softened

1 egg yolk

½ teaspoon grated lemon rind

1 teaspoon lemon juice

1 ½ teaspoons grated orange rind

2–4 tablespoons orange juice

1. Cream sugar and butter. Add egg yolk, lemon rind, lemon juice, orange rind, and 2 tablespoons orange juice.
2. Gradually stir enough of remaining orange juice into frosting to achieve spreading consistency.

LANE CAKE
1 9-inch cake

One of the most elaborate of southern cakes was the Lane Cake, named after Emma Rylander Lane of Clayton, Alabama, who gave the original recipe under the name "Prize Cake" in her cookbook *Some Good Things to Eat*, published in 1898. Filled with fruit and nuts, laced with bourbon, and then covered with mountains of white frosting, the cake became a holiday favorite, almost replacing the traditional English fruitcake.

Note: *According to Emma Lane, this cake "is much better . . . made a day or two before using." It gives the flavors a chance to mellow and the filling, of course, keeps the cake moist. It is best, however, to make only the layers and filling in advance. Put them together and place in the refrigerator in an airtight container for 48 hours. Allow to come to room temperature before frosting.*

Cake:

⅜ cup butter

⅜ cup white hydrogenated shortening

2 ¼ cup sugar

3 ¾ cups cake flour

3 ¾ teaspoons baking powder

¾ teaspoon salt

¾ cup milk

¾ cup water

2 ¼ teaspoons vanilla

6 egg whites (¾ cup)

1. Preheat oven to 350°F. Grease and flour 3 9-inch round cake pans. Have all ingredients at room temperature.
2. Cream together butter, shortening, and sugar at low speed until light, smooth, and fluffy.
3. Sift together flour, baking powder, and salt. Mix milk, water, and flavoring. Add flour mixture to creamed mixture alternately with liquid, beginning and ending with flour.
4. Beat egg whites at high speed until stiff peaks form; fold into batter. Divide batter equally among prepared pans. Bake 25–35 minutes or until no imprint is left when touched lightly in the middle. Cool 10 minutes in pans, then turn out and complete cooling on cake rack.

Filling:

8 egg yolks

1 cup sugar

½ cup butter or margarine

¼ cup water

½ cup bourbon whiskey or brandy

¾ cup raisins, finely chopped

¾ cup grated coconut

¾ cup chopped pecans

¾ cup finely chopped maraschino cherries

1. Combine egg yolks, sugar, butter, and water in heavy saucepan. Cook over medium heat, stirring constantly, until mixture coats spoon and has begun to thicken(165°F). Do not allow to boil. Remove from heat and stir in remaining ingredients. Let cool, then assemble cake.

Frosting:

2 cups sugar

½ cup water

2 tablespoons light corn syrup

2 egg whites (⅓ cup)

1 ½ teaspoons vanilla

1. Mix sugar, water and corn syrup in heavy saucepan. Boil slowly without stirring until syrup spins a 6- to 8-inch thread (242°F). Keep saucepan covered first 3 minutes to prevent crystals from forming on sides of pan.
2. While syrup is cooking, beat egg whites until stiff enough to hold a point. Pour hot syrup very slowly in a thin stream into stiffly beaten egg whites, beating constantly. Add vanilla and beat until frosting holds its shape. Frost sides and top of cake.

Although the original recipe called for three layers and both filling and frosting, many present-day southern cooks favor a simpler version, making a two-layer white cake, using half of the filling between the layers and piling the rest on the top of the cake, allowing some to drizzle down the sides. For a two-layer cake, use ¼ cup butter, ¼ cup white hydrogenated shortening, 1 ½ cups sugar, 2 ½ cups cake flour, 2 ½ teaspoons baking powder, ½ teaspoon salt, ½ cup milk, ½ cup water, 1 ½ teaspoons vanilla, and 4 egg whites (½ cup).

Please see "A Note about Eggs," p. 307.

LADY BALTIMORE CAKE
1 8-inch cake

Another, even better-known Southern cake owes its fame to *Lady Baltimore*, a novel written by Owen Wister in 1906. Wister today is remembered chiefly as the author of *The Virginian*, the novel that made the cowboy a popular hero, but to his contemporaries all his stories were delightful, and often appeared in serial form before being published as books. Numerous culinary writers have taken it for granted that *Lady Baltimore* must be a historical novel about early Maryland, but in fact it is set in Charleston, South Carolina, and is simply a story of a man and a girl and a cake named Lady Baltimore.

One is left, then, with the question of where Wister first heard of a cake with such an unusual name. It has often been suggested that it was created by Alicia Rhett Mayberry, a former Charleston belle, but in 1930 she stated that, as far as she knew, Wister first was served the cake in the Women's Exchange tea room where he frequently ate his lunch. The suggestion seems eminently sensible, since that is exactly how the narrator, in the novel, meets the lovely lady.

Cake:

⅜ cup butter

⅜ cup white hydrogenated shortening

1 ½ cups sugar

2 ¼ cups cake flour

3 teaspoons baking powder

¾ teaspoon salt

½ cup milk

½ cup water

1 ½ teaspoons almond flavoring

4 egg whites (½ cup)

1. Preheat oven to 350°F. Grease and flour 2 8-inch round cake pans. Have all ingredients at room temperature.
2. Mix, bake, and cool as for Lane Cake (recipe on page 247).

Frosting and filling:

2 ½ cups sugar

1 tablespoon light corn syrup

1 cup water

3 egg whites

1 teaspoon vanilla

½ cup chopped walnuts

¼ cup chopped raisins

¼ cup finely chopped figs

Note: *The figs and raisins are traditional, though Wister himself mentions only nuts in the novel. Chopped dates may be substituted for the figs if desired.*

Please see "A Note about Eggs," p. 307.

1. Combine sugar, corn syrup, and water in a heavy saucepan and heat to 242°F or until an 8-inch thread spins from spoon. While syrup is cooking, beat egg whites at high speed until stiff enough to hold a peak. Pour syrup slowly over egg whites, beating constantly. Add vanilla. Continue beating until mixture will hold its shape.
2. Combine nuts and fruits in small bowl. Add just enough frosting to bind, and use between layers. Cover top and sides of cake with the remaining frosting.

LORD BALTIMORE CAKE
1 9-inch cake

Since the Lady Baltimore Cake is made with only the whites of eggs, it was perhaps inevitable that someone would come up with a companion piece that made use of some of the leftover yolks. It is, of course, the Lord Baltimore Cake.

Cake:

¼ cup butter

¼ cup white hydrogenated shortening

1⅔ cups sugar

5 egg yolks (⅜ cup)

2½ cups sifted cake flour

2½ teaspoons baking powder

1 teaspoon salt

1 cup milk

1 teaspoon lemon extract

½ teaspoon vanilla

1. Preheat oven to 350°F. Grease and flour 2 9-inch round cake pans. Have all ingredients at room temperature.
2. Cream together butter, shortening and sugar until light, smooth, and fluffy. Sift together flour, baking powder, and salt. Beat egg yolks until thick and cream-colored.
3. Blend beaten egg yolks into butter and sugar, then add flour mixture alternately with milk and flavorings, beginning and ending with flour.
4. Pour into prepared pans. Bake 25–30 minutes or until no imprint is left when touched lightly in the middle. Cool 10 minutes in pans, then turn out and complete cooling on cake racks. Fill and frost with the frosting recipe on the next page.

Frosting and filling:

2 ½ cups sugar

1 tablespoon light corn syrup

¾ cup water

¼ cup syrup from maraschino cherries

3 egg whites

½ teaspoon lemon extract

½ teaspoon orange extract

¼ cup toasted coconut

¼ cup chopped pecans

¼ cup chopped almonds

¼ cup finely chopped maraschino cherries

Note: *To toast coconut, heat oven to 350°F. Place coconut in an ungreased pan and bake, stirring occasionally, 5–7 minutes.*

Please see "A Note about Eggs," p. 307.

1. Combine sugar, corn syrup, and water in a heavy saucepan and heat to 242°F or until an 8-inch thread spins from spoon. While syrup is cooking, beat egg whites with electric mixer until stiff enough to hold a peak. Pour syrup slowly over egg whites, beating constantly. Add lemon extract and orange extract. Continue beating until mixture will hold its shape.

2. Mix coconut, pecans, almonds, and cherries with about a third of the frosting. Use between the layers and on top of cake. Frost sides with remaining frosting, and add a thin layer to top of cake if desired.

CHIFFON CAKE
1 10-inch cake

The Chiffon Cake was invented (for no other word will do) in 1927 by an insurance salesman whose name, coincidentally, was Henry Baker. Baker, a Californian, added "salad oil" to what was essentially a sponge cake batter, and kept his secret for twenty years, baking cakes for Hollywood stars and other notables. Finally he sold his formula to General Mills, and the Chiffon Cake was introduced to an enthusiastic public in May of 1948. It takes its name, of course, from the soft diaphanous fabric, probably by way of the Chiffon Pie (see chapter 12).

Variation: *For an Orange Chiffon Cake, omit vanilla and lemon rind, use* orange juice *in place of water and add* 3 tablespoons grated orange rind. *For a Pineapple Chiffon Cake, omit vanilla and lemon rind, use* pineapple juice *in place of water and add* ½ cup well-drained crushed pineapple *with the juice.*

2 cups flour

1 ½ cups sugar

3 teaspoons baking powder

1 teaspoon salt

½ cup vegetable oil

7 eggs, separated

¾ cup cold water

2 teaspoons vanilla

2 teaspoons grated lemon rind

½ teaspoon cream of tartar

1. Preheat oven to 325°F. Mix flour, sugar, baking powder, and salt. Make a well in the dry ingredients and add, in order, oil, unbeaten egg yolks, water, vanilla, and lemon rind. Beat with a spoon until smooth.
2. Measure egg whites (1 cup) into a large mixing bowl and add cream of tartar. Beat with electric mixer until whites form very stiff peaks. Pour egg yolk mixture gradually over beaten whites, gently folding just until blended.
3. Pour into an ungreased 10-inch tube pan. Bake at 325°F for 55 minutes, then at 350°F 10–15 minutes or until top springs back when touched lightly. Invert and let hang until cold.

CHAPTER 12

PIES & TARTS

Pie, meaning a dish with a pastry crust, so often touted as typically American, actually has deep etymological and cultural roots in the British Isles. The word first appears in English in the fourteenth century. It is not related to any word in any of the other languages of Europe except for the Gaelic *pighe*, which has the same meaning and appears at about the same time. Etymologists argue over whether the English word was derived from the Gaelic or vice versa, but it doesn't really matter, for in both languages the culinary pie is named for the magpie, a large, chattering bird with striking black-and-white spotted plumage, known in the Middle Ages simply as a "pie." The magpie is a hoarder with the odd habit of carrying off any brightly colored object to its nest. Early baked pies contained a similar jumble of ingredients—meat and vegetables or meat and fruit (as in mincemeat)—as motley as the plumage of the bird. (The magpie's variegated coloring also gave the English language two other related words: "pied," meaning particolored, as in the pied piper; and "piebald," meaning spotted, especially for a pony.)

The earliest English pies were probably much like turnovers, consisting of a pastry crust wrapped around a filling, and small enough to hold in the hand. Such a self-contained meal would have been a great convenience in the Middle Ages, for not even the highest-born diners had forks or plates. Knives, often used in pairs, functioned as serving implements and personal eating utensils, while truly liquid dishes like stews called for bowls and spoons. But solid food, even dishes covered with sauces, could only be placed on slabs of stale bread called trenchers; these bread trenchers finally gave way to wooden trenchers—rough square or round plates, with a circular depression in the middle—but the transition was not complete until the sixteenth century.

As time went on, pies became larger and deeper. Little Jack Horner's Christmas pie was evidently of pretty good size, and the rhyme is believed to date from the 1500s. The crusts of early pies were often called "coffins." Macabre as it sounds to the modern ear, at the time the word only meant basket or receptacle. Eventually meat pies and fruit pies separated and the latter, sweetened, were served as desserts. Apple and gooseberry became British favorites.

Though pies had quite simple beginnings, they could also be very elaborate productions. The "four and twenty blackbirds baked in a pie" of the nursery rhyme had a basis in real life. Epulario, an Italian chef whose cookbook was published in 1516 and translated into English in 1598, gave detailed directions for baking such a pie.

To Make Pies That the Birds May Be Alive in Them, and Flie Out When It Is Cut Up

Make the coffin of *a great pie or pasty*, in the bottome thereof make a hole as big as your fist, or bigger if you will, let the sides of the coffin bee somewhat higher than ordinary pies, which done put it full of *flower* and bake it, and being baked open the hole in the bottome, and take out the flower. Then having *a pie the bigness of the hole in the bottome of the coffin aforesaid*, you shal put it into the coffin, withall put into the said coffin round about the aforesaid pie *as many small live birds as the empty coffin will hold*, besides the pie aforesaid. And this is to be done at such time as you send the pie to the table, and set before the guests: where uncovering or cutting up the lid of the great pie, all the birds will flie out, which is to delight and pleasure show to the company. And because they shall not bee altogether mocked, you shall cut open the small pie, and in this sort you may make many others, the like you may do with a tart.

Another Renaissance chef suggested a similar prank; in that version the pie contained frogs, guaranteed to frighten the ladies.

But most pies remained simple, and edible, dishes. One that played a strange part in the development of the English language was the umble pie. Umbles were the internal organs of the deer, traditionally the servant's portion. While the noble huntsman and his guests feasted on roast venison, the kitchen help made merry with an umble pie. A play on words was inevitable. By the nineteenth century some wit had coined the phrase "to eat humble pie" and it became a part of the language.

The American colonists produced pies with great enthusiasm, right from the very beginning. Ours was a young, hardworking country, and manual labor produced mighty appetites. Pie was often served not only for dinner and supper but also for breakfast. The abundance of fruit, both wild and cultivated, made two-crust pies the rule, but both cream and custard pies were known, though they were more often referred to as puddings or pudding pies.

The nineteenth century ushered in a splendid innovation. One day, late in the 1880s, Charles Watson Townsend of Cambridge, New York, was dining at a local hotel, and asked for some vanilla ice cream on his piece of pie. Later he requested the same combination at Delmonico's famous restaurant in New York and Delmonico's promptly dubbed it "pie à la mode."

The first really new pie of the twentieth century was the chiffon pie, introduced in the 1920s. It is said that it was the brainchild of a young professional baker and that it was at his mother's suggestion that he named it for the filmy, floating fabric so popular at the time.

Parfait pies, made with ice cream, date from the 1950s, the outcome of a promotion sponsored by a nationally known flour miller and a manufacturer of fruit-flavored gelatins. To the French, a *parfait* (meaning perfect) is a frozen mousse, but the pies more likely took their name from the American version, elegant frozen desserts piled in layers in tall parfait glasses.

MAIDS OF HONOR
12 tarts

Maids of Honor are an English specialty. The tiny tarts have long been associated with Richmond, near London. Legend says that they were named for the ladies-in-waiting who served the aging Queen Elizabeth I at the royal palace that once stood at the end of Richmond Green. Elizabeth did spend her last years at Richmond and the local bakers have done much to promote the tale, but the real story is more interesting.

Tarts known as darioles (the word first appears in French, but the origin is unknown) were identical to the luscious little Maids. They had been made in both France and England for a good two hundred years before Elizabeth came to the throne. They were also known in Spain, where, in 1508, Garci Rodríguez de Montalvo's *Amadís de Gaula* [*Amadís of Gaul*] was published. The origins of the story are in doubt, but the printed version was at once the last of the medieval romances and the first modern novel. Translated into French and then into all the other languages of western Europe, *Amadís* was read by everyone who could read; a whole generation of the nobility modeled itself on both its language and its manners.

At the beginning of the novel Montalvo introduces a character named Darioleta; her name is derived from the sweet darioles and she is the maid-servant of Elisena, daughter of King Garinter. Elisena falls in love with Perión, King of Gaul, and Darioleta arranges secret trysts for the lovers. The influence of *Amadís* was so strong that Darioleta became a word in French, *dariolette*, a servant willing to assist her mistress in conducting illicit love affairs.

Amadís and Darioleta were as well known in Elizabethan England as in France. The obvious origin of the resourceful maid Darioleta's name led to renaming the little darioles Maids, adding "of Honor" because Darioleta had served a princess—or perhaps in irony, because a *dariolette*'s deeds weren't, after all, too honorable.

6 tablespoons butter or margarine, chilled

2 tablespoons hydrogenated shortening, chilled

1 ½ cups flour

¼ teaspoon salt

1 tablespoon sugar

3 to 4 tablespoons ice water

3 egg yolks

½ cup sugar

½ cup ground almonds

1 tablespoon grated lemon zest

½ cup light cream or half-and-half

1. In a large bowl combine butter or margarine, hydrogenated shortening, flour, salt, and sugar. Cut together with pastry blender or two knives until mixture looks like bread crumbs. Pour 3 tablespoons of ice water over the mixture all at once, toss together lightly, and gather the dough into a ball. If dough crumbles, add ice water a half-teaspoonful at a time until dough just adheres. Put in a plastic bag and chill.

2. Preheat oven to 400°F. *Thoroughly* butter and flour 12 muffin cups (2½ inches across), rapping on table to knock out excess flour. Set aside.

3. Roll dough to 3/16-inch thickness, or large enough to cut out 12 3-inch rounds. Ease rounds into muffin cups without stretching. Press firmly in place. The tarts are traditionally shallow, and pastry will not come up to top of muffin cup. Place in freezer to chill while making the filling.

4. Put egg yolks, sugar, almonds, lemon zest, and cream into a mixing bowl and beat with a fork till smooth. Divide mixture evenly among the 12 tart shells, and bake 15–20 minutes, until crust is brown and filling is almost set. Remove tarts from pans and cool to room temperature on a cake rack.

CURRANT JELLY TARTS

The name currant refers to two entirely different fruits, and the British are extraordinarily fond of both of them. The first currants to be brought to the British Isles were a variety of tiny dried grapes from Greece called raisins of Corauntz, or in later French, *raisins de Corinth*. They became an essential part of English baking and the name got shortened and slurred until it had become "currants." Then, around 1600, cultivated bushes of the genus *Ribes* were introduced into England, probably from the Netherlands; they bore small, tart, red or black berries. The English decided that the tiny fruits must be the source of the dried currants and promptly christened them by that name. One wonders how they could think a fruit so tart when fresh could be so sweet when dried, but, as so often is the case, the name persisted even after the mistake was realized.

Fresh currants can be used for puddings and pies, but they are at their best in jams and jellies. They are seldom seen in supermarkets, except in their preserved form, but if you can locate them at a farm market or roadside stand, they are well worth buying to make a wonderful jelly, which in turn can be used for Currant Jelly Tarts, perfect for a tea table. For recipes using dried currants, see pages 7 and 17.

Note: *These are perfect to serve, along with Maids of Honor, for an English tea. They can, of course, be filled with commercially made currant jelly.*

Jelly:

3 ½ quarts red currants

1 cup water

7 cups (3 pounds) sugar

1 pouch (3 fluid ounces) liquid pectin

1. Remove large stems from currant clusters. Crush berries one layer at a time in a large pan. Add 1 cup water. Cover and simmer 10 minutes, stirring occasionally. Spoon into dampened jelly bag or several thicknesses of cheesecloth. Let drip into a container to catch the juice. Complete extraction of juice by

gently pressing or squeezing the bag. Measure juice to make 5 cups. If measure is slightly short, add water to pulp in bag and squeeze again.

2. Pour measured juice into a large 6- or 8-quart kettle. Open pectin and stand pouch in cup or glass. Measure sugar and stir into juice (kettle must be no more than a third full). Place over highest heat and bring to a full boil, stirring constantly. At once stir in pectin. Stir and bring to a *full rolling boil* (a tumbling boil that *cannot* be stirred down) and boil hard 1 minute, stirring constantly.

3. Remove from heat. Skim off foam and ladle jelly into hot jelly glasses. Quickly seal by pouring ⅛ inch hot paraffin onto hot jelly surface. Allow to cool, then put on lids or cover glasses with circles of aluminum foil. Store, covered, in a cool, dry place.

Pastry:

½ cup butter or margarine, softened

¼ cup sugar

¼ teaspoon salt

1 egg

1 ½ cups all-purpose flour

1. Preheat oven to 425°F.

2. With an electric mixer blend butter, sugar, salt, and egg. Add flour and continue mixing until flour disappears and dough has formed a ball. Chill in freezer 15–20 minutes.

3. Divide dough in half. Roll out one portion to ⅛-inch thickness. With a 2 ½-inch round cookie cutter or small glass cut out 9 rounds of dough and fit each into a miniature (1 ¾-inch) muffin cup. Prick lightly on sides of tart only. Repeat with second half of dough.

4. Chill in freezer 15–20 minutes, then bake 10–15 minutes, or until browned. Tip out of pans at once, and allow to cool. Fill with currant jelly just before serving.

SHOO-FLY PIE
1 9-inch pie

The pie-loving Pennsylvania Dutch often found themselves short of baking supplies in the late winter and early spring. The dried apples and various "put up" fruits of summer were gone. Milk and eggs were scarce, as the cows had not yet "freshened" (calved) nor had the hens begun to lay again in earnest. About all that was left in the pantry were flour, lard, and molasses. From these sparse ingredients they fashioned Shoo-Fly Pie and found that their families liked it so well that soon they made it all year round. The unusual name is presumed to come from the fact that pools of sweet, sticky molasses sometimes formed on the surface of the pie while it was cooling, inevitably attracting flies. In this version, corn syrup replaces some of the original molasses, producing a filling more in tune with modern tastes. Though not at all traditional, topping a slice of shoo-fly pie with vanilla ice cream makes a delicious addition.

    1 cup flour
    ½ cup light brown sugar
    ¼ cup hydrogenated shortening
    1 teaspoon baking soda
    1 cup boiling water
    ⅔ cup light corn syrup
    ⅓ cup dark molasses
    1 unbaked 9-inch pie shell (recipe page 278)

1. Preheat oven to 375°F. Combine the flour and brown sugar in a bowl. With two knives or a pastry blender cut in the shortening until the mixture resembles coarse meal. Set aside for topping.
2. In a deep bowl, dissolve the baking soda in the boiling water. Add the corn syrup and molasses and mix. Pour the mixture into unbaked pie shell and sprinkle the crumbs evenly over the top.
3. Bake in the middle of the oven 10 minutes. Reduce heat to 350°F and continue baking for about 25 minutes, or until the filling is set and does not quiver when the pan is gently shaken from side to side. Do not overbake. Cool to room temperature.

FUNERAL PIE
1 9-inch pie

The Pennsylvania Dutch considered store-bought raisins a luxury, one of the few food items that they could not produce themselves. But raisins did have the advantage of being available all year round.

Mourners who came from a distance to attend a funeral had to eat somewhere before they began the long drive home, and the hospitable neighbors who arranged these dinners wanted to feed them well. Raisin pie appeared so often for dessert on these occasions that serving it became a custom, and finally it acquired a new name, Funeral Pie.

2 cups raisins
2 cups water
½ cup brown sugar
2 tablespoons cornstarch
½ teaspoon cinnamon
¼ teaspoon salt
1 tablespoon vinegar
1 tablespoon butter or margarine
Pastry for double 9-inch crust (recipe page 278)

1. Preheat oven to 425°F.
2. Combine raisins and water in medium saucepan; boil 5 minutes. In a small bowl blend sugar, cornstarch, cinnamon, and salt. Add to raisins and cook, stirring until clear. Remove from heat and stir in vinegar and butter or margarine. Cool slightly.
3. Turn cooled filling into pastry-lined pan. Cover with top pastry (see page 278 for fitting top crust) or lattice strips. Bake 30–40 minutes or until golden brown.

JEFFERSON DAVIS PIE
1 9-inch pie

Jefferson Davis, the only president the Confederacy ever had, will never be forgotten in the South. A number of states still celebrate his birthday, sometimes as the Confederate Memorial Day, and his estate, Beauvoir, near Biloxi, Mississippi, is beautifully maintained and open to visitors.

Just as southern cooks like to name their cakes for famous men, so, too, they name their pies. The best-known of these namesakes is the Jefferson Davis Pie, a rich, luscious creation typical of Southern single-crust pies. There are numerous variations; this one contains spices, dates, and nuts.

> 3 egg yolks
> ⅔ cup sugar
> 1 tablespoon flour
> ½ teaspoon salt
> ½ teaspoon cinnamon
> ¼ teaspoon nutmeg
> 1 ⅓ cups light cream or half-and-half
> 1 teaspoon vanilla
> 1 cup cut-up dates
> 1 cup chopped walnuts or pecans
> 1 unbaked 9-inch pie shell

1. Preheat oven to 350°F.
2. With electric mixer on medium speed beat egg yolks, sugar, flour, salt, cinnamon, and nutmeg until very thick. On low speed, blend in light cream or half-and-half and vanilla. Stir in dates and walnuts or pecans.
3. Pour into unbaked pie shell. Bake 50–60 minutes or until top is golden. Serve when cool. Refrigerate any remaining pie.

PRESIDENT TYLER PUDDING PIE
1 9-inch pie

John Tyler has two unusual distinctions. He had more children than any other U.S. president (eight by his first wife and seven by his second) and he is the only president whose death was totally ignored by the federal government.

In 1839 the newly formed Whig party held its first national convention. The Whigs chose William Henry Harrison, an aging war hero who had defeated a small force of Indians at the Battle of Tippecanoe twenty-eight years earlier, as their presidential candidate. Then, to balance the ticket with the aim of attracting Southern votes, they nominated Tyler, a former senator from Virginia, for vice president. Campaigning almost solely on the slogan "Tippecanoe and Tyler Too," the Whigs won handily. Harrison died one month after his inauguration and Tyler thus became the first vice president to succeed to the presidency. He managed to make the Constitution work and to establish genuine presidential authority, rather than merely filling the role of acting president as his enemies would have preferred. Nevertheless, since he opposed almost everything the Whigs supported but was not accepted by the Democrats, Tyler became a president without a party. At the end of his four years in office he simply threw what little support he had to James Polk and retired to his plantation.

Always a states' rights man, Tyler closely observed the events that preceded the Civil War. At first he opposed secession and was largely responsible for arranging the Washington peace conference of 1861. After that effort had failed, however, Tyler urged immediate secession at Virginia's convention held later that year. Elected unanimously to membership in the provisional Confederate Congress and to the House of Representatives under the permanent Constitution, Tyler died before he could take that office.

Unlike the Jefferson Davis Pie, for which no one claims any actual connection to the beloved leader for whom it is named, the

Pudding Pie, according to President Tyler's numerous descendants, was a family favorite, frequently served in the White House. A number of variations exist.

½ cup white sugar

1 tablespoon flour

½ cup light brown sugar

3 eggs

1 teaspoon vanilla extract

¼ teaspoon salt

½ cup milk

¼ cup butter or margarine, melted

½ cup flaked or shredded coconut

1 unbaked 9-inch pie shell

1. Preheat oven to 375°F.
2. In a large bowl combine white sugar and flour and mix well. Add brown sugar, eggs, vanilla extract, and salt and mix. Add milk and butter and mix again. Pour half of filling into pie shell. Sprinkle coconut evenly over surface and add remainder of filling.
3. Bake 40–50 minutes or until golden brown and set. Refrigerate until chilled, about 2 hours. Serve, refrigerating any remaining pie immediately.

CHESS TARTS
8 4-inch tarts

Chess tarts, another Southern favorite, have puzzled many a curious cook. The unusual name has prompted folk etymologies that range from the unlikely to the ridiculous. It has been suggested, for example, that the tarts, small enough to be held in the hand, were favored by men deep in a chess game and loath to stop even for refreshments.

Actually, chess is a corruption of cheese. Cheese tarts, with a filling much like modern cheesecake, were made in England as early as the fifteenth century. Southern cooks in colonial times left out the cheese but retained the name, creating almost inevitable bafflement.

Note: *For Chess Pie, pour filling into an unbaked 9-inch pie shell and bake at 375°F 40–50 minutes or until crust is brown and filling is set.*

Pastry for a double-crust pie

1 ½ cups sugar

1 tablespoon flour

1 tablespoon cornmeal

4 eggs

¼ cup butter or margarine, melted and cooled

¼ cup milk

3 tablespoons lemon juice

2 teaspoons grated lemon zest

Sweetened whipped cream (optional)

1. Preheat oven to 375°F.
2. Divide pastry into 8 equal pieces. Roll out each to ⅛-inch thickness and ease gently into a 4-inch tart pan. Trim off excess, then hook very edge of pastry over the rim of the pans, to prevent shrinking and sliding. Chill in freezer while making filling.
3. In a large mixing bowl combine sugar, flour, and cornmeal. Add eggs, butter, milk, lemon juice, and zest. With an electric mixer blend until smooth.
4. Place tart pans on cookie sheet and fill with lemon mixture. Bake 10–20 minutes, until crusts are brown and filling set. Cool thoroughly. Spread with sweetened whipped cream before serving, if desired. Refrigerate any remaining tarts.

FRANGIPANI PIE
1 9-inch pie

The Frangipani were a noble Roman family powerful enough in the eleventh and twelfth centuries to meddle in the affairs of popes and emperors. In the sixteenth century a lesser Frangipani went to France and set himself up in the perfume business. Two hundred years later the name came to be applied to a pastry cream or filling flavored with crushed almond macaroons. In France frangipani (or frangipane) was used as a filling for tarts or between the layers of little cakes; brought to America, probably by the Louisiana French, it became a full-fledged pie.

Incidentally, and again recalling perfume, the Frangipani name has also been given to a particularly fragrant variety of pear and to a tropical tree sometimes known as the red jasmine.

Variation: For a simpler Frangipani Pie, add 1 teaspoon almond extract with butter and omit crushed almond macaroons. Sprinkle ¼ cup sliced almonds over the sweetened whipped cream.

⅔ cup sugar
¼ cup cornstarch
½ teaspoon salt
3 cups milk
4 egg yolks, slightly beaten
2 tablespoons butter or margarine
1 cup crushed almond macaroons, divided (recipe on page 201)
1 baked 9-inch pie shell
Sweetened whipped cream

1. Stir together sugar, cornstarch, and salt in saucepan. Blend milk and egg yolks; gradually stir into sugar mixture. Cook over medium heat, stirring constantly, until mixture thickens and boils. Boil and stir 1 minute. Remove from heat; blend in butter or margarine.

2. Immediately pour into baked pie shell; press plastic wrap or waxed paper onto filling. Chill pie thoroughly, at least 2 hours. Sprinkle top of pie with ½ cup macaroon crumbs. Spread with sweetened whipped cream and sprinkle with remaining crumbs. Serve at once. Refrigerate any remaining pie.

CONCORD GRAPE PARFAIT PIE
1 9-inch pie

Concord grapes are named for Concord, Massachusetts. Ephraim Wales Bull, a noted amateur horticulturist in the mid-nineteenth century, was dissatisfied with the wild grapes that grew in abundance throughout New England. Though a number of varieties existed they were all too small and too strong or "foxy" in flavor to be much good for anything but jelly. Aware of the work that others had done in hybridizing fruits, he patiently began to work on the none-too-promising *Vitus labrusca*, the northern fox grape. Ten years and three generations of grapes later he had the famous Concord strain.

Bull exhibited his new grape on September 3, 1853, and began to sell the vines for five dollars each. The first year he made $3,200, but then nurseries began to propagate their own vines by cuttings and he received almost no further income. He died embittered and his gravestone reads, "He sowed, but others reaped."

1 envelope unflavored gelatin

⅓ cup sugar

1 ¼ cups unsweetened Concord grape juice

2 tablespoons lemon juice

1 pint vanilla ice cream

1 baked 9-inch pie shell (recipe on page 278)

Sweetened whipped cream

1. Combine gelatin and sugar in a large mixing bowl. Mix well and set aside. Bring grape juice to a boil and add to gelatin mixture. Stir. Add lemon juice and stir again. Add ice cream by spoonfuls, stirring until melted. Chill until mixture mounds slightly when spooned.
2. Pour into baked pie shell. Chill until firm. Cover with sweetened whipped cream.

ORANGE CLOUD PIE
1 9-inch pie

Variation: *Frozen tangerine juice can be used in place of frozen orange juice.*

The imperial Romans probably were familiar with citrus fruits, but that knowledge, like so much other, was largely lost during the Dark Ages that followed the fall of the empire in the west. When the Europeans again discovered oranges, lemons, and limes, it was through the Arabs, who brought the plants from the east.

The English word orange is taken from the Arabic *naranj* by way of the French *orange*. The initial "n" was evidently absorbed by the article *une* while the influence of the French *or* for gold changed the "a" to "o." In English the use of the word as a name for the fruit is older than its use as a name for a color; to the Anglo-Saxons orange and red were both just *read.*

The tangerine, too, has close ties with the Arab world. It takes its name from Tangiers, where the Europeans first tasted it; in the east it would be considered just another form of mandarin orange.

The first attempts to create an orange pie were not particularly successful. Delicious as orange juice is to drink, it lacks the tartness of the ever popular lemon. Commercially prepared frozen orange juice concentrate, introduced in the 1940s, made possible an intensity of flavor never before available. This Orange Cloud Pie, a favorite in the 1950s, is actually a chiffon pie.

1 envelope unflavored gelatin

¾ cup sugar

¼ teaspoon salt

1 cup water

3 eggs, separated

¾ cup (6-ounce can) concentrated frozen orange juice

1 baked 9-inch pie shell

Sweetened whipped cream

1. Combine gelatin, ½ cup of the sugar, salt, and water in top of double boiler, mixing well. Place over direct heat until gelatin is dissolved, stirring constantly. Add gradually to slightly beaten egg yolks and return the mixture to top of double boiler.
2. Cook and stir over hot water until mixture coats a metal spoon. Remove from heat; add orange juice and blend. Chill until mixture begins to thicken.
3. Beat egg whites until foamy, then add remaining ¼ cup sugar a tablespoonful at a time, beating after each addition. Continue to beat until stiff peaks can be formed. Fold into orange mixture gently but thoroughly and turn into baked pie shell. Chill.
4. Just before serving, spread pie with sweetened whipped cream.

KEY LIME PIE
1 9-inch pie

Note: *Fresh Key limes are virtually unobtainable outside of Florida. Bottled Key lime juice can be purchased at specialty shops, or the juice of Persian limes can be substituted. Key Lime Pie can, if preferred, be served in a baked regular pie shell.*

Please see "A Note about Eggs," p. 307.

Limes came to Florida with the *conquistadores.* When Columbus returned from Spain in 1493 on his second voyage to the island he had named Española (Hispaniola), he brought with him oranges, and, very probably, limes, for they were flourishing on the island by 1520. From there they spread gradually across the West Indies, westward to Mexico, and northward to the Florida Keys, where the trees were found growing wild by Americans in the 1800s.

The Key lime is quite different from the dark green Tahiti limes or Persian limes later commercially grown in both Florida and Mexico. It is small, yellow-skinned, and round, and its juice has been called both sourer and more complex.

Sweetened condensed milk became widely available in the United States following the Civil War. It was welcomed in the Florida Keys, where fresh milk spoiled quickly in the high temperatures, and not too many people bothered to keep cows. Some inventive person, whose name will probably never be known, combined the new product with the juice of the Key lime and discovered that it immediately thickened. With the addition of eggs it became the distinctively different Key Lime Pie.

Crust:

⅓ cup butter or margarine
1 ½ cups fine graham cracker crumbs
3 tablespoons sugar

Filling:

4 egg yolks (from grade A, unbroken eggs)
1 can (14 ounces) sweetened condensed milk
1 cup Key lime juice (see note)
Few drops of green food coloring (optional)
Sweetened whipped cream

1. Heat oven to 350°F. Melt butter or margarine and add to crumbs. Add sugar and mix well. Press into a 9-inch pie pan. Bake 10 minutes and allow to cool.
2. In a medium bowl, beat egg yolks until thick. Gradually add condensed milk, lime juice, and green coloring, if desired, beating until mixture thickens.
3. Pour into cooled pie shell and chill in refrigerator for several hours. Serve covered with whipped cream.

GRANNY SMITH APPLE PIE
1 9-inch pie

Note: *This type of single-crust apple pie, often called a French Apple Pie, can, of course, be made with other types of apples, but the tart Granny Smith is perfect with the sweet topping.*

There really was a Granny Smith. Her name was Maria Ann Smith and she was an elderly widow living on a farm near Sydney, Australia. One day, while working in her garden, she noticed an apple seedling. She decided to save the little tree even though she had no idea what kind of apples it would bear. She could only vaguely recall having dumped a bunch of rotten apples in that part of the garden some years earlier, and, besides, apples do not come true from seed.

The tree grew and finally bore large, beautiful, bright green apples, with a wonderful tart-sweet flavor. Granny Smith's neighbors, impressed, began to ask for cuttings. By the time she died, in 1870, her tree was well known locally; twenty-five years later Australia's early agricultural experts had decided that "Granny Smith's Seedling . . . would be worth a trial." As it turned out, the apple, which ripened in late March, had wonderful keeping qualities in addition to its superb flavor.

In time shipments began to the northern hemisphere, first to the British Isles and then to the United States. American consumers are notoriously conservative when it comes to apples, preferring the well-known varieties, but the Granny Smith was enthusiastically received. American growers began almost at once to plant Granny Smiths, and now the apple is available all year round.

¾ cup white sugar

1 ¼ cups all-purpose flour, divided

½ teaspoon nutmeg

½ teaspoon cinnamon

6 cups thinly sliced, pared Granny Smith apples

1 unbaked 9-inch pie shell

½ cup firm butter or margarine

½ cup light brown sugar

1. Preheat oven to 425°F.
2. Stir together white sugar, ¼ cup flour, nutmeg, and cinnamon; mix with apples and turn into unbaked pie crust.
3. With a pastry blender or two knives, cut butter and light brown sugar into remaining 1 cup flour until crumbly. Gently pat over apples. Bake 50 minutes. Cover topping with aluminum foil for the last 10 minutes of baking if top browns too quickly. Serve warm.

BLACK BOTTOM PIE
1 9-inch pie

Note: *Please see "A Note about Eggs," p. 307.*

A Dictionary of Americanisms defines "black bottom" as a "relatively low-lying section [on the outskirts of town] inhabited by Negroes." The term first appears in print in 1915 but is probably far older. Black Bottom Pies began appearing in cookbooks around the turn of the century.

In the 1920s a dance called the Black Bottom had a brief period of popularity. It probably originated in black culture, and, in turn, it inspired a sundae of the same name, made of chocolate ice cream and chocolate syrup.

Crust:

¼ cup butter or margarine

1 ¼ cups fine gingersnap crumbs

Filling:

½ cup sugar

2 tablespoons cornstarch

½ teaspoon salt

2 cups milk

2 eggs, separated

2 teaspoons unflavored gelatin

3 tablespoons cold water

2 tablespoons rum, *or* 2 teaspoons rum flavoring

1 ½ ounces unsweetened chocolate, melted and cooled

¼ teaspoon cream of tartar

⅓ cup sugar

Sweetened whipped cream (optional)

Semisweet chocolate (optional)

1. Preheat oven to 325°F. Melt butter or margarine and add to gingersnap crumbs. Mix well and press into a 9-inch pie pan. Bake 10 minutes and allow to cool.

2. Stir together ½ cup sugar, cornstarch, and salt in a large saucepan. Blend milk and egg yolks and stir into sugar mixture. Cook over medium heat, stirring constantly, just until mixture boils. Pour out 1 cup of the mixture and set aside.

3. Soften gelatin in cold water; stir into remaining hot custard. Stir in rum or rum flavoring. Chill, stirring occasionally, until mixture mounds slightly when dropped from a spoon. Meanwhile, combine cooled melted chocolate and the reserved custard mixture. Pour into baked crumb crust.

4. Beat egg whites and cream of tartar until foamy. Add ⅓ cup sugar, 1 tablespoon at a time, continuing to beat until stiff and glossy. Do not underbeat. Fold remaining chilled mixture into beaten egg whites. Spread on top of chocolate mixture. Chill at least 4 hours or until set. If desired, garnish with sweetened whipped cream and sprinkle with shaved or grated semisweet chocolate.

PASTRY FOR 9-INCH SINGLE-CRUST PIE

1 cup all-purpose flour

½ teaspoon salt

⅓ cup plus 1 tablespoon hydrogenated shortening
  or ⅓ cup lard

2–3 tablespoons cold water

1. Measure flour and salt into large mixing bowl. With pastry blender or two knives, cut in shortening until the mixture resembles coarse crumbs. Sprinkle with water, 1 tablespoon at a time, mixing until all flour is moistened and dough almost cleans side of bowl. More water can be added, ½ teaspoon at a time, if necessary to make the particles adhere.

2. Gather dough into ball and shape into a flattened round on lightly floured board. With a floured rolling pin, begin to roll dough, lifting occasionally to prevent sticking. Roll dough to 11-inch circle. Fold pastry into quarters; unfold and ease into pan without stretching.

3. With a knife trim overhanging edge of pastry from rim of pan. Pressing lightly, hook edge of pastry over rim, to prevent shrinking and sliding. Chill in freezer 15–20 minutes.

For single-crust pie:
  Fill and bake as directed in recipe.

For double-crust pie:
  Double all ingredients. Roll half of dough and ease into pan, trimming edge as above. Fill as desired. Roll second half of dough. Cut slits so steam will escape, then fold into quarters. Lightly moisten rim of bottom crust with cold water. Place top crust over filling and unfold. Trim overhanging edge of pastry ½ inch from pan. Fold edge of top crust over edge of bottom crust and press firmly to seal. Bake as directed in recipe.

For baked pie shell:
  Roll out pastry for single-crust pie and fill pie tin as directed above. Prick bottom and sides of shell thoroughly with fork before chilling. Bake at 475°F 8–10 minutes or until lightly browned.

STIRRED
OR
SHAKEN

CHAPTER 13

BEVERAGES

Water, the universal beverage, was for millennia the only drink generally available to humans over the age of infancy. Milk from domestic animals became important about ten thousand years ago when the agricultural revolution changed men from hunters and food-gatherers to herdsmen and farmers. Strangely enough, beer and wine are believed to be just as old: fermentation is a natural process and probably was discovered quite by accident in many different places. The Egyptians and Mesopotamians were skilled brewers; they had some knowledge of wine but produced much more beer. It was left to the Greeks to grow grapes in abundance and turn wine making into an art. The Romans, famous borrowers, learned from the Greeks, and soon vineyards were to be found throughout their great empire.

Coffee, tea, and chocolate are all much newer. The coffee tree grows wild in Ethiopia. Coffee was recognized as a stimulant, and, long before the invention of the beverage, the beans were pounded with animal fat and shaped into balls, which bands of warriors carried as part of their rations on long-distance raids. In fact, coffee is still used in this way in some parts of Africa by people making long and difficult journeys. Coffee plants were cultivated in Yemen on the Arabian peninsula, possibly as early as the sixth century, and it is believed that the fruits were allowed to ferment to make a kind of "coffee wine." This practice was discontinued when Mohammed forbade the use of alcohol, and for a time coffee was considered to be only a medicine.

Much later, probably in the fifteenth century, it was discovered that a delicious nonalcoholic beverage could be made from the roasted beans. Coffee drinking spread rapidly throughout Arabia and was introduced into Turkey in 1554. In 1615 Venetian traders began selling coffee in Italy.

The beverage quickly became popular throughout Europe, and coffeehouses sprang up in major cities. London alone had five hundred by the beginning of the eighteenth century. The coffeehouse served not just as a place of refreshment but as a kind of club where, before the advent of the telegraph, telephone, and modern newspaper, information and news of every kind could be exchanged. Coffeehouses also provided semiofficial gathering places for men of the same profession, who would regularly patronize a particular coffeehouse where they could be found conveniently by clients or friends. Political views were aired, opinions sounded, alliances made, and bargains sealed, all free from the sometimes judgment-warping effects of alcohol. Among the most noteworthy of all the coffeehouses was that opened by Edward Lloyd on Tower Street in the late seventeenth century. It became a popular meeting place for the underwriters who insured ships and was the beginning of Lloyd's of London, the great international insurance market that finally became a corporation.

With coffee in such demand, the Arabic world could not maintain its monopoly forever. The Dutch managed to obtain a few seeds and began to grow coffee in Java about 1696. The story of the introduction of coffee plants into the Americas centers on Gabriel Mathieu de Clieu, a young French officer who, in 1723, stole a plant from the Jardin des Plantes in Paris, kept it alive during a particularly difficult Atlantic crossing, and then planted it in Martinique. The plant and its descendants flourished, spread throughout the West Indies, and eventually reached the mainland of South America, which quickly became the center of coffee production.

Tea drinking is older than coffee, but reached the west later. The earliest certain reference to tea is found in the *Erh Ya*, an ancient Chinese dictionary written about 350 B.C. Its use spread slowly from the interior province of Szechwan where it was first cultivated. Tea drinking was encouraged by Buddhist priests who hoped to combat drunkenness (sake wine was already well known); Buddhist missionaries introduced tea into Japan.

The Dutch brought the first tea to Europe in 1610. It reached Russia in 1618, France in 1649, and England and the American colonies about 1650. At first, the English were hardly impressed. They were already practically addicted to coffee, and it was only very gradually, over the next two centuries, that tea replaced coffee as the national drink. Factors besides taste contributed to the change. As modern methods of communication made the business aspect of the coffeehouses obsolete, clubs and pubs eventually assumed their social role. Moreover, times were changing in other ways. The new tea shops welcomed unescorted ladies, an innovation that would have been unthinkable in the all-male domain of the coffeehouse. Finally, when the tea industry became firmly established in India in the mid-nineteenth century, the price of tea dropped dramatically, so that even the poor could afford tea, while they never could have afforded coffee.

Anna Russell, the seventh duchess of Bedford, began the custom of afternoon tea in 1840. She had tea and cakes served at five o'clock to ward off what she called a "sinking feeling." The phrase has evoked many smiles, but actually in fashionable circles, dinner was served so late in the evening as to make an intervening fourth meal a necessity.

It was the heat of our scorching American summers that brought about the creation of iced tea. It has often been reported that Richard Blechynden, an Englishman vainly trying to sell hot tea at the St. Louis World's Fair of 1904, was all but ready to give up until he poured the scalding drink over ice and began to sell "iced tea." The story could be true, but even if it is, the resourceful Blechynden would only have been copying an American custom as yet unknown in Britain. Cookbooks in the United States were including recipes for iced tea (or "ice tea") as early as the 1860s.

Chocolate was first made by a far more ancient group of Americans, the Aztecs of Mexico. They called it *chocolatl*, cocoa water, and drank it mixed with vanilla and spices but unsweetened. The *conquistadores* took the beverage back to Spain, where it was sweetened (a great improvement), and gradually the new drink spread to neighboring countries. In 1657 chocolate was introduced in London by a French shopkeeper, but at a price that only the wealthy could afford. Fashionable chocolate houses appeared in London, Amsterdam, and other European cities. The drink was again improved, about 1700, by the English this time, with the addition of milk.

Inevitably, though, man has lavished more care and attention on alcoholic drinks than on nonalcoholic beverages. Distillation, the process that increases the alcoholic content of a beverage, was discovered many different times by many different peoples. The Romans may have known the art; certainly the alchemists of te early Middle Ages distilled wine and called the seemingly magical liquid they produced *aqua vitae*, water of life.

The Italians were the first to put their knowledge of the distillation process to practical use. By the year 1000 A.D. a crude brandy called *acquavite* was being produced in some abundance. Soon other countries followed suit. The English word brandy (originally brandywine) comes from the Dutch *brandewijn*, burned wine. Cognac, the finest of all brandies, is produced in a clearly defined region in France centering on the town of Cognac. Armagnac, another fine French brandy, is made in Gascony.

The Irish, possibly as early as 1100 A.D., were using beer to make *uisgebeatha* (Gaelic for "water of life," from the Latin *aqua vitae*) which in turn became *whisquy-beath, whiskeybae,* and finally whiskey. The art was introduced into Scotland, and the Scots made it their own, producing the renowned Scotch whisky. (The Irish and American product is known as whiskey; Scotch and Canadian whisky is always written without the *e*.)

Hundreds of years later the Scotch-Irish on the American frontier discovered that corn could be mixed and distilled with the more usual rye or barley, producing excellent results. The new product, always associated with Bourbon County, Kentucky, came to be called Bourbon whiskey or, more simply, bourbon. The county, of course, had been named for the royal house that dominated all of Europe for generations.

Gin originated in the Netherlands in the seventeenth century; it was called *genever* from the juniper berries used to flavor it. English soldiers fighting in the European wars at the end of the century took an immediate liking to the new "Dutch courage," shortened the name to gin, and introduced it into England. Queen Anne gave gin distilling a major boost when she raised the duties on the imported product and lowered the excise tax at home. "Gin palaces" sprang up in the rapidly growing English cities, replacing the rustic taverns. Sadly, gin became the drug that made the horrors of the early Industrial Revolution a little easier for the poor to bear, a situation graphically recorded in William Hogarth's engravings.

Rum, like gin, dates back to the seventeenth century. First made in the West Indies, it was called "kill-devill" and described as a "hot, hellish and terrible" liquor, fit only to blind the plantation slaves to their appalling misery. Made from sugarcane juice or from the molasses left over from sugar production, it later came to be called "rumbullion," a word of obscure origin, which in turn was shortened to rum.

The Spanish, who had introduced sugarcane to the New World, and the French, also, began to make rum. Since the islands in the Caribbean were infested with pirates, it was inevitable that rum would forever be associated in legend with these plunderers. Gradually some attention was paid to flavor and aroma, and eventually rum became a drink a gentleman could enjoy in moderation.

Human beings are quixotic; having learned to make drink stronger, they then began to search for ways to mix it with other appealing liquids to make it weaker and more pleasant to drink. A number of mixed drinks come from the Old World, but cocktails are an American invention.

The origin of the term is obscure, but it began appearing in print in the early 1800s. In the exuberant and often rough and tumble world of the infant United States, numerous concoctions were created and often given fantastic names. Among the many that flourished were the Stinkibus, the Stone-fence, the Timber-doodle, the Bust-head, the Ching-ching, the Deadbeat, the Deacon, the Moral Suasion, the Phlegm-cutter, the Split-ticket, and the Vox Populi. Mercifully, most of these have vanished, but their places have been taken by a myriad of others.

GIN RICKEY
1 serving

Cocktails that sprang up in the post–Civil War period were often named for well-known persons or places. The Gin Rickey takes its name from a Washington lobbyist, Colonel Jim Rickey. He may have been only a "Kentucky colonel," and his first name may have been Joe, not Jim, but it does seem that he was a regular patron of Shoomaker's, a popular Pennsylvania Avenue bar frequented by congressmen and other public officials.

Although the lime was familiar to sailors of the time, it was still a novelty to bartenders. One day when the colonel appeared at Shoomaker's, the bartender who always served him squeezed a lime into a tall glass, added cracked ice, gin, and seltzer water, and handed it to the popular lobbyist. Rickey, delighted, demanded another, and the pleased bartender named his new drink for the colonel. Much later, lime rickey would be used as a name for a soft drink.

1 ½ ounces gin
¼ lime
Club soda, chilled

1. Put several ice cubes in tall glass. Add gin.
2. Squeeze lime above drink and drop into glass. Add soda to fill and stir.

GIBSON
1 serving

The Gibson, really only a Martini cocktail garnished with small white onions, is named for illustrator Charles Dana Gibson, creator of the turn-of-the-century "Gibson Girl," the ideal woman of that era, whose image appeared in *Life*, *Harper's*, and other magazines. Gibson ordered a Martini (named for the brand of vermouth, from the Italian firm Martini and Rossi), usually served with an olive, from bartender Charles Connolly of the Players in New York City. Connolly, out of olives, served the drink instead with two tiny white onions. There was, in fact, nothing spectacular about the garnish; the drink caught on only because Gibson was immensely popular. The regal, almost haughty, "Gibson Girl" fascinated a generation, and anything associated with her creator was considered the height of fashion.

1 ¾ ounces gin
¼ ounce dry vermouth
1–2 pickled cocktail onions

1. Stir gin and vermouth with ice cubes. Strain into chilled cocktail glass.
2. Garnish with onions.

DAIQUIRI
1 serving

The Daiquiri is named for the town of Daiquiri, near Santiago, in Cuba's mountainous Oriente Province. American engineer Jennings S. Cox, the supervisor of the area's copper mines, invented the drink one day in 1896 when unexpected visitors from the States arrived in Daiquiri. Lacking gin, he mixed the local rum with lime juice and sugar, and the drink was an immediate success.

The Spanish-American War brought a vast influx of Americans to the island and Cox was a genial host to many high-ranking officers. When the war ended the drink was introduced at the Army and Navy Club in Washington, D.C.

> 1 ounce light Puerto Rican rum
> 1 teaspoon superfine sugar
> Juice of 1 lime

1. Combine ingredients and shake with ice.
2. Strain into chilled cocktail glass.

FROZEN DAIQUIRI
1 serving

The Frozen Daiquiri, which achieved its fame and notoriety at
La Floridita in Havana, is the crowning achievement of Constante
Ribailagua, *cantinero* and later owner of the well-known Cuban
bar. Ernest Hemingway, who moved to Cuba in the thirties, was
Ribailagua's good friend and the bar's most noted patron. His pas-
sion for the Frozen Daiquiri knew no bounds and he included both
Ribailagua and the *Floridita* in his posthumously published novel,
Islands in the Stream.

2 ounces light Puerto Rican rum

1 teaspoon superfine sugar

1 teaspoon maraschino liqueur

2⅔ cup crushed ice

Half a lime

1. Combine rum, sugar, liqueur, and ice in chilled container of
   blender. Squeeze lime above mixture. Blend on high speed 5 seconds, or until slushy.
2. Pour into chilled cocktail glass. Serve with two short straws.

STRAWBERRY DAIQUIRI
4 servings

The advent of electric blenders made possible an infinite number of Daiquiri variations, as different fruits were added to the
original ingredients. Strawberry Daiquiris are perhaps the
favorite.

6 ounces light Puerto Rican rum

2 ounces lime juice

1 package (10 ounces) frozen sliced strawberries, unthawed

1 ⅓ cups crushed ice

1. Combine all ingredients in chilled container of blender. Blend
   on low speed 10–15 seconds, until slushy.
2. Pour into chilled cocktail glasses. Serve with two short straws.

CUBA LIBRE
1 serving

The Spanish-American War, fought in 1898, involved the United States deeply in the affairs of Cuba. Although the U.S. had steadfastly insisted that it had no designs on the island, Americans stayed behind for a number of years following the war. During that interval they invented the Cuba Libre.

Cuba Libre means "free Cuba," and the drink, the handiwork of the United States Signal Corps, is believed to have been invented in August 1900. Coca-Cola, a prime ingredient, had been invented almost fifteen years earlier; it quickly became a success and by the turn of the century was available to American soldiers in Cuba.

It took Prohibition, however, to bring the Cuba Libre to the attention of the American public. Visitors from the United States flocked to Cuba in search of good times in general and liquor in particular. By the time the ban on alcohol was lifted in 1933, the Cuba Libre was already well known to many Americans and it soon became a popular drink in the United States.

Half a lime
1 ounce light Puerto Rican rum
Cola drink, chilled

1. Squeeze lime into tall glass partially filled with ice cubes; save lime shell. Add rum.
2. Add cola to almost fill glass. Stir and add lime shell.

TOM COLLINS
1 serving

The Tom Collins, originally the John Collins, seems to have been the inspiration of an Irish headwaiter by the latter name who worked at Limmer's Hotel in London in the nineteenth century. The name was changed to Tom Collins when it became customary to make the drink with Old Tom Gin. Although this sweetened gin is rarely used today, the drink remains a Tom Collins, or, more simply, a Collins.

> 2 ounces gin
> 1 teaspoon superfine sugar
> ½ ounce lemon juice
> Club soda, chilled
> 1 slice orange (optional)
> 1 slice lemon (optional)
> 1 maraschino cherry (optional)

1. Shake gin, sugar, and lemon juice with ice.
2. Strain into very tall glass partially filled with ice. Add soda to fill. Stir quickly. Garnish with fruit as desired.

SCREWDRIVER
1 serving

The Screwdriver seems to have been created quite spontaneously during the early 1950s by American engineers working in the Middle East oil fields. Adding vodka to small cans of orange juice, they stirred the mixture with their screwdrivers.

> 1 ounce vodka
> Orange juice, chilled

1. Put vodka into tall glass partially filled with ice.
2. Fill with orange juice and stir.

BLOODY MARY
1 serving

The Bloody Mary was created in the 1920s at Harry's New York Bar in Paris. Vodka, newly arrived in the west from Russia and Eastern Europe, inspired a French bartender by the name of Fernand "Pete" Petiot to concoct a blend of tomato juice, vodka, and seasonings. American entertainer Roy Barton christened the drink "Bucket of Blood" after a nightclub in Chicago. (The original Bucket of Blood was a saloon in Havre, Montana; by the 1890s the grisly name was being used for any seedy drinking establishment.)

Petiot left Paris in 1933 for New York and the King Cole Bar at the St. Regis Hotel, where the drink caught on under the less sanguine name Red Snapper. It is not known exactly when other bartenders began calling it the Bloody Mary, but its fame spread rapidly and it has remained popular, especially as a drink served at brunches. The Bloody Mary from whom the drink got its final name was, of course, Mary Tudor, the English queen remembered for her bloody persecutions of the Protestants.

> 1 ounce vodka
> Dash pepper
> Dash celery salt
> Dash Worcestershire sauce
> 1 drop Tabasco sauce (optional)
> Tomato juice, chilled

1. Put first five ingredients into tall glass partially filled with ice.
2. Fill with tomato juice and stir.

ROBBIE BURNS
1 serving

Since the Scots are extremely proud of their whisky-making ability, it was perhaps inevitable that cocktails would be devised that call for scotch whisky and are named for famous Scotsmen. Two of the best-known are the Robbie Burns and the Rob Roy.

Robert Burns (1759–1796) needs little introduction. An erratic genius who died tragically young, he was Scotland's greatest poet, and his birthday (January 25) has become a national holiday, celebrated with haggis (which needs a great deal of introduction, but is essentially a sheep's stomach stuffed with other organs, suet, and seasoned oatmeal and then boiled) and great quantities of both whisky and national pride.

1 ½ ounces scotch	Dash orange bitters
½ ounce sweet vermouth	Dash Pernod

1. Stir ingredients with ice cubes.
2. Strain into chilled cocktail glass.

ROB ROY
1 serving

Rob Roy (1671–1734) is less well known than his compatriot Robert Burns; indeed, he might be totally forgotten if he had not been made the hero of one of Sir Walter Scott's novels. Born Robert MacGregor (Rob Roy was a nickname meaning "Red Robert," referring to his red hair), he was a Highland chieftain who was outlawed, perhaps unfairly, and then spent the rest of his life raiding his neighbors for both fun and profit.

1 ounce scotch	Dash Angostura bitters
½ ounce sweet vermouth	1 maraschino cherry

1. Stir scotch, vermouth, and bitters with ice cubes.
2. Strain into chilled cocktail glass and garnish with cherry.

SCARLETT O'HARA
1 serving

Cocktails have sometimes been named for fictional heroines. Undoubtedly, the most familiar is Scarlett O'Hara, the headstrong beauty of Margaret Mitchell's *Gone with the Wind*. The name seems essential to the character today—Scarlett and Rhett have entered the pantheon of famous lovers, as inevitable a pairing as Romeo and Juliet and Anthony and Cleopatra; but as it happens, there could easily have been no Scarlett. Margaret Mitchell at first intended to name her heroine Pansy. She had been Pansy throughout the first draft of the novel. Then, at the last minute and with the manuscript due, Mitchell began to have second thoughts. She considered Storm, Robin, Angel, and several other names before finally settling on the now world-famous Scarlett.

> 1 ounce Southern Comfort
> 1 ounce cranberry juice
> Juice of ¼ lime

1. Stir ingredients with ice cubes.
2. Strain into chilled cocktail glass.

SHIRLEY TEMPLE
1 serving

Inevitably, for the sake of those unfortunate children who are dragged, willy-nilly, to adult gatherings, someone would come up with a nonalcoholic "kiddy cocktail." It is, of course, the Shirley Temple, named for the child star of the thirties, whose popularity coincided with the post-Prohibition era of fashionable drinking.

1 ounce grenadine syrup
Ginger ale, chilled
1 maraschino cherry

1. Pour syrup into cocktail glass.
2. Fill with ginger ale and garnish with cherry.

WASSAIL BOWL
22 (½-cup) servings

The custom of the wassail bowl comes directly from the Anglo-Saxons who conquered Roman Britain in the fifth century. Waes-heil, "be well" in Old English, was a pledge drunk between friends. The correct response was *drink-heil*, "drink well." Frequently, pieces of toasted bread were floated on top of a beverage; as they were considered a choice portion, the salutation itself came to be termed a "toast."

In medieval England the wassail bowl was usually associated with the holiday season. Wealthy households brought out a huge bowl, often of silver, not only at Christmas but also for the New Year and Epiphany, and filled it with drink. The poor would go from door to door, cup in hand, begging in rhyme for a ladleful. Wassailing became another word for caroling.

The traditional beverage, consisting of heated ale, roasted crab apples, beaten eggs, sugar, and spices, was often called lamb's wool. It has been suggested that the apples tended to disintegrate into globs that did, indeed, look like lamb's wool; it seems much more likely, however, that the name comes from the Gaelic *la mas uball* (pronounced la ma zool), the day of fine apples, a drink originally associated with November 1, the great Celtic holiday of pagan days.

12 small apples

¾ cup sugar

Water

1 teaspoon ground nutmeg

2 teaspoons ground ginger

2 sticks cinnamon

6 whole cloves

6 allspice berries

2 750-ml bottles cream sherry

64 ounces ale

4 cups sugar

12 eggs, separated

1 cup brandy

Note: *Please see "A Note about Eggs," p. 307.*

1. Preheat oven to 375°F. Core apples and pare upper half of each. Place apples upright in ungreased 9 x 13-inch baking dish. Pour 1 tablespoon sugar into the core of each apple. Pour water (¾ inch deep) into baking dish. Bake uncovered until tender when pierced with a fork, 30–40 minutes. Spoon syrup in dish over apples several times while roasting.

2. Combine 2 cups water and spices in a large saucepan and simmer for 10 minutes. Add sherry and ale and stir in sugar. Heat, stirring, but do not boil.

3. In a large bowl beat egg whites until stiff peaks form. In a separate bowl beat egg yolks until pale and thick; fold in stiffly beaten egg whites.

4. Strain half the ale and sherry mixture over the eggs. Pour into a warmed punch bowl. Bring the remaining hot mixture to a boil and strain into the punch bowl. Add brandy and apples.

NEGUS
10 (½-cup) servings

Note: *To make twists of lemon rind, use a sharp knife or twist cutter and thinly peel only the colored portion of the rind into ½-inch-wide strips.*

Heated drinks were popular in England. Perhaps the often cold and rainy climate made them especially appealing. The Negus, named for its creator, Colonel Francis Negus, appeared in the eighteenth century. Negus was an officer who served in the European wars of the early 1700s; later he held various posts in the royal household and became a member of Parliament.

On one occasion, after a convivial dinner, the bottle was passing rather more rapidly than good fellowship seemed to warrant. A hot political discussion involving a number of prominent Whigs and Tories rapidly became combustible, and Negus narrowly averted a fracas by recommending the dilution of the wine with hot water and sugar. Attention was diverted from the point at issue to a discussion of the merits of the mixture, which ended with the compound being nicknamed "Negus." The name became current in Negus's regiment, the Suffolks, but in the hard-drinking eighteenth century, the drink was soon relegated to the breakfast table or to children's parties.

1 bottle (750 ml.) sherry or port
3 teaspoons superfine sugar, or more to taste
Juice of 1 lemon
2–3 large twists lemon rind
½ teaspoon vanilla
1 ¾ cups boiling water
Ground nutmeg

1. Heat wine by placing opened bottle in large container of hot water. Do not warm over direct heat.
2. When wine is thoroughly heated, pour into preheated pitcher. Add sugar, lemon juice, lemon rind, vanilla, and boiling water.
3. Stir, add additional sugar if desired, and stir again. Strain into wineglasses or punch cups. Sprinkle each serving with nutmeg.

BISHOP
14 (½-cup) servings

The Bishop came to England from the Netherlands in the early 1700s. Probably introduced by Dutch sailors, the drink combined heated wine, citrus juices, and spices, and was an immediate favorite.

Early versions were heavily sweetened—one recipe favored in the American colonies called for a pound and a half of sugar to one bottle of wine—but tastes change, and today the sugar is virtually eliminated.

2 oranges
24 whole cloves
2 bottles (750 ml. each) red wine
2 tablespoons sugar or honey

1. Preheat oven to 350°F.
2. Bake whole, unpeeled oranges in preheated oven about 10 minutes, until golden. Remove from oven, allow to cool slightly, and stud each orange with a dozen cloves.
3. Place oranges in large glass or earthenware bowl. Stir in wine and sugar. Cover and let steep 12 hours.
4. Cut one orange into quarters and squeeze juice into wine. Reserve other orange for garnish. Heat wine mixture in top of double boiler or over very low heat until just hot. Pour into preheated pitcher or punch bowl. Add whole orange. Serve in wineglasses or punch cups.

FISH HOUSE PUNCH
48 (½-cup) servings

Punch came to England at the beginning of the East India trade in the 1600s. Sailors introduced the new drink and it was an immediate success, both at home and in the fledgling American colonies. It has often been stated that the name comes from the Hindi word *panch*, meaning five, for the number of ingredients; but, in fact, early recipes for punch called just as often for four ingredients (spirit, water, sugar, and citrus juice) as for five, nor was there any uniformity even when a fifth ingredient was added. It has also been suggested, perhaps more correctly, that the word may actually come from puncheon, a word now obsolete, though used at the time for small casks of liquor.

Punch recipes are easy to invent, and they have proliferated during the last three hundred and fifty years. Probably the most famous of all punches is Fish House Punch, noted both for its potency and unusual name.

Fish House Punch was devised (or, as they would say, "built") by members of Philadelphia's oldest men's club. The club had simple origins. In 1732 a small group of wealthy gentlemen, among them William Penn's secretary, agreed to spend a day together every now and then, fishing along the Schuykill River and then cooking their catch for dinner, with no wives or servants present. The original name of the club was the Colony in Schuykill, changed to the State in Schuykill after the Revolution. As the club became more formal, a clubhouse was needed, and in time this progressed to three buildings, the "State House," the "Castle," and the "Fish House," down by the river bank. It is for the latter, of course, that the punch is named.

1 ½ cups superfine sugar

1 quart fresh lemon juice

2 quarts light or dark rum

2 quarts cold water

4 ounces peach brandy

1 quart cognac

1. Place sugar and lemon juice in large punch bowl. Stir to thoroughly dissolve sugar.
2. Add rum, water, brandy, and cognac, stir, and allow to ripen at room temperature for at least 2 hours, stirring occasionally.
3. Place a solid block of ice in bowl, to cool and dilute mixture. If still too strong, add more water. Serve in punch cups.

GROG
1 serving

Grog is named for a British admiral, Edward Vernon, whose nickname, "Old Grog," stemmed from the heavy grogram (grosgrain) cape he habitually wore at sea. A buccaneer to the Spanish, he was a hero to the British when, in 1739, he took the Spanish harbor of Porto Bello (in present-day Panama) with only six ships. The exploit earned him particular admiration in the thirteen colonies, where the "Spanish menace" still loomed large, and Lawrence Washington, George's older brother, renamed the family home Mount Vernon in honor of the daring admiral.

Crews on board British ships were less admiring in the following year when, hoping to combat drunkenness, Vernon ordered that the men's customary ration of rum be cut with water. The resulting mixture became known, disparagingly, as grog. In America the name came to be applied to a hot drink spiked with rum.

1 teaspoon superfine sugar

Juice of ½ lemon

1 slice lemon

Several whole cloves

1 (1-inch) piece cinnamon stick

1 ounce light or dark rum

Boiling water or hot tea

1. Place sugar and lemon juice in preheated 8-ounce mug. Stir to dissolve sugar.
2. Stud lemon slice with cloves and add to mug, along with cinnamon stick and rum.
3. Fill mug with boiling water or hot tea.

TOM AND JERRY
2 servings

The Tom and Jerry, a nineteenth-century favorite, has become a holiday drink. It owes its name to a novel by Pierce Egan, *Life in London, or the Day and Night Scenes of Jerry Hawthorn, Esq. and His Elegant Friend Corinthian Tom* (1821). Egan, a professional sports-writer, knew London low life well; in some ways his works antici-pate Charles Dickens. His characters in *Life in London* are a pair of dissolute but likable young rakes, and the book was instantly pop-ular. Its sequel, *Finish to the Adventures of Tom, Jerry and Logic*, put the names in the order in which they are remembered today.

Soon "to-Tom-and-Jerry" meant to drink and indulge in riotous behavior, like the young bloods of the Regency period, while a "Tom-and-Jerry shop" became a synonym for any kind of low, dis-reputable drink shop.

Just how Tom and Jerry came to be the name of a drink is uncer-tain, but the recipe appeared in 1862 in *How to Mix Drinks*, by Jerry Thomas, the flamboyant American bartender who called himself a "mixologist." The name of the drink then was transferred to a kind of ceramic mug, and the two names became inseparably linked.

In September 1965, CBS aired a new cartoon about a cat and a mouse. The cat's name was Tom; as might be expected, the mouse was Jerry. The cartoon, in which the main characters are non-speaking, has been shown all over the world, and the "Adventures of Tom and Jerry" seem destined to continue well into the future.

2 eggs, separated

1 ½ ounces light or dark rum

⅛ teaspoon baking soda

2 teaspoons superfine sugar

1 ½ ounces brandy

3–4 ounces hot milk or boiling water

Ground nutmeg

Note: *Please see "A Note about Eggs," p. 307.*

1. Beat egg whites in small bowl until stiff peaks form.
2. In another small bowl, beat yolks until foamy.
3. Fold yolks quickly into whites. Sprinkle ½ ounce rum, baking soda and sugar on top of egg mixture. Stir well.
4. Preheat two 8-ounce mugs and divide egg mixture between them. Add equal amounts of brandy and remaining rum to each mug.
5. Pour hot milk or boiling water into each mug and stir. Sprinkle nutmeg on top.

IRISH COFFEE
1 serving

Irish Coffee was invented in the 1930s by Joe Sheridan, chef at the Shannon airport. At that time the facilities of the airport left a lot to be desired; passengers disembarking from international flights had to walk a good distance across a runway that was often swept with wind and cold rain. Sheridan, a kindly man, wanted to offer visitors a drink that would both warm and cheer, and his Irish Coffee was an immediate success. Its fame spread quickly to Britain (where it is sometimes called Gaelic coffee) and, after World War II, to the United States, where it was introduced in San Francisco by newspaperman Stan Delaplane.

1 ½ ounces Irish whiskey
1 teaspoon sugar
5–6 ounces fresh hot black coffee
Heavy cream or sweetened whipped cream

1. Pour whiskey into preheated 8-ounce stemmed glass or coffee cup. Add sugar and coffee and stir.
2. Pour cream over back of a spoon to float on top, or add a generous dollop of sweetened whipped cream.

MOCHA
4 servings

Mocha is an ancient city in the small country of Yemen, located at the southwestern corner of the Arabian peninsula. Originally the center of the coffee trade, Mocha first gave its name to the superior coffees grown in the area, then to any top quality coffee, and finally to a mixture of coffee and chocolate used either as a beverage or as a flavoring.

¾ cup boiling water
1 tablespoon instant coffee
2 ounces unsweetened chocolate
¾ cup cold water
⅓ cup sugar
⅛ teaspoon salt
2 ½ cups milk
1 teaspoon vanilla extract

1. Pour boiling water over instant coffee. Stir to dissolve and set aside.
2. Put chocolate and cold water in saucepan. Place over low heat and stir until chocolate is melted. Add sugar and salt. Simmer 3 minutes, stirring constantly. Gradually stir in milk. Add coffee and heat, but do not boil. Stir in vanilla.

A NOTE ABOUT EGGS

Sporadic outbreaks of salmonella have occurred in recent years in the poultry industry in the United States, leaving many cooks uneasy about using raw eggs or partially cooked eggs. Scientists from the U.S. Department of Agriculture seem to be on the verge of solving the problem, but, in the meantime, there are some sensible precautions that can be taken.

Certainly the easiest solution is to use the liquid eggs available in most supermarkets (in the refrigerated section, usually next to the egg substitutes). They are pasteurized and entirely safe. Equally safe are the powdered egg whites often available in cake decorating supply shops. For the egg yolks needed for Béarnaise Sauce and Hollandaise Sauce, Harold McGee, in *The Curious Cook*, gives a somewhat complicated but workable way of destroying salmonella while still leaving the egg yolk in a liquid state. Sometimes the simplest solution is to substitute a commercially prepared product, such as bottled dressing for Caesar Salad.

SELECTED BIBLIOGRAPHY

General References

Encyclopedia Britannica. 24 vols. Chicago: Encyclopedia Britannica, 1965.

The New Encyclopaedia Britannica. 32 vols. Chicago: Encyclopaedia Britannica, 1990.

The Oxford English Dictionary. 2d ed. 20 vols. Oxford: Clarendon Press; New York: Oxford University Press, 1989.

Chambers, Robert, ed. *The Book of Days: A Miscellany of Popular Antiquities in Connection with the Calendar.* 2 vols. Reprint of the 1862–64 edition. Detroit: Gale Research Company, 1967.

Eliade, Mircea, ed. *The Encyclopedia of Religion.* New York: Macmillan, 1987.

Evans, Ivor H., ed. *Brewer's Dictionary of Phrase and Fable.* New York: Harper and Row, 1959.

Hastings, James, ed. *Encyclopaedia of Religion and Ethics.* 13 vols. New York: Charles Scribner's Sons, 1908–26.

Johnson, Allen, ed. *Dictionary of American Biography.* New York: Charles Scribner's Sons, 1927.

Mencken, H. L. *The American Language: An Inquiry into the Development of English in the United States.* New York: Alfred A. Knopf, 1936.

———. *The American Language: Supplement I.* New York: Alfred A. Knopf, 1945.

———. *The American Language: Supplement II.* New York: Alfred A. Knopf, 1948.

Morris, William and Mary. *Dictionary of Word and Phrase Origins.* New York: Harper and Row, Publishers, 1962.

Robert, Paul, ed. *Dictionnaire alphabétique et analogique de la langue française*. Paris: Société du Nouveau Littre, 1973.

Stephen, Sir Leslie, and Sir Sidney Lee, eds. *The Dictionary of National Biography*. 27 vols. London: Oxford University Press, 1937.

Strayer, Joseph R., ed. *Dictionary of the Middle Ages*. 13 vols. New York: Charles Scribner's Sons, 1982.

Walsh, William S. *Curiosities of Popular Customs*. Philadelphia: J. B. Lippincott Company, 1897.

Wentworth, Harold, and Stuart Berg Flexner, eds. *Dictionary of American Slang*. New York: Thomas Crowell Company, 1975.

Culinary References and Histories

Note: Most useful here were the volumes of the Time-Life Foods of the World series; they are now out of print, but will remain a valuable resource for culinary writers for decades. To the following list must be added the vast collection of antique cookbooks (part of the John Crerar collection) now housed in the libraries of the University of Chicago.

Aresty, Esther B. *The Delectable Past*. New York: Simon and Schuster, 1964.

Beard, James. *Beard on Food*. New York: Alfred A. Knopf, 1974.

———. *James Beard's American Cookery*. Boston: Little Brown and Co., 1972.

Bennington, Lee Edwards. *Oh Fudge! A Celebration of America's Favorite Candy*. New York: Henry Holt, 1990.

Berkhout, Edda Meyer. *Best of German Cooking*. Tucson, Ariz.: HP Books, 1984.

Brillat-Savarin, Jean Anthelme. *The Physiology of Taste; or, Meditations on Transcendental Gastronomy*. New York: Boni and Liveright, 1926.

Brothwell, Don and Patricia. *Food in Antiquity: A Survey of the Diet of Early Peoples*. New York: Frederick A. Praeger, 1969.

Bullock, Helen DuPrey, and Helen McCully, eds. *The American Heritage Cookbook and Illustrated History of American Eating and*

Drinking. New York: American Heritage Publishing Company, 1964.

Dictionnaire de l'académie des Gastronomes. Paris: Prima, 1962.

Escoffier, Auguste. *Memories of My Life.* Translated by Laurence Escoffier. New York: Van Nostrand Reinhold, 1997.

FitzGibbon, Theodora. *The Food of the Western World: An Encyclopedia of Food from North America and Europe.* New York: Quadrangle/New York Times Book Company, 1976.

Fussell, Betty. *I Hear America Cooking.* New York: Viking, 1986.

Garmey, Jane. *Great British Cooking: A Well Kept Secret.* New York: Random House, 1931.

Hale, William Harkin. *The Horizon Cookbook and Illustrated History of Eating and Drinking through the Ages.* New York: American Heritage Publishing Co., 1968.

Hartley, Dorothy. *Food in England.* London: MacDonald and James, 1954.

Lang, Jenifer Harvey, ed. *Larousse Gastronomique: The New American Edition of the World's Greatest Culinary Encyclopedia.* New York: Crown, 1988.

Mariani, John F. *The Dictionary of American Food and Drink.* New York: Ticknor and Fields, 1983.

McGee, Harold. *The Curious Cook: More Kitchen Science and Lore.* San Francisco: North Point Press, 1990.

———. *On Food and Cooking: The Science and Lore of the Kitchen.* New York: Charles Scribner's Sons, 1984.

McNeill, Florence Marian. *The Scots Kitchen: Its Traditions and Lore with Old-Time Recipes.* London: Blackie and Son, 1936.

Montagne, Prosper. *Larousse Gastronomique: The Encyclopedia of Food, Wine and Cookery.* New York: Crown, 1961.

Morton, Frederic and Marcia. *Chocolate: An Illustrated History.* New York: Crown, 1986.

Schriftgiesser, Karl. *Oscar of the Waldorf.* New York: E. P. Dutton and Co., 1943.

Simon, André L. *A Concise Encyclopaedia of Gastronomy.* New York: Harcourt Brace and Co., 1952.

Simon, André L. and Robin Howe. *Dictionary of Gastronomy.* New York: McGraw-Hill, 1970.

Solomon, Jon and Julia. *Ancient Roman Feasts and Recipes Adapted for Modern Cooking.* Miami, Fla.: E. A. Seemann Publishing, 1977.

Tighe, Eileen, ed. *Woman's Day Encyclopedia of Cookery.* New York: Fawcett Publications, 1966.

Wheaton, Barbara Ketcham. *Savoring the Past: The French Kitchen and Table from 1300 to 1789.* Philadelphia: The University of Pennsylvania Press, 1983.

Whitman, Joan, comp. *Craig Claiborne's* The New York Times *Food Encyclopedia.* New York: Times Books (Division of Random House), 1985.

Williams, Richard L. *Time-Life Foods of the World.* 27 vols. New York: Time-Life Books, 1968–71.

Wilson, C. Anne. *Food and Drink in Britain from the Stone Age to Recent Times.* New York: Barnes and Noble, 1974.

INDEX